Footloose & Fearless @ Fifty +

Denise O'Leary

Cover design by Nicola Erdpresser

Photos available to view:
http://www.deniseoleary.co.uk

CONTENTS:

MEXICO

OAXACA

Hung like a hammock high in the hills above the Sierra Madre of Mexico lies the tiny city of Oaxaca. It's so remote, that when Cortez and the Conquistadors came looking for gold and found none, they left it alone and it was allowed to carry on as it always had done. Today, it is quiet, respectful, regal and in total harmony with the surrounding nature. It still has a soul untouched by the ravages of consumerism and by the diseases of the West. No one smokes, no one drinks and no one is obese. They still have their own dialects and no one speaks English – not good for me as I speak nothing else.

So what was I doing in Latin America? It started last summer when my boyfriend bought me a book of short stories by one of my favourite writers; Gabriel Garcia Marquez – master of magic realism. One was about a man who fell overboard in the Gulf of Mexico and washed up in Cartagena in Colombia. How was that possible, I thought, when Colombia had no Caribbean coast? I consulted my atlas and there it was, a huge coast line and I thought how great it would be to visit that country and that part of the world.

Five months later, and not for the first time, I'd yet again finished with the boyfriend of 11 years which was still going nowhere. I'd never been afraid of ending a relationship if it hadn't worked out (including a much loved husband) but I'd stayed too long this time. Never mind that it had taken until my 40s to find who I thought was the love of my life, it was still no reason to stay when he clearly, no longer, was the love I wanted. When you cease to cherish your partners company, no matter how lonely being single seems, it was still better to leave. How often do we stay too long simply

7

because the idea of having to start again is just so daunting?

And so there I was - metaphorically paralysed by a bitterly lonely and cold winter with just the same boring four walls for company, staying in alone on Saturday nights watching old films or bad new one's thinking, "is this it for the rest of my life?" I couldn't bear the idea that I had nothing to look forward to and I would just drift into middle age and endless solitude. I'd gone from being something of a socialite; revelling in new company, to being a recluse. I'd even reached the stage when going out was just too much bother. I'd toss up the option of meeting with friends and not even being able to get ready. I had a wardrobe of party dresses gathering dust and high heeled shoes barely worn. I was desperate for something to happen but also knew that if something was going to happen, I would have to *make* it happen.

Quite frankly, I was exploding with frustration. I didn't even have a job to break up the day. Despite having just finished a degree course, at my age, there wasn't much on offer and I was reduced to living on what was left of my student grant and watching my savings vanish. I was too young to grow old and dying to live and I'd simply cracked and packed. In a moment of madness or magic, I'd found a tenant for my house, booked all of my flights, a few cheap places to stay through airbnb, hostelworld or booking.com and that was that. People, just like me, get up every day and say they are going to change their lives but they never do. This time, I was determined to make a dream a reality and that is all it took – I just made the decision and didn't even pause to look back in case the grass of the past suddenly became greener.

I had no idea what to take so just packed my favourite silk, linen and cotton dresses (all from charity shops) and six pairs of shoes in varying degrees of sophistication; from my old worn out moccasins, to the fancy gold ones, to the stilettos - none of them remotely practical but all of them gorgeous – glamour at any price. If I was going to be alone, I would

8

prefer to at least be having a well-dressed adventure.

And so to Oaxaca, the first stop on my three month trip that would take me to the Pacific beaches of Mexico; the cities, towns and Caribbean beaches of Colombia; both the oceans of Costa Rica and finally, to the metropolis of the Western world - New York.

The flights from Heathrow via Houston had been the usual nightmare of transfers, border control queues, dying for a cigarette and lack of sleep. The adrenalin of adventure had allowed me to float above the worries gnawing at my ankles, but as we came into land, no matter that I silently counted down from ten and shouted Geronimo (as I had done since a child to give me the courage to do things like dive off the top board), I could feel butterflies beginning to rage in my stomach. Couldn't I have found an easier alternative to abject loneliness than casting myself off alone half way across the world? I hadn't really considered just how much courage this had taken and how much more I would need to see me through, but I really hoped that it wouldn't let me down.

Arriving late at night, I had no idea how I would get from the airport to the town and with no Spanish; not even a dictionary or a phrase book, I couldn't even ask anyone. The arrogance of the English speaker who expects everyone to know their language is ridiculous. No one spoke a word and instantly, I was in trouble and that was how it would continue. Luckily, there were two girls from Dallas, there to buy fabric, who spoke the language and soon we were speeding into town in an old collective mini-van which, as promised, dropped me at my hostel Zipolite in the southern part of town.

Slightly set back from the road, the hostel; wedged between a mechanic's garage and a shop, was once probably a splendid town house laid out around a little tiled courtyard, but those days were long gone. It was now faded and forlorn with peeling yellow and blue paint and bare light bulbs. But for all that, it still had a little fountain gurgling away, a few potted plants and the young girl who opened the door to me seemed proud to be a part of it. She helped me up the stairs with my bag and showed me to my room - barren save for a bed, a table, a chair and a broken window covered over with a plastic bag which opened onto the court yard. I instantly imagined being robbed in the night and wondered if maybe I should have spent more than £7.50 per night but I was too tired to really care. After travelling for nearly 24 hours, all I wanted to do was sleep.

****

With coffee, is the way I like to start my day, and despite having brought my stove top coffee pot (not as ridiculous as it sounds), I couldn't see anyway of using it, so very early the following morning I went out to search. It was all so wonderfully foreign and WARM. I walked the block but there were no coffee shops or indeed any shops open, but what there was, in the street next to an old church, was a wooden cart with three enormous metal vats and a stack of paper cups. I'd never been afraid of sampling the fare of street vendors, so went to investigate.

One of the vats contained what I knew to be the locals' favourite - thick syrupy hot chocolate, one that smelled of "coffee" and one of thick hot white stuff. I'm dairy intolerant so didn't want milk (what my alternatives might be hadn't really registered – usually it's soya milk) but as I couldn't communicate with words, I stood there, mooing like a cow. What I must have looked like I can only imagine, but they seemed to think it was really amusing and with big smiles, they shook their heads – no, it wasn't milk.   What it was, I still have no idea, but I bought a cup of both for next to no money and headed back to my room to imbibe – it was interesting, but not like any coffee I'd ever had before.

Next, I needed to clean myself up. Bathrooms are a wonderful thing but my room didn't have one. I've shared bathrooms many times before and lived in hope that they will at least be clean and sturdy. At Hostel Zipolite there was only the one with a flimsy haphazard shower cubicle, a sink with wonky taps, a tiny mirror and a stained toilet. Luckily I got in there early after it had just been cleaned and before the floor was swamped and the bucket overflowed with used toilet tissue. I didn't linger long especially as every other guest seemed to be a migrant worker and being in a hurry, banged impatiently on the door. When I unlocked the dodgy bolt, they all seemed shocked or surprised to see a tall blonde gringo woman coming out, dressed in an old and faded but still stylish black wrap around dress that I'd designated as my dressing gown. Once again, I wondered if perhaps I should have paid a bit more to at least ease me in gently to my new surroundings...

Refreshed as was possible, I wanted to log on to my super new, super mini laptop, to let those who care, know that I'd arrived. I'd packed and planned in a hurry – this time last month, I wasn't going anywhere. As a recent "mature" graduate, I'd been applying for jobs but really, who wanted someone of my age?

I dug out my adaptor plug; I looked at the round pins on the plug and then I looked at the straight holes in the wall. It was never going to work and bearing in mind I had an entire bag of chargers for phone, camera and everything else you could think of (including straighteners without which, my hair has all the sophistication of a 10 year olds, and an Epilady for removing all that unwanted other hair), all plans of sight-seeing were void. I had to sort the plug situation and sort it fast.

After a couple of hours going this way and then that and then this way again (clearly lost) and always ending up back on 10th November Street, passing the same bemused people again and again (I was dressed in yellow and black silk harem trousers and hardly went unnoticed), I found the tourist information office where someone did in fact speak English.

11

Unfortunately, she couldn't help and it was back to wandering, becoming more and more desperate. I wondered if I could just change all my plugs to two pin ones and thought I'd email my brother Sean who knows about this sort of thing and that's when I ran into another problem. I went into an internet café and tried to log onto my email account. It didn't recognise my location and told me that it would send a password to my FLAT mobile phone.

Problems seemed to be piling up and I'd only just arrived. Luckily Facebook wasn't so cranky and just showed me photos of "friends" to identify. Seconds later, I was logged in and able to communicate. That problem was at least solved. I decided to try the tourist booth on the edge of the main square manned by two young men who spoke perfect English and within minutes, I'd found an adaptor. I was so happy, I wanted to kiss the shop assistant. She had no idea what it meant to me.

Re-connected and re-invigorated, I set out to see the city – I can never relate the scale of a map to real life, but Oaxaca is really tiny and everything is within one mile – the Cathedral, all the churches, markets, shops and restaurants – magnificent. There were churches everywhere which proves that where Cortez failed, priests didn't – they weren't looking for gold, they were there to give their version of it; in the words of God. And what a legacy they left – the churches were breathtaking. The ornate facades have crumbled slightly, but inside, they were so beautiful no one could help but wonder at the existence of an Almighty. Santo Domingo de Guzman in particular, is a building of sheer Masonic majesty and has stood there for over 500 years.

The city is like a time capsule and looks much the same today in architecture and produce as it would have done in the 16th century. It is a testament to tradition and the importance of preserving cultural identities and ethnic differences. It was so different to the London I'd left which is constantly metamorphosing into something more modern as if in a race.

And I felt as if I too was in a race, speeding around and seeing nothing, like a whistle stop tourist. Finally, I sat in the square, took the time to look around and realised that I was in a truly remarkable place that I'd first heard mentioned over 30 years ago. Suddenly I was looking through calmer eyes and simply realising where I was and how much there was to explore – everything.

Food in Oaxaca is supposed to be unique and the indoor/outdoor markets and street stalls come highly recommended. Mercado de la Mercad reminded me of the big produce market in Barcelona's Las Ramblas. Stalls were piled high with chickens the colour of the sun, sides of beef more blue than food colouring red, piles of shell fish, pastries, breads, chorizo, sweets, vegetables of every description and indoor barbecues where you could pick your steak and watch it cook - that's if you could see through the billowing smoke to which all the customers seemed impervious.

I had no idea what to try from the myriad on offer so allowed myself to be enticed by a smiling, plucky, young girl – how often do we just need a helping hand? She showed me minced beef which yes, I could eat, but seemed discombobulated when I pointed at the tacos etc and shook my head (I have a wheat and grain intolerance as well – not much fun in a land almost anywhere). She smiled beatifically and then she bade me sit down. She set to work frying the mince and then ladled swathes of yellow stuff that looked like plasticine all over it and then brought it over, (with the obligatory tacos) and yes, you've guessed it – cheese, but not like any cheese any of us would know and which, of course, I couldn't eat.

So there I sat, at a taco stall, trying to pick the beef out of what seemed like wallpaper paste AND she over charged me! I know they're poor and in comparison, I am rich, but I was on a sparse budget. Luckily, afterwards, when still trying to find real coffee and once again, failing, I met a local man who seemed beguiled by my plug story and treated me to a bowl

13

of instant "coffee" which was so weak, it was almost transparent.

Back out on the streets, in the late afternoon heat, I noticed how much pollution there was. Old decrepit cars, buses and trucks spluttered through the city belching toxins poisonous enough to make your eyes water and your lungs ache. The city seemed to be where old vehicles, especially VW Beetle cars, came to die. The exhausts were broken or missing and they just leaked fumes. No one seemed that bothered by it and for the few days I was there, neither did I but it did jar that somewhere so akin to nature could allow its pure air to decay.

That's not to say that it was all like that. There are many pedestrianised areas with leafy squares for just quiet contemplation or coffee shops and restaurants to enjoy throughout the day. There was a certain peace about the inner city and whilst they all had to make a living, living itself was more important than the making of money. It had a sense of honour and respect long gone in many places elsewhere and maybe that was because the people had been allowed to retain their own beliefs and not to be consumed by consumerism.

Breathing lightly, I headed home and so the first day was almost over and having found the only booze shop in town, I climbed the narrow, wobbly, metal staircase to the roof with my bottle of Chilean Red to celebrate the day. I might as well own up – I like a drink; I've drunk grown men under the table most of my life (including half of the Corfu Mafia but that really is another story), and all in all, it is one of my greatest pleasures. Which is just as well, because when there isn't much else to do, I could always enjoy myself. In fact, a word of warning to anyone who is thinking of travelling on your own; you have to be happy with your own company because you will more than likely spend vast tracts of time on your own.

14

And so there I was, up on the roof and I felt so good. I'd made it. I'd done it – my dream had come true and even though I was on my own, I wasn't lonely. I felt like a queen surveying her kingdom and as I watched the little lights of the little city come on, lighting up the surrounding hills like a Christmas tree, one thing I was sure of – it was a whole lot better than sitting at home on my own, fretting about my future.

****

I was awakened early with the peel of church bells and the crowing of cockerels. Feeling slightly more normal, I took a second look at my enormous bag which could seat two comfortably but which had lost a wheel in Houston where my flights connected. The old song, if anyone remembers it, "One wheel on my wagon, and I'm not rolling along" popped into my head. I thought: "Am I really prepared to lug this thing on one wheel over 5000 miles?"

Luckily and surprisingly (the budget again), I decided not to and so out I went again. Same trousers, same streets, same bemused faces, same tourist booth and after circumnavigating the town, I finally found a bag with two wheels. It was perhaps a little bigger than I needed – in fact on closer inspection, it would fit my 13 year old god daughter Rosa in. But never mind, it would do and choice was non-existent. And that was where I really discovered what everyone in Oaxaca did – they worked in the service industry and Gandhi would be so proud of them! One person opened the door of the shop and greeted me, two other people served me, another took my money and lastly, another described to me the exact details of the item AND the guarantee even though it was completely obvious I didn't understand a single word he said. And it was the same in every single shop and cafe and I was so pleased to see it – machines don't buy things, they just make more profit for the owners.

So, enormous bag on wheels safely stowed, I thought it was time I really ate something substantial. I'd passed a barbecue chicken shop earlier – huge racks of those yellow chickens – that's the quality of the food in Oaxaca, and so I headed back there. I pointed to "¼", was waved to a table and not long after, an enormous plate of perfect chicken, rice, salad and all manner of chilli sauces arrived and I am not even embarrassed to say, I ate like a pig. I was happy, they were happy and when I offered them what I thought it cost – next to nothing, they even gave me half of it back! If I could eat in a place like that every day, I would never cook again.

Almost too full to walk, I headed back into town with my (now) fully charged camera to really see what Oaxaca had and discovered the north of the city, which was basically the half a mile above the main square. It was Valentine's Day. I was surprised to find that they celebrated it but they certainly did. Everywhere, there were women selling flowers and enormous clouds of balloons all declaring love. There was such an innocence of affection it was simply heartening. One young couple sat on the steps of a church, the girl holding a 3ft teddy bear and they were just so in love. I asked if I could take their photo and it was as if that was the only excuse they needed to proclaim what was obvious – they would spend the rest of their lives together. It was all so uncomplicated.

And then I walked. The streets on the periphery were lined with shambolic shops and businesses but nearer the centre, everything was neater, more colourful and more expensive. Plastic tablecloths were replaced by linen, ramshackle grocers by artisan bakeries and gaudy baubles by exquisite jewellery. All roads led to the Plaza de la Constitucion, more commonly known as the Zocalo – the main square at the centre. Heavy stone walled buildings were fronted by spacious shaded porticos offering sanctuary from the midday sun. This was where the well-heeled of all nationalities grazed and gazed. Being February, it was warm but not hot, yet a languid torpor seemed to envelop everything for those few afternoon hours.

16

Nobody, including the vendors, was really interested in the pushy sale of textiles for which Oaxaca is famous – rugs, shawls, tablecloths and carpets. There was no frantic Souk-like sales pitch, just tiny old ladies selling lace, deeply lined Indian ladies with skin as tough as the leather goods they sold and little stalls selling all kinds of toys, tiny kitchen utensils I knew not what for, manned by men and children who seemed just happy to be there. The whole place oozed serenity and in a street away from the market where a new road was being laid, there was no roar of pneumatic drills, just workmen, dressed as they had always dressed; in straw hats, loose white cotton clothing and sandals, literally hewing kerb stones from bare rock and everyone, almost without exception, showed a simple courtesy that would make a misanthrope smile. Even back at the hostel, the girl, having realised morning coffee was something of a problem for me, led me into the back room, showed me a little two plate electric cooker and between us, we understood that I could use it. Not so daft to have taken my coffee pot after all.

The only thing left for me to do was to buy my bus ticket for the Pacific town of Puerto Escondido. I found the station easily enough – it was very close and marked on my now dilapidated map. The ticket lady couldn't understand why I only wanted just the one ticket. Where was my husband? She seemed aghast that I didn't have one and then amazed and shocked when I explained, with invented sign language, that I was travelling on my own. It wasn't the first time I'd met with this response and it would never be the last. Women, they think, do not travel on their own – ever.

I hoped that maybe I'd changed her way of thinking about the solo female traveller. We're not mad and any woman (or man) can do it. You just have to want to change your life enough. And should you choose to start your adventure in Mexico, start it in Oaxaca. It's a wonderful place and even though hardly anyone spoke English and I spoke no Spanish, I think we all had an experience to share.

17

OAXACA TO PUERTO ESCONDIDO

I was up early and then just sat in my room worrying about the bus journey ahead. I wasn't normally a nervous traveller but for some reason I couldn't calm myself. When I'd started travelling alone thirty years ago, I was confident and fearless, but not anymore. It was a strange feeling to know that I'd changed and that a trait of my personality, not used for eight years since I'd been on my lone trek to India, simply wasn't the same as I remembered and expected it to be. Was that what getting older was all about?

I tried not to think about it lest it undermined me further but couldn't help taking it a stage further. With youth, there was a blissful ignorance of things that might and could go wrong. With age, there was the expectation that ANYTHING might and could go wrong. My problem wasn't just a lack of confidence in everyone else; it was also a lack of confidence in me. I simply didn't trust things to go as planned – what if I got lost (why would I, the station was two streets away), what if I'd got the wrong time and missed it (why would I – it was written on the ticket), what if Mexico was just somewhere that nothing went as planned and timetables meant nothing?

In the end, I arrived at the bus station an hour early. It was already half full so either they were thinking the same as me or they had nowhere else to go. Shocked and surprised, bang on time at 10am, I boarded the mini bus with my super new huge bag and began the 250 mile journey south to the Pacific Ocean. I was just thinking how much Mexico reminded me of India, when we pulled into a town which had the same three wheeled tuk tuk taxis. If it wasn't for the music, Mexico and

19

India would be very similar – the same poverty, the same desperate street sellers, the same skinny cows, donkeys and goats grazing on the verges and the same absolutely appalling roads. There were pot holes everywhere which slows the traffic to a crawl and then, for some ludicrous reason, there were speed humps!

So I settled down for what was supposedly a seven hour journey, (how was that possible to cover only 250 miles?) and suddenly I wished I'd had a pee before we'd left. No matter, I was sure we'd stop for lunch but no – it was as if our macho driver was on a mission to prove that he could drive the whole way without stopping – for anything. Thankfully, the weaker of us demanded a stop or two and he looked at us as if we were utter failures – never mind that he got out and peed too...

And so the Sierra Madre. The mountains just went on and on and on and on. Just when you think you must be descending, up you go again; hour after hour and it was just a two lane road where overtaking should be banned but isn't. In the other direction came big old trucks laden with people with what looked like all their belongings – it was like watching a movie set in the dust bowl years of the USA – whole communities on the move. Luckily our driver wasn't a complete maniac and finally, we arrived at the little seaside town of Puerto Escondido. We were all uncomfortably hot and it was only when we stopped, that the driver turned on the air conditioning – that's one way of saving on his petrol allowance and making a little money on the side I suppose.

We were unceremoniously dumped at the side of the road and once again, I got out my mighty Rough Guide to Mexico. I approached a burly policeman with a very curiously shaped and very long thumb nail (?) and pointed at the map. I thought he'd understand that I wanted to know where I was and he'd just point it out. No. So I looked at my language section in the back of the guide and said "donde este?" Why I said that I don't know because he began to tell me in such an earnest way that I didn't have the heart to tell him I had no idea what he was saying and just nodded and motioned "right at the next corner", said "muchas gracias" and smiled. He smiled back with the obligatory gold tooth and off I went with my unfeasibly heavy bag.

I don't know how hot it was but after a few yards, I was pouring sweat like a cartoon character. The same harem trousers, usually so cool, stuck to my legs like cling film. I was hot. I was really hot. The pavement was full of high kerbs and steps and no place for a three stone bag on wheels. Why I didn't get a cab, I don't know – well I do; it would be the old budget thing again, never mind if I lost another wheel or two... I came across a couple of completely stoned dudes and asked if they spoke English and to my utter relief they did and gave me directions. The road flanking the sea seemed to go on forever and being the afternoon, most things were shut for the siesta. Everything seemed new, clean, bright and white – not the old relaxed fishing village I was expecting.

When finally I arrived at the Hotel Monte Cassino (£11 per night), I think I may have been delirious with heat and dehydration, but I managed to garble that I had a reservation. The young man who looked remarkably like Antonio Banderas (good) asked why I hadn't called ahead and he'd have picked me up. Words utterly failed me. He told me how pretty I was (it must have been my wild expression), and despite being at least 20 years younger, asked if he could kiss me and offered to carry my bag.

I said no to the kiss but yes to the bag and he physically buckled under the weight of it. He lent it against the wall; it fell over and almost broke the gate. We both looked at that gargantuan bag and probably thought the same thing – what the hell has she got in there? (Of course, I knew - apart from all the electrical goods and the coffee pot, there was my diary, travel books and novels – I was yet to lighten my load with a Kindle or a smart phone. There were also 500 vitamins and a sub section of toiletries; three different types of spot cream to avoid that unsightly flare up, night and day creams, pre and after sun lotion, cleanser, toner, eye makeup remover – the list went on. They weighed more than my clothes but if I was to keep up appearances, ALL were strictly necessary. Does anyone want to look their age?)

Anyway, there was no way either of us was going to lug that bag up a flight of stairs, so he put me in the only ground floor room he had – never mind that it had two double beds and was clearly designed for four. We simply didn't care. He dumped the bag in the room, gave me the key and I headed straight for my very own bathroom and a COLD shower. They never have hot water, never, ever, ever. But this time they did, and ONLY hot water – unbelievable but who cared. I washed three days of grime off and prepared for the next leg of my adventure.

I was only supposed to stay for two nights but I just knew I needed longer. My room was super comfortable, the hotel was small and quaint with an upstairs sun terrace and a colourful, calming courtyard and I just wanted to relax. The Italian owner, Mario, said that I could stay as long as I liked and then we got talking. What a legend! He's a fit and spry 75 but looks way younger and very much like the actor Christopher Walken. He's Italian but was sent to military school in England when he was nine, later studied architecture and at the age of 23 went to Benin as an engineer with absolutely no experience and it just went from there; working all over Africa, getting caught in wars and god knows what and surviving. He was one of those people who were totally full of outrageous but true stories and we talked the night away – he didn't even mind me slipping out to buy a bottle of very warm wine – he did however think I was insane to drink it – "serve at room temperature" had a totally different meaning in the 40 degree heat of Mexico...

****

The hotel didn't do breakfast but instead, they directed me to, of all things, a perfect Italian coffee shop – Vivaldi's. The cafe sat on the wide, empty tourist thoroughfare parallel to the beach. I chose an outside table on the terrace and in the early morning sunshine, looked out to the sea with the little town behind me. Like all towns in boiling hot places, it was all painted white and rose up into the surrounding hills. It was full of little shops selling all sorts of souvenirs; small medium and huge, all wonderfully painted but which I simply couldn't carry. It was fairly empty in February and not what I was expecting. I suppose I thought it would be full of alternative people seeking adventure, fun and sun but, probably, they'd all gone back to work or college after the winter breaks and before Easter and summer. What I was left with were the people who could afford to stay on – mostly retired Canadians. Some never went back. So, with excitement as unlikely as snow, my only option was to find interesting people. One such man, Aldy, replete with straw hat, gnarled countenance and very blue eyes happened to be sitting next to me and so we got talking.

Maybe I'm lucky in my encounters or maybe I just choose the people who *look* the most interesting, because he was also incredible. He'd been a sailor who was caught in a hurricane with 40 foot waves crashing through the windows and nearly capsizing the boat. He'd got the bends whilst deep sea diving and had never fully recovered and he'd also been a worker in a chicken factory – he said KFC modify their chicken so much it doesn't even have feathers anymore and they can't even call it "chicken". That's right folks, coming to a table near you. We agreed that big business will lie, deny and only when absolutely necessary, pay up.

I meant to go to one of the many beaches, but got talking to Mario again and once the beer started flowing, I wasn't going anywhere. We talked all afternoon, just like I used to and I was reminded of how much I missed it. We talked love, life and passion. He told me about his stormy relationship as a youth and I told him about my wild erratic one of eleven years. We both agreed that in the end, endless passion just wears you out. Sadly, his wife had died six years ago and without her, he felt pointless; like a seaside town at the end of the season when everyone has gone and suddenly, there was no purpose. I hoped that maybe I'd managed to cheer him up and promised to write a new blurb for his hotel listing.

There wasn't really much to do at night other than eat – fried everything with rice salad and of course tacos and no matter that Aldy had taught me to say "no tacos", (sin pan) they still turned up wrapped in a cloth to keep them warm. But never mind, with my warm wine, my super laptop and cable TV, I remembered that there was nothing I liked to do more than write and so I got to work.

****

Day three and I was determined to swim in the Pacific – after all, that was the reason I was there. I put on my new dashing red bikini (yoga and zumba meant that thankfully, my body hadn't let me down the way my men had), slathered Factor15 tinted body lotion over my very white body, wrapped a 20 year old trusted Indian sarong around me and headed off.

I walked across the road to where the fishing boats lined up, stepped onto the baking sand and wandered around the cove to the three mile long Zicatela Beach, home to the Mexican "Pipeline" – waves so big that you can surf through the tubes. Nothing much was going on; the few cafes and holiday bungalows in the distance were closed and it all seemed a bit forsaken. But between May and August when the surfing championships take place, it would be completely different and full of international surfer dudes looking effortlessly cool. I might have felt slightly out of place if I'd turned up then, but as it was deserted, I felt fine.

Even though the waves weren't massive, they still sounded like a jet fighter flying overhead and all I wanted to do was throw myself in. I wondered if it was safe to swim. I was

24

reminded of my favourite film when Robert Duvall says "If I say it's safe to surf this beach, it's safe to surf this beach". I asked a surfer and he looked at me as if I was mad. He went into great detail about the undertow, how a wave could come from nowhere and knock me over and I'd be disorientated and would have to hold my breath until I figured out which way was up, and how people drown all the time and how he wouldn't let his daughter swim there and that really, I'd be much better off going around the headland to the safer beaches.

I went in anyway and it was GREAT! The waves were huge; knocking me over, dragging me under and spitting me out, time after fantastic time. I hadn't seen waves that big since a couple of days prior to a hurricane hitting Palm Beach when the lifeguards were practically begging me not to go in. I swam there too.

Ragged and happy, I emptied out the sand which had gathered like two unsightly logs in my bikini bottoms and laid down to sunbathe without realizing that the surf had washed off all my rubbishy sun tan lotion. So there I lay, baking in the baking heat, and along came a really good looking man who waded into the surf, pulled his T shirt up around his shoulders, a la James Dean and started to pull on his dick. I wasn't sure if I was seeing right, but there he was, wagging it at me and grinning! Maybe I should have taken it as a compliment, but it seemed like time to go and it was just as well, because by the time I'd walked back to the hotel, my legs looked like chorizo – oh how I laughed. I was reminded of the Russians in Goa who would lay on the beach the colour of the whitest dinner plate and leave the colour of raw beef. My skin was so hot, you could have fried eggs on it.

Weirdly, that didn't put the Antonio Banderas look-alike receptionist off – he thought it was "cute" and asked if he could take me to the beach on his day off – tomorrow. Why not, I thought, I didn't have anything else to do. So moving swiftly on, he didn't take me to the beach around the headland which he'd told me was so lovely, instead he took me to Marinaro beach practically opposite. This was where the fishing boats moored and with their outboard motors haphazardly leaking petrol and oil, it wasn't the cleanest beach he could have chosen.

Regardless, he asked a couple of fishermen tending their nets to look after our bags and insisted that we went for a swim. He asked me about my husband and my children and when I said I had neither he looked at me with what - deepest sympathy or pity or just plain confusion as if this was the worst thing that could ever happen. "But why", he asked, "when you are so pretty?" It was beyond his comprehension that this was my choice rather than a cruel blow that I would never get over.

He was quite a sweet bloke but clearly wanted more from me than I wanted to give and really, all I wanted was to body surf. So there he was, treading water and serenading me (?), when a huge wave would crash over him and I'd turn and be whisked off into shore, leaving him bobbing about with a surprised look on his face. He kept asking me for a "hoog", – a hug, telling me that he had a son but was divorced and trying to do the right thing and how happy he'd be if I let him take me out to dinner. Maybe he thought that if I didn't have a husband, I was clearly having no sex and he could put that right for me and then be on a one way ticket to England. Hoog or not, I thought, I really didn't have anything else to do and so accepted his invitation – to dinner that is. He was overjoyed and tried to hold my hand all the way back.

He didn't turn up and Mario told me that rather than being an admirable single parent, he was already on his second wife – the cook at the hotel who had seen him fawning over me! Unbelievable. I toyed with the idea of going out to a few bars Aldy had recommended but I couldn't bring myself to breeze in, as I once had done, sit myself down and wait for people to come and talk to me. It's one thing being in your 20s, 30s and 40s but somehow, it's just not the same in your 50s when you seem to become invisible. And so, my last night in Puerto Escondido was again spent in the excellent company of super Mario. He seemed relieved that he didn't have to regale me with the same stories everyone else expected of him as a living legend and instead, we had real conversations about his life here and now.

We talked like old friends or new lovers, confiding secrets, dreams and regrets. At one point, I wondered if I should just stay in Puerto Escondido rather than explore the coast, but in the end, I just thought that it would be too easy. The whole point of me being away travelling, was to write my journal, have a huge adventure, test myself and ultimately change and grow from the experience. "It's never too late to be who you might have been", as George Eliot quite rightly said.

And so after four days in Puerto Escondido, I once again loaded up my enormous bag, gave Mario a huge hoog, promised to go back if I didn't like it elsewhere and set off to wave down the bus, pay the equivalent of £1.70 and headed off on the 50 mile journey east along the coast to San Agustinillo.

SAN AGUSTINILLO

Three of us got off at the abandoned, dusty crossroads and the three of us shared a taxi along the dirt track into the tiny town. They were German girls from Hamburg who, of course, spoke perfect English. I had already booked at the Posada Paloma and they too went in to see if there was a room – there wasn't – the circus was coming to the next town, Mazunte, and everything was booked. Thank god I'd planned ahead.

The hotel was new and gorgeous; a big open air reception and bar, with little steps up to the terrace, all painted with blocks of colour from aubergine to orange. Numerous hammocks rocked in the breeze and the most verdant plants grew everywhere. The lovely animated lady on reception, Maricella, showed me to my room and what a beautiful room! A lavish mosquito net cloaked the double bed, it had a tiled floor, ceiling fan, little desk and chair and hooks to hang all of my clothes on - and I had a lot.

Outside of the room, on the veranda was another table and chair replete with a little bookcase stuffed with novels and travel books in every language you could think of. Even the shared open air bathroom was a joy of bold green and pinks and it's not often I will ever say that. I don't think I'd been as happy with a room since the fort in Jaisalmeer in Rajasthan. At £15 per night, it was the most expensive thus far but there were no cheap rooms there. There was no cheap anything. You could almost say that it was an up market town.

The weirdest thing though, all the guests at the hotel seemed to be retired Canadians even though this was billed as a more cosmopolitan town. Dixie, the 60 something lady in the next room said that the towns either side of San Agustinillo were the party towns which were all right if you liked dread locks and tattoos and I wondered if indeed, they might be more my type of towns. I thought they would be more like Goa and Dixie even said that they were full of hippies who came in the 60's and never went home – exactly like Goa. That's not to say that I was a hippie, more that I liked laid back non-judgemental people who liked to eat the lotus.

I was only booked there for three days but just knew, once again, that it was a room I wanted to spend more time in, so I spoke to Maricella, (who it turned out, had studied mime in London) and she said she'd see what she could do. Later, Fabian the unfeasibly good looking half Mexican, half French, blue eyed owner told me that I could stay in his house for an unfeasibly enormous price. I said it was too much, he said it was a big house, I said I only need a room and finally, we agreed that he'd find me something else for two days and then I could go back for a further two days. Dixie said "didn't you tell him you're really good company?" We hadn't spoken so much and I was surprised at her lovely compliment, proving that you never can tell what people will make of you.

It was time to explore so still being slightly sunburnt, I donned my black 1950s style swimsuit replete with little skirt, and off I went. I crossed the road, walked down the steps between the buildings to the beach and there it was. I was astonished at just how glorious it was. Palm trees swayed along the entire length of it (maybe a mile or so), big waves pounded around the bay and there was hardly anyone in sight other than a few fishermen and their boats moored up for the day. I walked the length of it passing all sorts of cabanas, new and old, and many little restaurants, mostly empty, which perched on the edge.

Doubling back along the one street through town, everyone was so friendly. The locals languidly tended their shops which housed just the bare necessities – a few sacks of rice and flour, exhausted vegetables, dusty wine bottles and tins, and yet all, without exception, boasted an enormous rumbling Coca Cola fridge bursting with sugary cold drinks of every colour with a few beers stashed at the back. I doubted that they could believe what had happened to their town. Workmen were laying new pavement, others were rigging up street lighting whilst others were adding finishing touches to their new homes. Less than 20 years ago, it was just a fishing village with a road running behind the beach and a small crop of houses climbing up the hill behind.

That is essentially what it still was but with more houses/guest houses rambling further up the hill offering far more luxury than the locals could probably have imagined. The old cantinas were still there but slowly being edged out by more sophisticated tastes and wallets. The food was still mostly sea food or chicken, but it was now fashioned into more elaborate dishes of Italian and French design. Some restaurants needed to be booked whilst others stood empty, shifting with the season's fancy. There weren't many bars and nothing raucous went on. Basically, it was a wholesome town, with wholesome people and the lights were quite literally, out by 10pm.

There was even a vegetarian restaurant – not that I'm a vegetarian but I really needed some pure goodness and that's exactly what I had – a veritable mountain of salad with quinoa. I asked a fellow diner about San Agustinillo and he said that he'd been going there for years and whilst Mazunte and Zipolite were being expanded and ruined, this town couldn't get any bigger because it was hemmed in by cliffs.

And there was one other crucial issue – fresh water. There wasn't enough. So like all those ancient abandoned cities strewn across the earth for lack of water, this was one town that *couldn't* get any bigger. It was only when I thought about the limitations of the simple need for drinking water, that I realised that Canada, with all of its FRESH water, would be the last habitable place on earth and they'd be mounting the stockades in the not too distant future. When I told the Canadians that, they laughed. But I wasn't joking.

****

My veritable vat of breakfast coffee came from a gleaming industrial espresso machine which the young girl (who doubled as the cleaner), took great delight in managing. She looked about 13 years old but as she had her own baby and husband, I presumed she was older. She seemed so proud of her job and to be working in such beautiful surroundings. Nothing was too much to ask. Such a refreshing change from home where some shop assistants seemed to think they were doing you a favour.

It was time for another swim but this time, taking no chances, I slapped on factor 30 sun cream and headed back across the road to the beach. Weirdly, the waves were bigger there than they were on the "surfer" beach I'd left behind, but maybe it was just the time of year. The bay was made up of long beaches, broken by rocky outcrops and had condors circling silently above on the warm airy thermals. I found a bay with whopping waves and other swimmers (apparently, you can't be sure there aren't rip tides), dumped my stuff and waded in.

The waves were huge! It reminded me of when I and my brother Sean were little kids and we'd swim like dolphins in waves too big and seas too rough for our own good, but somehow survived. This was similar. I felt like a piece of tumbleweed, being hurled, rolled, dragged under and finally chucked out on the shore. When the waves broke, it was like a liquid avalanche; deafening, fierce, unstoppable and totally wild. It's curious that we associate the colour red with danger when often, it is the white terror that is more deadly. I loved it and must have been in there for an hour until the skin on my fingers looked like prunes. And it was a good job I liked swimming so much, because there wasn't much else to do...

32

I wondered what I expected? Somewhere like Goa I suppose where it would be full of my type of people – travellers looking for some fun and adventure in a land completely different to the one they had come from; people looking for a totally new experience of culture in every possible way; from aromas, to food to colours to religion to tradition – in fact everything and once they'd found their spot, stayed put and returned year after year. But it wasn't like that in San Agustinillo. People, mostly Canadians, went to Mexico to get out of the cold and do pretty much what they would do at home – not much.

They weren't there to celebrate and embrace Mexican life at all. Some of them even stayed in purpose built "condo's" within gated communities so that they didn't have to mix with the locals. They just kept themselves to themselves. The Canadians at Posada Paloma seemed content to sit outside their rooms playing cards. One of them just sat alone looking at his iPad until it was time to go to bed at 9pm. I wondered if it's what he expected. I also wondered if they'd all seen those old movies when Mexico was portrayed as some exotic home from home except with cocktail parties and gorgeous people all out to have a good time on the cheap in the sun and expected it to be the same.

I know Dixie and her husband Ken didn't – they were well travelled but it did seem peculiar that for many others, there was no adventure intended, they just wanted to relax out the winter, eat and sleep – very early. They were really nice people but I found it a bit weird. They were not even there to meet people, seemingly happy with the people they already knew. And almost in proof of this point, I got talking to a Canadian in a restaurant who came from Quebec and it was like wading through custard. I was sure I was asking interesting questions about architecture, culture, language, heritage etc and he just didn't respond. In the end, I gave up, ate so much chilli sauce I swear it was coming out of my eyes and just went back to my room where at least I didn't have to TRY to talk to anyone.

Instead, I sat outside my room until the mosquitoes drove me inside and gave up on the idea of finding some fun. There was nothing for it except to do some reading, writing and of course, some drinking. When all the lights were out, I headed to the bathroom and closed my door to stop bugs getting in. As soon as I heard the final click of the door, I knew I'd made a mistake – I'd locked myself out!

What was I to do? I tried to jimmy the bottom of the window frame off with a tiny coin I'd found on the floor so that I could reach around the mosquito gauze to the key on the table, but all I managed to do was break off a piece of the wood. Luckily, I could still hear movement in the next room so tentatively knocked the door. Dixie came out and on hearing my plight, was keen to help – this was EXCITEMENT! So armed with her knife, which also didn't work, and then her torch, we wandered around the deserted, dark, reception looking for help but finding none. She asked if I had a phone and she could ring Fabian – yes, I did have a phone – in my room.

In the end, she leant me a sheet and pillow from their spare bed – she even offered the bed but it all seemed too much like "*The Walton's*", the three of us saying good night with a little harmonica beep at the end. So I went and slept out in the open air of the bar in a hammock, cocooned in the sheet to stop me getting eaten alive by bugs and that's where I was when Ramos, the so called night receptionist, burst through the door like a rampant bear. He raided the beer fridge and filled his rucksack (?) and on seeing me wrapped in the sheet like some sort of ghostly apparition, nearly fainted. Luckily, up close, he recognised me and let me back into my room.

****

In the morning I appealed for clemency, forgiveness, understanding and sympathy and got all four – apparently, Ramos should have been there and it was HIS entire fault.

Obviously I was happy to go along with that one. Who knew what the next night would bring but the following day, the circus was coming to Mazunte, the next town along. I almost wondered if I should have brought my juggling clubs but realised that would have been even more insane that bringing all the other necessary nonsense I had with me.

THE CIRCUS COMES TO MAZUNTE

After three days in my paradise room, it was time to move out for two nights. Fabian told me I could leave some things with him so that I didn't have to lug everything with me – good idea. But even so, when I left, my bag still weighed a ton. He'd booked another room for me and told me to just climb the steps. STEPS. I was reminded of arriving in Vaschist high in the Himalayas and having to climb "steps" which turned out to be huge great boulders which even Sherpa Tensing would have baulked at.

These steps weren't quite as bad, but still, they snaked all the way up the hill past other little houses hewn from the rock and patches of fenced off land where they grew their crops and kept their ducks and chickens. Even so, when I finally arrived at El Recinto del Viento, looking wild eyed and exhausted, no one told me I looked cute. They just sat me down, gave me cold homemade lemonade and once I'd recovered, the lovely Aline showed me around.

The house was built by hand and with love. Just like the old style palapas cabins it was styled on, it stood on stilts, was made from brick, wood and bamboo and had a palm leaf roof. There were steps up to the heavy bare wooden door which opened onto the living area – a wide open space strung with hammocks and save for a waist high wall, was completely wide open to the elements. The palm roof hung down to provide shade from the ever present sun allowing the fresh breeze to zephyr through.

There was a big old wooden table and chairs, a little Christmas tree still in situ and at the far end, a small patio filled with plants and cushions and a view of the ocean crashing below. To the right, behind a bamboo wall was the cosy kitchen. It almost surprised me that there was electricity and a calor gas cooker which, incidentally, I could use and so once again, the lunacy of bringing my own stove top coffee pot didn't seem quite so ridiculous. Further on, there was a little shower room and separate toilet, also open to the air and seemingly hewn from rock. It was so at one with the surrounding nature, it might as well have grown there. It was wonderful.

The couple – Aline and Miguel had been building it for 17 years and they too belonged to nature. They both exuded serenity and had a slow graceful way of movement where time was taken to appreciate everything. Aline showed me upstairs and gave me a choice of rooms – one on the Pacific side with little light and one at the back with more. She said that the wind changed direction at night and came from the hills. Thinking of hot stuffy nights, the room at the back, with a big opening to the east was the one I chose. There was no glass in the window, just a wooden panel cut from the bamboo which could be opened or indeed, closed. The simple wooden bed was draped with the obligatory mosquito net and an equally simple table and chair sat beneath the window. Once again, I was delighted.

Still in awe of everything, back downstairs, a tall attractive woman appeared from an en suite room I hadn't even noticed. She had a mound of grey hair plaited to her waist, glowing brown skin, an aura of tranquillity AND she spoke English! She was Canadian (weren't they all) but she was different. She was French speaking, had travelled all over the world taking photos and there she was, having driven down the thousands of miles for some karmic sun.

We instantly liked one another. She had that easy feel and smile about her and reminded me of the German Baroness Carla, I'd become friends with in India – they even wore the same suede moccasins. She said she was going to walk into

Mazunte and did I want to go – of course I did. I hadn't had a good conversation in days and so we set off in the blazing heat (sun creamed up of course – me not her – she was the colour of caramel) for the next town along.

Ten years ago, my nephew Barrie described Mazunte as a small hamlet with a couple of cabanas on the beach. Not anymore it wasn't. It was like a proper little town, not exactly pretty as all the buildings were mostly new and made of concrete and catered for all of the new young people who'd opted for a different life style, but it was welcoming. Who knows how the word spreads. But those people were from all over Mexico and Europe. One girl who sold the equivalent of cheese straws on the beach, came from Benecasim which is like the Glastonbury of Spain i.e. it has a music festival rather than a Tor, and she said that she didn't want to raise her kids wanting all the rubbish synonymous with living in the West – computer games etc etc etc. And her look was one of sheer calm and reverence for the life she now found herself living and they all seemed to be like that.

It made me think about the life we're all expected to live; get a good education, a good job and settle into the system of house, mortgage, family and the endless task of living to earn rather than living to learn about the alternatives. The people there had voted with their feet and simply walked away. They were lithe, lean, taut and tanned. They had bright white eyes and bright white smiles. They were uncontaminated by the consumer disease of the West. They didn't really drink or smoke cigarettes – they just seemed to have a real empathy with the Earth and nature and they exuded happiness, tranquillity and confidence. After all, how much money do you really need when all you buy is the food that you don't grow or rear yourself?

So we wandered to the little beach, which wasn't as good as "our" beach in San Agustinillo – the waves were smaller and it was full of people. And as if by magic, she just happened to have a little something with her. Marijuana is legal in Canada for medicinal purposes – the state grows it on huge farms – she worked on one and said half the population had a prescription. Who would have thought that Canada would be so liberal? So we smoked it and the whole day took on a totally new direction. We talked about everything, shifting on tangents as diverse as faces. There was only a year between us in age so we shared a lot of cultural history and influences. I just couldn't believe my luck – only the day before, I was wondering how much time I could spend on my own listening to other people and there I was with an exceptional, fascinating person who was as interested in talking as I was. Originally from Quebec, she now lived in a place called Nelson in British Columbia which sounded like possibly the best place to live in Canada.

So there we were, sitting in the shade working up a thirst when she suggested we get a Mojito from the best rum stall in town. Was I hearing right? Was my new friend seriously suggesting we go and get a drink in the middle of the afternoon – I was there like a shot (of rum) and it was so good. It must have been at least a litre, cold as Christmas and as strong as Samson – eureka!

We could see the circus beginning to set up, so we got ourselves prime positions at the front of the stage. The school brass band kicked off first and it was so traditional. A big tuba umpa umping, trumpets, trombones and saxophones and they were so proud and happy to be playing there for all the strangers (in both senses of the word) and then the mayor gave a short speech. I almost wanted him to be in full military regalia replete with epaulets but he just wore trousers and a short sleeved shirt - maybe those days were gone.

This was a Circe de Soleil type circus rather than one with animals, and the performers, like the dreadlocked, tattooed people of the town, came from all over Europe and Mexico. There were clowns, although without speaking Spanish, the words which accompanied their performance were lost to me but the trapeze and the juggling wasn't (damn – I should have brought my clubs...). Many small children sat cross legged at the front of the make shift stage but I wasn't sure if it was what they or their parents expected. "Circus" probably still conjured images of The Big Top and animals and with neither on offer, after awhile the children started to wander off to the food stalls dragging their parents with them.

I too had a sense of disappointment and it was almost a relief when the sun set and the insects came out. With no super duper chemical deet to rub on, I was soon eaten alive and thankfully we had to walk back (in the pitch black) with only a low crescent moon, once again, hung like a hammock, and a million stars to light our way. When we finally reached "home" we bought a couple of beers, had more smoke, talked for another hour or so and then we retired – Andree to her ground floor room and me up the twisting wooden stairs, again in the dark, wondering how I'd ever find my way and not break my neck.

I finally found the light switch (not on the wall where you might expect it but hanging from the ceiling), found my way in through my mosquito net, laid down on my bed and contemplated the stars through the glassless window, listened to the cicadas croaking to one side and the slam of the pacific to the other and realised that what I'd thought was paradise (the beautiful room of Posada Paloma) wasn't – this was – having someone to communicate with on every level in perfect surroundings.

The other thought I had was that as we wondered the streets, lots of people were smiling at us in a strange way and it suddenly occurred to me that what we were, to them, was a couple of older, reverent (not irrelevant) women who had been sleeping on beaches and embracing that life, long before they were born and there we were, in the same place at the same time, leading an alternative life too. All that, and it was still only 9.30pm and as I listened to the waves, it sounded like a piano player's fingers running over the keys to

41

disappear into the distance and then begin all over again. The ocean is such a scintillating sound to fall asleep to but cicadas are not and in the morning, I changed my room for the ocean side.

****

Pochutla is a dusty little town 20 miles inland that you only went to if you needed a bank. But on Monday's, farmers from everywhere around crowded in, set up their stalls and offered their goodness from beetroots the size of your head, spring onions the size of light bulbs, pineapples as bounteous and ornate as a Mayan palace, radishes the size of a heart, those big yellow chickens as in Oaxaca and coffee stalls which ground brown and black beans to a powder of fine aromatic intoxication. Andree and a fellow Canadian were going, so of course I went along too.

The road there, just like all the other roads, was long and pot holed and piled up with vehicles in varying states of dilapidation. Either side, the countryside was laden with crops. Even the hillier scrub land was dotted with sheep or goats. It seemed that nothing was left to waste. The town was, as described, a dusty old lop-sided worn out shanty of peeling and neglected buildings. The only modern facades belonged to the many banks from all over Europe and North America. Without tourists, I doubted there would be more than one or two. There were also dozens of pharmacies each with their own consultation room, selling either over priced branded products or cheaper generic drugs. Health care is free in Mexico and later, we were to see just what that had to offer.

We headed into the market, splayed out through the streets at the centre of town, as if we were kids in a wonderland. I just couldn't get over the size of everything. It was as if it had all been genetically modified to be huge but it wasn't. That was just what nature could do on its own. It was similar to Oaxaca except the people were different. The Amerindians

42

were nowhere to be seen and instead, the people were small and compact and seemed to be more aligned with the Spanish settlers. They also seemed to be gruffer and rather than smile, they just bundled things up and threw them at you. We loaded our bags up anyway and then I loaded my belly with yet more rotisserie chicken and then disaster. Andree miss stepped and twisted her foot.

Nobody wants to be that poor holidaymaker wearing a great big plaster cast and phoney smile and Andree was no exception. She didn't think it was broken so her friend fetched the car and I know it's not very considerate, but all I could think was "Oh no, don't tell me we won't get to the booze shop!" Were all Canadians calm in a crisis? We got to the wine shop, and we loaded up there too.

Back at the house, Andree with help, climbed the many steps – not a good place for someone who can't walk. She seemed so upset. She said she wouldn't be able to do any of the things that we planned and was worried that I'd get bored and leave for another town as I'd originally intended to. I reassured that I wasn't going anywhere. Talking is more important to me than walking – I can do that anywhere. Especially when you consider that I'd been dying for conversation for so long at home that I'd taken the drastic step of transporting myself to another continent in order to find some. I wasn't about to walk out on the precise person I'd been looking for for a very long time. I even suggested that she come with me onto Colombia and beyond but she had her car to think about and it just wasn't going to happen.

So, immobile, there wasn't a lot of movement there in paradise. Personally, being bone idle, that didn't bother me a bit. Instead of going for long walks as we'd planned, what we did was head down the steps to the beach, she'd sit with her foot in the surf whilst I'd dash off and crash through the waves and in between, we'd talk. About anything we liked.

She told me that Mexicans didn't really swim in the sea – they

43

preferred pools or lagoons. I couldn't imagine, with a huge great ocean, why that could be true. And then I looked – the waves were so big, as a child you could never withstand it – you'd be mown down like skittles and simply dragged out to sea. She also told me that when she was living in a little village in Africa, the town hall – basically a mud hut with a palm leaf roof, was deliberately made low so that no one could stand up straight and dominate the meeting – could you imagine, say, the United Nations, if they all had to sit and crouch and discuss, rather than swaggering and thumping lecterns?

When the sun got too hot, we headed for the shade, smoked a little something pure and strong and then we headed for one of the bars along the beach just out of the sun's rays and we'd either have a coconut water which is literally, the top sliced off of a whole green coconut with a little straw pushed through which, when we'd finished, they chopped in half and gave back to us to eat, or we'd have a cold beer or we'd have a mojito. It was so pleasant not to have to make too many decisions. I once had to make over 200 decisions a day and it was such hard work, especially as 30 grizzly men relied on me to get it right. You can imagine the relief then, when simply what to drink, was the main decision of the day. Bliss really.

And there in the shade, we swapped stories of our lives – she'd won a beauty pageant in Canada – she'd be the curvaceous good looking Bridget Bardot type model, draped over the bonnet of the most expensive car. She'd also had exhibitions of her photographs and art work all over Canada – I saw them and they were spectacular. And I told her about my dad telling me that my great great grandfather was the King of Ireland and I, naturally, deduced that I was a princess and from that point forward, lorded it over everyone – I wasn't popular at school. She laughed out loud at that one and I had to say "I'm serious" and she said "I know!" I also told her of my writing, my plays and my poetry and my days as a fearless motorbike courier in London making it in a man's

44

world.   Between us, we seemed to have achieved quite a lot in the maverick market. She read my tarot cards for me and it all made sense – she's like one of those earth mothers who has seen the light.

****

After two nights up at the "Special House of the Wind", I was back down the steps to the Paloma for the next two nights. It was just as beautiful as I remembered and it was like going home. I like being sociable but like everyone else (I presume), we all need our own space and at the other place, it was the home of a family and it FELT like the home of a family. I called back up to see Andree and once again we sat outside on the little wall and talked with such openness it was like talking with a very old friend. Until she spotted a scorpion coming towards us, that is. Fernando, who looked like a native Indian and probably was – long lush black hair and dark eyes - came to the rescue and just put a glass on top of it, paper beneath it and released it out onto the hill, just like you would an (inoffensive) spider anywhere.

He told of us about the enchanted Pueblos all over Mexico and that the government sponsor them to keep the magic of Mexico flowing. He also said that if you are bitten by a scorpion and live, if you are bitten again, your body resists the poison but your mind is taken on a magical intoxicated journey and rather than fearing a scorpion, you embrace it. How wonderful to think that free thinking was still encouraged – provided it didn't lead to dissent...

Weirdly, I felt that I couldn't dominate Andree's time and that inside the House of the Wind, they would be missing her, so after awhile, I was back down the steps to home. And then a really weird thing happened. When I appeared, Dixie gave me a great big welcome home hug and we all started to talk; about books, the plays I'd written, travelling and god knows what, and I had a really great time! Funny how first impressions can be (and often are) entirely wrong. Don't

45

judge a book by its cover, we are told, but if we didn't, why do publishers spend so much money getting the cover right? God knows what they thought of me at first – god knows what anyone makes of me at first, but we all changed our minds that night.

****

In the morning, it was back up to the steps to collect Andree and take her to the beach where we once again talked for hours. Maybe it was the thought that we'd maybe never see one another again that allowed us to be so honest and open about our lives. We talked boyfriends, past and recently present, husbands, being married, feminism and the indignity at having to buy our own drinks – at that one she howled with laughter – she thought exactly the same as me and said that her daughter was a stripper and made an absolute fortune and was in no way exploited – she had a beautiful body, didn't mind showing it off and men most certainly didn't mind paying to see it – what could possibly be wrong with that? It's like saying that it's wrong to be an athlete or cash in on your brain. They are all gifts; there to be used.

We parted in the early evening but not before she had ordered garlic prawns for me – a feast I was to have nearly every day thereafter. I returned to Paloma for a last night of serenity and peace and a convivial Canadian evening brimming with wine and conversation – at least they liked to drink, especially Dixie who I was really growing quite fond of.

****

I had been wondering what my bill would be? I was supposed to leave an online review at airbnb.com for them but thought I'd wait to see if I'd been charged for breaking the window (and a glass). Nothing! I was so happy that they hadn't blamed the damage on me even though it was entirely my fault. I used their wi fi one last time and chatted to the lovely

46

receptionist Maricella. She was divorced with three children and I asked her if, when she looked at her children and saw her ex-husband in them, did she feel resentment. No, she said, because he was so handsome and so were her children! Finally, we ALL hugged and I was out on the street and back up the steps to the House of the Wind and my airy room at the front, refreshed by the wind from the ocean.

It was then back to the dusty old town of Pochutla, to get Andree's foot x-rayed. She couldn't drive so we went in the collectivo van which was an experience in itself. This was a canvas covered mini truck with two bench seats along the sides and standing room in between. It was great fun swaying about, jammed between an entire cross section of people from farmers in work clothes to gold strewn tourists talking about the house they intended to buy. It was also laughably inexpensive although we had to get a taxi from the bus stop to the hospital.

Mexicans are proud of their health care and wagged a dismissive finger at what was on offer in the States. I presumed that meant that what was on offer would be first class but it wasn't. The hospital was a relatively new concrete monstrosity like many hospitals world-wide, but as soon as we walked through the door, it was chaos, bedlam and filth. Sick people just waited in vain for attention; strung out on stretchers or slumped in chairs and then I suddenly thought – that was what it was like in England the last time I looked. Weird the way it is all put into perspective.

I didn't even want to go in there and preferred to wait outside except that I wanted to use the toilet. Surely they'd be clean, but no. In parts of Mexico, toilets are as filthy as they are in some of the filthiest places in the world and it doesn't make any difference whether you are in a hospital, a restaurant or a bar and NEVER presume anyone has washed their hands after using one. Half of the time, there isn't even a sink, let alone water and soap. I'm no cleanliness fanatic but there is something about public toilets that always compels me to wash.

Andree, after an hour of being shunted around (she had health insurance - how long it would have taken if she hadn't), found out it wasn't broken. She was told to rest it and it would heal in a week or so. As if by magic, we both suggested, simultaneously, that we could drive back to Oaxaca together in her car – me to catch my plane to Mexico City and her to see the sights. I wondered if it did happen, would it be like a Thelma and Louise type of adventure except without the dead bodies and the cliff hanger of an ending...

****

The little daughter's birthday arrived there at the House in the Wind and so did her entire extended family, so rather than being like a guest house, it was more like an over-crowded airport lounge, with people everywhere, one bathroom for all 12 of us, scorpions and boa constrictors in the garden and bugs as big as bats in the house. In the morning, we were all there in the kitchen making our coffee with an assortment of gadgets from my stove top, to filter machine and Andree's filter drip top holder. It was like a huge chaotic cafe with Elena, the tiny waist-high maid of indeterminate age from 40 to 60, frying golden coloured omelettes and smiling all the time. She owned an organic corn farm outside of town but there wasn't much to do between harvests and, watching corn grow, I presumed, was as boring as watching paint dry.

Elena was very happy up there surrounded by children and so was Aline's mum who was down from Mexico City. When I asked if she would like to come more often and stay longer she said that yes, she would, but only when they'd built an apartment with a kitchen and air conditioning that she could call her own. Somehow, I just couldn't imagine that blending in. The noise alone would drown out the gentle hum of nature which just goes to prove, you can't have everything. But with all the noise going on in the house, I doubt you would have heard a plane landing. And with that in mind,

Andree and I slipped down to the beach hoping they wouldn't all be staying too long. I knew it was supposed to be more like a home-stay than a hotel but the claustrophobic atmosphere was beginning to grate.

SAN AGUSTINILLO – THE TRUTH SURFACES...

Mexico is alive with politics, a revolution beginning and ending on every corner and this little village was no different – there was trouble in paradise! Everyone who had gone to live there told a similar story going back 30 years when a few intrepid gringo souls drove down from the resort of Acapulco in search of authenticity and discovered the empty beaches braced by the Pacific and decided to stay.

At first, they blended in and lived in the same ramshackle palapas, renting them for peanuts from dirt poor fishermen. And then more came and then more. They offered big money for the land on the beach which no one really owned; they just lived there but claimed it as their own. So gradually, the fishermen, now flush with cash, claimed the land up the cliff and built new homes there and the gringos built on the beach. They said that it was good for the community because for once, they had spare money and more than just the fish they caught to eat. But it's the old story of poacher and game keeper, not seeing the wood for the trees and basically, simple politics.

So now there were all these city folk who had moved in to commune with nature and raise their kids along with the local kids, which all seemed to work fine, except that when I was traipsing up the steps past families living their lives, they didn't see me as an asset, they saw me as an intruder taking photos of their very intimate lives – I at least, didn't take photos. But others did.

New best friend and I were invited to see inside the new building on the beach (by the builder, not the owners). So we went inside and it was truly dazzling; enormous, beautiful and smack bang on the beach blocking not only the natural run of the mating turtles, but everyone's access. One of the (American) owners wrote about civil rights abuse around the world but surely, that was a civil rights abuse right there, right then in little San Agustinillo. We talked to our lovely hostess Aline and she said that everyone in the village objected to their ostentatious, solid concrete design, so the owners built them a library, took them all out to lunch (at least those without a conscience) and they got their building – it all sounded very familiar, seeing the way London was up for sale to the highest bidder.

But, it was my last few days in that idyll so I wasn't likely to dwell on politics. Instead, Andree and I did a lot of talking and smoking and then even more talking. She was so ready to laugh and what a laugh. She was so joyous and a perfect audience for me. When we talked of pregnancy (hers not mine – I never had the instinct for it), she told me that with both her girls, she was like a cat, had only six hours labour and a faultless birth with both. I said that in this day and age, I was surprised women still used their own wombs when surely they could put the fertilised egg into a pig or something, so saving themselves the bother and the pain. She laughed so much at that one I thought I'd have to call for help. She said that she thought women had babies so that the father would keep and provide for them. I said I'd rather live in a hut than be dependent on anyone.   She then said that if her bad ankle had a positive side to it, it was that it had slowed her up enough for us to just sit and talk and that it had inspired her to change her life. I hoped so.

****

A new man had come to town and to our house. He was a loud, moustachioed American who talked on the phone, day

52

and night. From what I could overhear, I thought he was a film maker but when I asked, he said no. He used to be a war photographer but after witnessing and cataloguing the Vietnam War and all of its atrocities, he had suffered post traumatic shock and had also lost his belief in his country. He simply couldn't believe that the land of his birth could be capable of such evil. He now lived in a meditation centre in Colorado and the idea was that you left after six years maximum but they'd let him stay on indefinitely, maybe because he had nowhere else to go. He was happy at the commune and I could see the benefits of a life where you could at least have a sense of belonging. He turned out to be generous and kind and even provided the ice cream for Andree's birthday in the coming days (long after I'd gone).

There was no wi fi there up the hill so as agreed, I returned to Posada Paloma to use theirs. I took Andree with me and she was knocked out by the colour and the sheer beauty of the place. It was now marketing itself as a coffee shop and with us sitting there, tapping and sipping away, it began to fill up and they said it had never been so busy which made us feel less guilty about using the free wi fi.

We cooked and ate together that night – the entire family had gone to the circus and so we had the house to ourselves – Andree and I that is. She suggested we play a game of cards but I said I wasn't a good loser and it might end in tears. She said I was all sharp edges whilst she was rounded and told me to open my arms to give as well as receive. And with that advice, terrified that the family would return and we'd be captured in a web of their noise, we took to our beds. I was so used to the ocean that I didn't even hear it by then.

****

The following morning, the family left and the musicians arrived carrying mandolins, lutes and guitars. Aline said that before the new concrete house on the beach had been built, people used to camp there and play around the campfire –

that too had been lost to so called progress.

Andree's foot was getting worse not better and hope of us driving to Oaxaca was fading. I was aware that this magical time was coming to an end and a hole in my heart was developing. It had been such serendipity that we'd met but I was afraid that this might be the only real friendship I'd make and hence, I'd be even lonelier in the future in "a taste of honey is worse than none at all" way. I found myself retreating back into solitude and later that day, when we were all at the circus, I left early and walked back in the dark alone, almost preparing myself for the rest of the journey. Alone. The paradigm had somehow shifted.

Fortunately, Pedro, a newly arrived musician, was sitting at the table with an array of bottles before him. He said they were all varieties of Mescal from the hallucinogenic to the liqueur and did I want to try some? Of course I did and suddenly, it didn't seem so bad to be on my own. I tried them all...

****

My last full day in San Agustinillo was taken up with trying to work out the best way back to Oaxaca. It seemed that it was to go back into Pochutla and take the overnight bus which left at 10pm and arrived at 5am. Aline rang and booked me a ticket but as usual, I didn't trust it to really happen. Rather than allow myself to fret about it and ruin the day, Andree and I again went to the beach. A big half car/half truck pulled up and some Mexicans got out. They looked in disbelief at the empty beach – how could that ever be "good" they must have thought, got back in again and drove off. I wondered if Mexicans just preferred a crowd and maybe it was anthropological – there was safety in numbers and it had stayed with them. And it's not just Mexicans; it's almost everyone except maybe the few discerning city folk who are so sick of being jammed in all day every day, that an empty beach is a vista. It certainly was for me.

The last supper I ate on my own – another plate of shrimps. Each day, I had been given an extra one so now my plate was overflowing. The man in the deserted bar next door even treated me to a Margarita – my first and last. I wondered if I'd been unwise to book all of my flights beforehand but it would have been too easy to just stay in one place if I hadn't and where was the adventure in that? But equally, where was the fun in wandering around on your own with no one to share your experiences with?

I once again climbed the steps to home. Andree had been overbooked and had been moved to a little building behind the house with its own little patio and it was to there that I went. To prepare for my journey, she showed me how my camera worked, although I wasn't paying that much attention... She'd already taken some for me and it was so obvious that hers and mine were taken by different people – one who knew what they were doing and one who didn't. She just told me to take more time and find the shot before I clicked the shutter.

And so our last night. Through our haze, we could hear music coming from the house and she suggested we went to join them. She was optimistic whereas I was expecting the worst – bad singing, bad guitar playing and a cacophony of percussion. But she wasn't like me – she saw only goodness whilst I would be more likely to roll my eyes and wonder if I'd be expected to knit my own wine. And the weirdest thing happened – I actually joined in and at one point, I was tapping on the table and even whistling (in tune, although there are many who would argue with that). It made me think; surely that was the way to live rather than watching some turgid TV show, full of wannabees and total twats with seemingly no prior experience and worse, no talent.

I also wondered if guitarists need passion to be a good player and if so, do they deserve to have as much passion as is physically possible? Should they be allowed free rein to roam the land, trying to talk a fair or dark maiden into their beds to keep the passion and the show going? Mescal Pedro certainly played with passion as did Miguel (our host) and the real joy was hearing Aline and her mum, singing traditional songs in a traditional house – I was so moved I even shared my last bottle of wine with them!

So who's to say who can come and settle and who can't? Once upon a time, Aline and Miguel were newcomers from Mexico City but at least they blend. The men in the big house on the beach don't blend and they don't bend – they even have a "panic" room for earthquakes, hurricanes and tsunamis. The only question is, how many will it hold?

****

And so to my last day. The sea had been so rough, it had been impossible to swim, surf or indeed do anything other than sit and look at it. Photos never do waves justice but Aline said the images remain in the memory and you don't need any other reminder. She also said that when the waves were that high, they are not for swimming in, only for looking at. I did walk though, from one end to the other and back again – it was such a great beach. I took photos of palapas to put things into perspective and I took a photo of Elena, the lovely tiny maid who hugged me so hard I almost cried. And when it was time for me to go, they ALL hugged me hard. I'd arrived as a guest and a stranger but once again, felt as if I'd left as a friend. We'd all sat around so often just talking, me to Aline, me to her mum and mostly, me to Andree.

I would miss Andree enormously. I hoped that she wouldn't be the only true friend I'd make on my epic journey but I knew that she would remain a truly remarkable person who would be extremely hard to replace, if indeed, that was possible. The last tarot card I picked with her was "abundance" and that was what she was and maybe, that was what she had given me – an abundance to be more open-armed with strangers.

Right on time, the taxi man arrived, loaded my huge bag onto his back and hacked down the path like the local that he was, while I tentatively stepped in the dark like the gringo that I was and once again, we set off for that dusty old town of Pochutla. He dropped me at the bus station where I sat sipping rum for purely medicinal reasons i.e. a 6 hour journey back up the mountains of the Sierra Madre to Oaxaca. The bus finally arrived loaded with people, chickens and god knows what and for some reason, which I had no intention of challenging out of either comfort or heroism, I was given the two seats at the front and as the full moon glowed down on me, we pulled out of town and headed north.

****

Six stomach turning, sleepless hours later, at 5am I was back in Oaxaca. At that time of the morning, there was no one around except a few bare foot souls, wrapped in blankets, sleeping in doorways. Testament to the fact that nowhere is without desperation of one form or another. Luckily, having walked every inch of that town before, I found the bigger bus terminal, found someone who spoke English (so that made four of them), he organised me yet another taxi and the next thing, I was on board my 8.30am flight to Mexico City.

We flew over miles of brown barren mountains with nothing on them; no people, no vegetation, no nothing and then we flew down into Mexico City itself which wasn't hung like a hammock, it was cast like a calamitous, chaotic, counterpane as far as you could see, with little buildings dotted like colourful Lego, interspersed with earthquake proof taller spires and tall purple trees. I was then into yet another cab heading for my hostel "downtown". It would be my home for the next three days.

MEXICO CITY

I was so tired, I didn't even care that the driver didn't seem to have a clue where he was going. He finally pulled up outside a "building", got rid of me before I might ask any more of him and I was left at the base of yep, another enormous flight of stairs leading up to Massiosare El Hostel which was billed as the penthouse of an historical building. There was a beautiful ornate concertina-door lift but of course it no longer worked, so I left my bag at the bottom with the concierge and climbed the four mountainous flights to the top and was greeted by the gorgeous Mexican but English speaking Gus – long wavy sleek black hair and eyes to match.

I warned him about the bag but he assured me he "worked out" and indeed, he must have, because he bounded up the stairs with it flung over his shoulder. He showed me to my small cell-like "room", my own little outdoor glass basin sink which stood on a wooden table (and emptied onto the floor behind it), my very own toilet which seemed to work, showed me the "roof terrace" which was a flat space with a few battered chairs and there was no getting away from it – THIS WAS A CHEAP HOSTEL!

The building was falling apart. It wasn't about to fall down – it was probably built 150 years ago when they were built to last, but it had fallen into decay for lack of money and just needed complete refurbishment. There were holes in the walls, water stains on the ceilings, threadbare carpets, electrical wires connected to nothing, broken tiles left where they'd fallen and whole corridors blocked off, but you know what? It really didn't matter. The energy of the young people who ran it was effusive and contagious. Everyone who worked there was so enthusiastic – Gus told me that he and the other co-owners loved Mexico City so much, they wanted to make it affordable to everyone. Again, they belonged to that growing tribe of people there (and elsewhere) who lived a caring sharing life untouched by materialism.

They'd personalised the place and slapped murals and slogans everywhere – the one outside my room said; "those who look inside dream, those who look outside are awake". There was a dorm room full of bunk beds for travellers on an even cheaper budget than mine and I was slightly surprised to see normal looking people like two young Norwegian girls fresh from Cuba and a young couple from Dresden (with three children – so admirable). But at £8 a night, what more could I possibly have expected or asked for?

And so there I sat, on my first day in Mexico City and the funniest thing was that I thought it would be really chaotic and noisy but it wasn't. When I'd told people that I was going to Mexico and Colombia, they asked why I'd picked the two most dangerous countries in Latin America. I didn't realise I had and I still don't think it's true. The sound of the city wasn't one of angry car horns, gunshots and sirens and the only real sound was that of music drifting on the air. I could have been anywhere in the world, so off I set to see more.

Where I was staying turned out to be the "electric district", not because it was full of night life and neon lights, but because it was full of shops that sold a multitude of electrical fittings. Basically, I was staying in the hardware store of town and everything had closed for lunch. Food is so important in Mexico, as it is in many other parts of the world, that they wouldn't dream of just grabbing a sandwich wrapped in plastic and eating it on the move. On every single street and down every alleyway, there were stalls and cafes selling everything you could think of and some things you couldn't. People, mostly men, just sat up on a stool, selected what they wanted and ate in situ. There were piles of used paper plates and plastic cutlery bulging out of black rubbish sacks and the further through the session they got, everything, including the massive bowls of chilli sauce get sloppier and sloppier.

I decided to try my luck at the chicken stall and was greeted with astonishment. I didn't know if it was because I was a woman jostling my way through a bunch of men who could have been extras in a Spaghetti Western, or if it was because I seemed to tower over them (and I'm no Amazon) or because I was wearing a pretty summer frock when they were in jackets or if it was my absolutely rubbish Spanish or whether it was just because they didn't expect to see what they presumed to be a rich gringo slumming it in their part of town. Probably it was all of those things, but once laden up with food, they made way for me and tried not to gawp at just how much I ate...

I decided to explore my part of town. Yes, it had its poverty but there were no beggars, the streets were clean and I felt safe albeit, there were policemen and security guards EVERYWHERE - even in the 7/11 stores the fridge doors holding the beer were kept locked! I wandered into a few local grocers and just like in Oaxaca, they teemed with shop assistants. Oddly, there were no prices on anything and rather than be conned or exposed as a cheapskate, I headed for a big supermarket instead. It had everything I needed; not quite to the standard of the markets I'd grown to love, but it was good enough and as always, laughably cheap except the wine. I will never understand how wine could be the same price there as it was in England when they imported it from countries on the same continent.

Back in my tiny Spartan room, being out on a landing and separated by thick walls, I didn't get wi fi so had to use the communal room. I don't know why I had become so averse to being sociable; something about never being able to find my tribe I suppose, but it really wasn't so bad. The ones who wanted to talk talked and the ones who didn't, didn't. The two Norwegian girls told me about their time in Cuba (good) and their time in Jamaica (bad) and later up on the roof, I shared a smoke with the young German couple who happily found answers to my questions about the transition that Dresden had made from being part of the East to being part of the West.

There just seemed to be a good vibe about the place and rather than worrying that they might be eyeing up my belongings as I sometimes did, I had little to worry about – what they had was miles better than what I had from iPhones to iPads and they seemed like a trusting and trustful group and the next day would be a new and exciting day when I would venture forth and discover Mexico City for myself.

****

The Massiosare El Hostel, for all its shabbiness and four flights of stairs, served breakfast. And I was there, at 9am for really good coffee, pastries, which I shouldn't eat (all those food allergies), and fruit. I got talking to an American man, Joel, who used to work in "finance" but who had since probably opted out. I mentioned that I hoped the magic of Mexico wouldn't disappear as America's commercial interests grew and he said why shouldn't all Mexicans have what we had? I said because what "we" had was rubbish which we neither needed nor wanted, sold to us by adverts and he looked at me as if I was mad. Remembering Andree telling me to open my arms to strangers, I didn't push it and instead, we agreed that Mexico was great.

Gus told me the best way into town was by Metro but it didn't seem far, so I decided to walk. Dressed in another floral summer dress, I stepped out only to see everyone else wearing coats. It was early March and it seemed warm to me – maybe they took longer to warm up. I started walking and I walked and I walked and I walked, heading into town to the Zocalo which, just like in Oaxaca was formally known as Plaza de la Constitucion. It is the third biggest city square in the world after Tiananmen in China and Red Square in Moscow and has been the main gathering point since Aztec times. The nearer to the centre I got, the more majestic it became. Shabby buildings gave way to restored architectural beauties. I could begin to imagine what the City must have looked like in colonial times circa l6th century, when money was no object – provided you were of the ruling class.

Surprisingly, the Zocalo wasn't that impressive. It was just large, grey and fairly empty of anything. The buildings and streets surrounding it, dating from the same time, didn't house grand galleries or companies but instead were home to tiny shops selling all sorts of tourist tat and tourist fare from nuts and sweets to watches and shirts. And there were huge great red logoed trucks delivering Coca Cola as if it was the greatest thing on earth and there in Mexico, you would think it was. Everyone drank it.

At the centre of the Zocalo was the cathedral built to symbolize the importance of Mexico to the Spanish empire but weirdly, it's not that impressive either, apart from the enormous organ and totally elaborate nave. I knew that Mexico City was supposed to be full of Aztec ruins and beautiful buildings, but it was the now that I found more interesting. For example, outside the cathedral, there were uniformed organ grinders playing music with a hand held out for money – was it similar to selling the Big Issue or regulated begging? And there were magazine stalls everywhere – taking a look at the covers, there were several devoted entirely to diabetes. I wondered what came first, the disease or the magazines to prevent it?

I didn't see ANY colossal people there, even though there was a lot of eating going on, but it was all wholesome fair. Well, I say wholesome – there were stalls selling parts of animals that I'd never even seen before. I presume it was tripe in the nicest possible way but it was all just so haphazard. The stalls were set up everywhere; they cooked the food there, they fiddled with the food there, they served the food there, but nowhere was there any sign of anywhere to wash their hands... Having said that, later on, when I discovered a stall selling rice i.e. a carbohydrate I could eat, with all manner of indistinguishable accompaniments, one of which was meatballs, I sat myself down and ate a bloody great plateful and it was so good, I ate another bloody great plateful and all for £2!

But back to Mexico City. There were entire malls, not huge, more like little indoor markets, selling only religious artefacts where you could buy life size plaster casts of Jesus – Jesus on the donkey on Palm Sunday, Jesus on the Cross, Jesus just being Jesus and many, many, many other saints and Mother Marys. They referred to "Guadalupe" - I don't know if that is a particularly religious town, but the last time I had anything to do with Jesus, I was under the impression he came from Nazareth but hey, I was in Mexico and when in Mexico... But I did wonder, were people buying those enormous ornaments for their houses or for their churches? I suspect that it was for personal use which took religion to a whole new dimension.

In Mexico City, there were also museums everywhere. I went into one displaying photographs, taken in the 1980's and it looked like the Mexico I expected – old fashioned, with "peasants" at play and the simple pleasure they exuded at fiesta time. The simplicity was still there but this was NOW – one girl's t-shirt said "I am addicted to my smart phone" and I bet she wasn't the only one. And then I came across Plaza Santo Domingo where there were stalls not selling food, but words. Scribes sat there, as they would have done for centuries, on wooden chairs, at wooden desks, with all sorts of paper and cards, to write a message for you – perhaps to a loved one or an official, and by their sides, were men playing games of dice and chess. The literacy rate in Mexico is now over 90% so I presumed people could write their own notes which made it even more of a pleasure to think that these men and women were kept in business not out of necessity, but out of respect for an era gone by.

64

There just seemed to be an abundance (there's that word again) of time and peace where no one was in a particular hurry and life was for living. Yes, there was a whiff of sewers now and again, but not as bad as Venice and the lack of sophistication was to be applauded. Wandering off onto the Calle Republica de Cuba (there is a street dedicated to just about every Latin American revolution), I came across an entire street dedicated to wedding dresses. And you should have seen them! They would make a Royal wedding seem bland and then there were the other shops where you would dress your bridesmaids, the shops where you would buy your trousseau and then the bakers for your cake, one so big, it filled an entire window.

It just seemed so wonderful that the traditions of yesteryear hadn't been trampled on by the relentless march to modernity that seemed to be infecting the rest of the world. All right, some would say religion can hold people back with its sometimes archaic practices but they don't say that when trying to preserve the traditions of Amazonian tribes, so why interfere with *anyone's* life?

And then almost finally, there was the fabulous government building of Education. Before the Mexican Revolution of 1913, it had been a convent but once the peasants had taken power from the colonialists, education was seen to be the most important asset anyone could have, so where else to set itself up, than in the grounds of an old colonial building. One of Mexico's most revered artists, Diego Rivera, was commissioned to paint murals on the walls depicting the revolution which in itself, was as education and something I wanted to see.

I walked up to the entrance and with my no Spanish was confronted by someone asking me something – this was a government building after all, with metal detectors not dissimilar to an airport. I was ready to give up when a lady approached and said "Do you want to see our murals?" "Yes!" I replied. And that was all it took. With art, no words are needed. There it was, the whole of the revolution set out on the walls. The colonialists were depicted as grotesque, bloated, decadent ugly caricatures, the army portrayed as brutal thugs and the peasants as oppressed but ultimately victorious. The colours were bold and vibrant with simple lines almost in themselves adding to the depiction of the simplicity and justification of why the revolution was so necessary. I could see the whole of the Mexican revolution from the fields to the factories – and it was still going on. And that was what was so great about Mexico. They keep saying "no"! I'd have photos too but, not for the first time, my camera packed up. Luckily, I was assured, it was only the memory card. I was asked why I hadn't thought to buy a new one. I had no answer. I didn't think I would *ever* need a new one.

On my way back, I cut through Alameda Park which is the city's main public recreational area; like Hyde Park in London or Central Park in New York except much smaller. It was full of Mexicans taking a walk, taking time to talk or just simply resting on a bench or on the grass. The trees were in blossom, the colonial marble statues glowed in the lazy spring sunlight and suddenly, I was aware of someone calling and chasing after me. I expected the worse but it was only a girl running to return the cardigan I'd dropped. And they say Mexico is dangerous. It is no more dangerous than any other capital city.

And so back to my hostel and you know what? I wouldn't rather have been anywhere else. I used the kitchen to cook up a mountain of vegetables and then sat in the communal room and communed. Gus wasn't there to answer my questions but another couple were and they were as equally gorgeous and helpful and just so proud of their city. They didn't even mind when I swapped the bright outside light bulb for the one in my room which gave about as much light as a birthday cake candle. And once back in my tiny BRIGHT room I scoured my guide book and wondered what sights and sensibilities the next day would bring.

****

For breakfast, I was delighted not the coffee, but with an English couple from my home town – London. Ephraim was jet black with hair that stood up in trowel shaped dreads – god knows what Mexico made of him, and his girlfriend Corrine. He was a cycle courier, surprised that I'd done the exact same job but on a motorbike. They were the first people from home I'd met and the familiarity was just great. You don't appreciate what it means to meet people from the same clued up capital city until you've left it. We shared the same humour and the same amazement at the differences we'd encountered. Joel, the American, came to join us and in conversation, he said that he was buying some land to build a house with a Mexican (the only way he can do it) but was worried that he might run off with the money. "At least you know where he lives", I quipped – he didn't get the joke but they did. That's the difference – a lot of the time, no one else gets English humour. Thank god we did. It's probably a very broad statement, but British people are, usually, so ready to laugh.

Not unlike the plug adaptor scenario in Oaxaca, that day I was on a mission to get a new memory card for my camera. Simple, you would think, but no. After walking for an hour to recommended shops, I finally found a proper photographic shop and I was back in business except I still couldn't get it to do anything so just asked a man with a huge camera draped around his neck if he could sort it out. Seconds later, problem solved, I asked him how he'd done it – he looked at me as if I was a complete idiot and said, "the function button". You'd never guess I'd studied photography for a year, but that was in the days of SLRs.

So once again I sallied forth and being Saturday, forget everything I'd said about Mexico City. It was total CHAOS! Everyone must have come to town and with something like 30 million people in the city, that's a lot of people. Cars clogged the streets, people clogged the pavements and street vendors clogged every open space. It was hard to believe what was on sale – if you could carry it, it was there. One old lady, skin of leather and varicose veins that looked like a relief map of the Sierra Madre was just sitting there selling nail clippers whilst other people sold knickers, socks, trusses (!) bags, plastic bubble blowing guns and god knows what. They just set up stalls anywhere and everywhere and they literally, lined every street and most of what they sold looked like junk they'd picked up off the street somewhere else.

Most museums in the city were free so I just wandered from one to another – having worked in the Natural History Museum in London, they didn't hold the same allure, but in the Cultural Museum of Mexico I was totally mystified. One of the exhibitions showed the ancient pyramids and their people and I thought crikey, they are EXACTLY like the ancient civilizations of Egypt! Turned out that they WERE the ancient civilizations of Egypt – I was in the equivalent of the British Museum except that they didn't plunder the world for their exhibits, they simply borrowed them.

But apart from all the strange goods for sale, what was stranger was the sheer number of food outlets; from the stalls, to the cafes, to the restaurants to the juice bars. Fruit and vegetables so fresh and pure were just pulverized on every street– I had a beetroot juice in a great big round cocktail glass and it was so fresh and formidable, it was like nectar. You could get anything you wanted and a lot of what you didn't.

Mexicans seem to eat all day – a little and often. I finally found a patisserie with cakes to shame Paris which also sold my favourite – rotisserie chicken. I went in, I sat down and I ate, but I was more interested in the devotion they paid to cake. One couple who must have been a grandmother and granddaughter took at least five minutes to choose. Theirs were the shape of wagon wheels and not dissimilar in size, stuffed with fruit and cream and the look on their faces as they sat down to eat was one of bliss – had it been Paris, they would have been too aloof to even acknowledge joy, but this was Mexico and passion was everywhere.

My final site was the Palacio de Bellas Artes, a beautiful Art Deco and Nouveau masterpiece, replete with a crystal domed roof which shattered light into rainbows. The building itself has a history of its own, initially sinking under its own weight and then being abandoned during the revolution but it was worth the wait. The light and space of this marble clad spectacle is as fine a monument to architecture as you will see anywhere in the world. It housed every form of art from paintings to photographs to opera and classical music and just standing in awe in the lobby was a privilege.

Heading home for the day, I just let myself drift with the crowd. I took my bearings from the sun and roamed streets full of performers much like in any cosmopolitan city – how do those people seem to levitate? Entertainment was everywhere from break dancers to traditional Mariachi bands dressed in sombreros and buckled boots; there to hustle the crowds for pesos. I was surprised to see, at the more expensive cafes or bars, a lot of older Mexicans smoking – both men and women even though it was shunned by the young.

Some habits are hard to break but in any case, I stopped for one of my own. I was just sitting there, on a wall, when a policeman, dressed from head to foot in riot gear approached me. My initial thought was, "Don't tell me he's going to tell me I can't smoke" (like in the utterly polluted city of Agra, home to the Taj Mahal) but no, he just asked me for a light, smiled and wandered back to his unit. I'd been aware of the riot police and their racks and racks of riot shields all day. I wasn't sure if they were expecting something in particular or anything in general. This being Mexico, I presumed it was the latter.

In the older parts of town, it was sad to see some of the

beautiful old colonial buildings falling apart, as if with the original owners gone, no one could afford or care to renovate them but maybe they belonged to a past that they wanted to forget. It was a real shame though because what they were being replaced with was faceless, nameless, concrete malls that blight the world. I just hoped that maybe, one day, the architecture would be appreciated for what it was rather than for what it represented, but until then, it is ignored. A pity.

Anyway, as I left the centre, I walked back through the "electric district" and it was just so magical. Nothing was thrown away and everything was recycled. There were tiny shops the size of my shed which refurbished electrical motors plus everything else you could think of and there were goods for sale that we in the "West" (not forgetting that Mexico IS in the west) would be ashamed of taking to the dump – like microwave ovens with bits missing. Do they still work without a door? Maybe, but stand well clear when operating....

And just to prove that things would carry on working long past any apparent sell by date – you should have seen the buses. I doubt any of them would pass a safety test; they listed to either side, they were all bashed up from crashes, they belched smoke, they were loaded down with people hanging out of the doors and yes, they were laughably cheap. But, curiously, not as cheap as the metro which was just 5 pesos a ride and could take you from one end of Mexico City to the other – that's 12p! I loved that city!

****

My last day in Mexico and I had two options, spend all day in the Museum of Anthropology which everyone raved about, or go out and have a day doing what Mexicans did. My guide book raved about the districts of Rosa and Codesa so I asked Gus – he was totally cool and I knew I could trust his judgement. If I wanted a typical Mexican day he said, I should ignore the recommendations which were only for

70

posing and instead, go to Coyoacan. So first, I went to the artisans market nearby and what a place. If I hadn't had to lug it all the way back to England with me, I would have bought one of everything and my house would very quickly have looked like a bright and beautiful Mexican cantina.

There were little pottery skulls (they were everywhere to celebrate the Day of the Dead later in the year), to superb silver studded sombreros, to puppets, purses, bags, jewellery, shawls, ponchos, hammocks, carpets, wall hangings, tablecloths, glass, the odd religious memorabilia, old ladies asleep at their stalls and even a man making guitars and cellos! I shouldn't really have bought anything but I really did need a new bag, purse and ring – I got them all and barely a barter in sight. I even bought a little picture – I asked how much? He said something which of course I didn't understand – I thought he said 200 i.e. £10 but what he actually said was 20 i.e. £1. How could I resist – he even threw in a couple of bookmarks, gratis.

After dropping my bags back to the room, I wandered into the Subway built by the French and exactly like the Metro except without any colour – it is purely functional but what do you expect for 12p a ride? (Incidentally, it cost the same to have a pee as it does to ride the subway – that one I simply could not make out.) I went nine stops south and with my trusty Rough Guide map, got completely lost. At one point, I was walking in totally the wrong direction and a young girl ran up to me and asked me where I was going – obviously there was absolutely NOTHING in that direction. I told her Coyoacan, she turned me around, and off I went again – and they tell you Mexico is a dangerous place.

As I approached, it was as if all roads led there and everyone was walking in one direction as if to an arena. Suddenly, the road emptied into a big old historic square set around public gardens and an ornate bandstand. It was filled with families on a day out. Restaurants and bars with linen covered tables spilled out onto the pavements, all manned by efficient waiters in long white aprons. It had the etiquette and neat formality of times gone by. It all looked like an elaborate film set of the 1950s. Everybody was in their Sunday Best and everyone was on their best behaviour. People queued at numerous churrio stalls (like long doughnuts), coffee shops, ice cream parlours and taco bars which were all jostling for space.

In an old converted warehouse there was yet another indoor market (I daren't look too hard in case I found things I liked more than my earlier purchases) and finally, there was a rotisserie chicken stand. I intended to sit in a restaurant and have a proper meal but with my non-existent Spanish I just didn't know what I might end up with - tripe in cheese or something equally indigestible.

But even the chicken joint was a challenge – I was trying to ask for a quarter. In the end, he asked me, in perfect English, if *I* spoke English! They didn't do quarters, he said, they did halves so without hesitation, I came away with half a chicken, rice, salsa sauce and he even threw in a spoon and all for 50 pesos - £2.50. It did make me think though – they just didn't cater for people like me – people on their own. I would have loved to have had someone to share it with, someone to point out little idiosyncrasies to and just someone to smile with at the communal bliss that unfolded around me, but I didn't.

So instead, I sat on a bench next to a young couple and watched many other young couples, sharing an ice cream, walking and talking and it was such a joy. This was what Mexicans did. They enjoyed themselves. There was no pomp, no ceremony, no rules, no nothing. They just got on with it. There were bands playing, there were people dancing, street performers entertaining and there was shade everywhere from the huge trees that surround the square. One of those trees was the huge purple flowered ones I'd seen from the plane and it was just so majestic. There was such simplicity of life in that country. They dressed up, they promenaded, they fell in love, they had kids, they had grand kids and life just went on. It didn't make me wonder who had got it right – I already knew.

And as the sun began to set, I wandered back towards my hostel and came across another Sunday soiree but as I ventured in, I realised straight away that it wasn't a jolly civilised affair. It seemed to be where the homeless and derelict assembled. I was eyed with amazement, interest and curiosity, but not in a good way – I felt like the intruder that I was. There are areas like that all over the world and Mexico was no exception. I got the message and went home, climbed the four flights of stairs for the last time, finally got my extra blanket from Gus and arranged for a taxi to take me out of there the next morning. Adios Mexico, hola Colombia!!!

COLOMBIA

BOGOTA ROCKS - WITH AN EARTHQUAKE

Three earthquakes in 30 years, and I got to feel it – welcome to Bogota! I arrived at night on a totally civilised flight from Mexico City. On arrival, all I wanted to do was have a cigarette but as soon as I walked towards the exit, a tall moustachioed man took me by the arm, took my huge bag by the handle and started leading me off. He was flashing a "tourist badge" and saying that it was fine to smoke in his taxi and that I didn't need to stand in line and wait for an ordinary taxi.

It was dark and I was tired but it just didn't feel safe and in the end, I just stopped and I just said NO! He seemed surprised at how adamant I was, but he took my massive declaration of non-participation seriously and just turned around, with enormous bag and walked me back and pushed me into a proper taxi.   "I want to smoke first", I almost screamed - this was getting on for eight hours! The taxi driver looked at me as if I was mad and just said, "it's OK to smoke in the taxi." Welcome to Colombia! It didn't even matter that he had no idea where he was going, and obviously, neither did I. I was happy. The address seemed to be missing a number, but when we pulled up outside the house which looked exactly like the photo on airbnb, there was Marcela waiting to greet me.

She helped me in with my bag to a wonderful big airy, tiled lounge which was scattered with cushions rugs and hammocks, she helped me up the varnished wooden stairs onto the varnished wooden landing and she helped me into my room, which was lovely but had bars on the windows – but that didn't mean it was dangerous (did it?). She made me some coffee and took me out into the garden and I was aware that all around the roof was barbed wire – but that didn't mean it was dangerous either (did it?).

Marcela, my host for three days, was a university lecturer, she'd lived in Germany and spoke English and was really sweet. She just wanted her guests to enjoy themselves. I thought I was the only one staying there, but there was also a German girl and a Dutch man. The Dutch man, Bram, said he'd walk me into town the following morning. And so after talking with Marcela and turning down her offer to go to the market at 6am, I retired to my room. I Skyped my sister Maggie who always looked up where I was on Google Earth so that she could show my mum – what a fantastic invention. She could see the very house I was staying in and the mountains behind! She asked about the weather – I showed her the super huge furry blanket on my bed – it was COLD.

****

Marcela just couldn't do enough to make my stay perfect. In the morning, she made me a huge pot of coffee (not as strong as I would had made it but then maybe it's me who's weird) and when Olga, the house keeper arrived, she made me a "maize" bread (I still can't eat it no matter what it's called) with fried onions and tomatoes, and sitting atop all of that, a slice of cheese, which I also couldn't eat (I was so tired of allergies!). I had to scrape the cheese off whilst she wasn't looking, wrap it with the bread in a napkin and put it in the bin – the cat was sitting there looking at me, I wondered if I should give it to her but something in my mind told me cats can't eat it either.

I thought I'd have the first shower for a couple of days – the hostel in Mexico City was great, but the idea of wobbly shower walls and the possibility of someone just wandering in had no allure whatsoever. And the funniest thing was that for about half of the world, plumbing and electricity just seemed to go together – live wires in the shower and plugs that sparked EVERY time I plugged them in – did we in England worry too much or were we right to be concerned? I washed the grime of Mexico City off and dressed for Bogota. It was cold and I was so glad Andree had given me a hoodie – I had no warm clothes whatsoever. I put on my baggy harem trousers, hid my empty money belt save for a debit card beneath them and me and Bram – the very tall Dutchman – began our walk into town.

It's 2600 metres above sea level, the air is thin, the pollution is thick and it is hard to breathe. Nevertheless, we walked and talked. He worked for an NGO looking into the environmental and social implications of the mining industry – no prizes for guessing that one of the biggest culprits was a British company.

It was appalling to hear what he had to say. When the mining companies found something that they wanted, in cahoots with the government, they sent in their own Para militaries claiming that the terrorist group, FARC, was operating. Bram said that FARC gave up years ago as did the people – the fight was just unwinnable. The mining companies then cleared the area, turned the indigenous people off their land and literally "ethnically cleansed" it and then helped themselves to the gold, gas and emeralds. They didn't even use the gold – it would only devalue it so they just put it in vaults for the future. I could weep. This had been going on for centuries and whilst a few people stamp their feet and stand up for the Amazon and everywhere in the world where minerals still exist, the people with the money just roll in with their bulldozers (what a word!), empty the earth and make an awful lot of money.

Please excuse the rant, but that's what "capitalism" is and that is what people are voting for without realising just how heinous it is. It's not about you and your house and your mortgage and your university fees; this is about raping the earth of everything it has and shouldn't have to give, until there is nothing left! Bram said he got threatening text messages all the time and he also said that the Colombian people had more or less given up the struggle and had become introspective, whilst the dispossessed had to move from rural to urban areas. With no education, invariably, the girls got pregnant and the boys just got sucked into the drug trade. It seemed like a very grim life with only the cartels, in collaboration with the government, making a very good living.

He left me on a corner, told me that even he'd been mugged and to be careful. I was filled with dread, dreaming of the safety of Mexico City. I walked on alone, towards the old part of town "La Candeleria", expecting to be attacked at any moment. But that was, of course, not what happened. Maybe I looked scarier than they did, but once again, I was helped all day. I'd give far too much money for coffee, for food, for whatever and they would just hand me back the notes they didn't need – with £1 equal to 4000 pesos, it was easy to lose a nought along the way.

So what's Bogota like? It's like a fiery ball of chaos cupped in the harsh hand of the mountains, whilst clouds tumbled over as if from an alchemist's jar. For 95% of the people, it's a grim place to live, poverty is everywhere and it is only the 5% who lived in the north of the city, who had any quality of life. It was cold, grey and wet. It looked slightly more sophisticated than Mexico, but it lacked the colour and verve. The architecture was a total jumble – beautiful old buildings from the 1600s sat beside the obligatory but obtrusive and sometimes ludicrous high rises of all sorts of shapes and the main square, devoted to Bolivar, who did much to fight off colonial rule, was full of pigeons and people feeding pigeons. I was reminded of Mary Poppins, "Feed the Birds", but it was pretty revolting especially when you consider that they are, more or less, flying rats.

There was the usual boring high street full of international brands but running off of it were lots of cobbled streets. To the east they were full of museums, theatres, the opera house, churches and a mini cathedral that looked like a very ornate wedding cake. At one point, I was walking past the parliament building and was told I couldn't walk on the pavement and had to walk in the road! There were police and soldiers everywhere – not that I minded, but it just didn't have a feeling of joy – anywhere. Maybe years of FARC trying to right the wrongs and failing, coupled with centuries of colonial rule, had simply worn them out.

I realised I was starving, not for the first time, and came across a restaurant with a "menu del dia" at 6500 pesos – even I could translate that. So I climbed the old wooden staircase into a lovely old cantina style room; simple wooden table and chairs and sat down. Obviously, there was the usual language barrier so I just pointed at someone else's lunch and swiftly, I was served a bowl of potato and pea soup followed by chicken, rice, vegetables and chips of both normal and sweet potatoes, a tumbler of mango juice – and all for £1.50!

I followed it with coffee in a square with music playing – not mariachis, but loud speaker type stuff and was surprised to think that I felt the earth move. I DID feel the earth move! Shock and a feeling of impending doom registered on everyone's face, but just as casually as it had arrived, it shuddered to a stop. A moment of realisation and then everything went back to normal and ladies in high heels continued to totter by, men and women selling everything on the side of the road continued selling, business men in sharp suits and sunglasses continued to trade, tramps continued to rifle bins and pee in the gutters and I continued home.

Despite the totally useless map of the city, I found my way and was delighted to realise that I was staying in a really nice neighbourhood. The shop keepers were all curious as to where I was from, they helped me, they laughed with me and in the little bar nearby, we even ended up nudging one another. Back at the house, Nicholas, the young man who lived in another self contained flat in the garden, asked me why English people never learned the language before they

81

went abroad – I ran him through just some of the countries I'd visited and it amounted to 20 languages – how many did he want me to learn??

****

I intended to go on a cycle tour of the city (I ride bikes all the time, so not such a shock) so once again, headed into town. Somehow, I got my calles (streets) and my carreras (avenues) mixed up and after walking for an hour, I was in totally the wrong side of town. The side of town Bram had warned me about. Threatening looking men and boys walked big dogs with muzzles that obscured their entire faces like something from a sci fi film about marauding gangs and the end of the world. I didn't know who was more surprised – them to see me wandering in their neighbourhood without a gun, or me to realise that I was totally lost and in the most dangerous part of town. The houses had turned into tumble down shacks, the pavement replaced by broken rubble and the road no more than a sand and buckled tarmac track. How I'd walked so far without registering this was testament to my optimism and ignorance, but when I did pay proper attention, I was terrified.

I was suddenly aware that passing cars were slowing down to look, other pedestrians were eyeing me with more interest than I wanted and random groups of boys were proudly guarding their turf. I didn't know what they expected me to do but what I expected, was to be mugged at any moment. Bram had told me that if I felt in any danger to just hail a taxi but in that part of town, there weren't any. Thankfully, I had a hoodie to hide inside. I tucked my hair into it and pulled up the hood right over my head, turned around and hurried back - not too fast as to seem scared, but more in a totally eccentric manner like a mad dog or an Englishwoman... I walked for at least 10 minutes before I felt vaguely safe and resolved never to be so unaware of my surroundings again but in a foreign land, that was not as easy as it sounded.

82

I was too late for the cycle tour, so I simply wandered a few streets away from the historic centre and discovered an area that was even worse than the one I had just stumbled out of. It was still the city centre, the capital city of Colombia but it was full of desperate, homeless, dirty, worn down, worn out people, trying to scrape a living; selling total rubbish, going through bins, sleeping rough and not a smile in sight. There was no music, no life, no nothing except misery. These were the indigenous people who had been driven from their rural homes into the city where they simply did not want to be and didn't belong. It was utter deprivation about which, no one gave a damn. There were no government benefits and their only hope was the charitable sector which was bursting at the seams. I wanted to photograph the abject desolation but I was just too scared and upset. No one should have to exist like that. And it was all because the rich needed to get richer. This was Bogota. This was Colombia.

Despite it still being the afternoon of my last day, I'd had enough and was completely depressed. I walked home and crawled back into my bed but nothing could shake those images loose. I kept wondering how people who lived there could possibly ignore what was happening. In the affluent north of the city, the partying was legendary as was the opulence but then that was true of many capital cities in Latin America (and elsewhere). I just hadn't seen anything in that league of hell before and never wanted to see it again.

As planned, myself and Marcela spent our last night together. Once again, we sat in the little garden. I got my brandy out and we talked and talked – about what I'd seen, politics, people and ultimately love – hers and mine. And once again, I found myself in intimate conversation with a total stranger and I wondered why we hadn't recognized ourselves as kindred spirits in the first place. But wasn't that so often the case (apart from Andree in San Agustinillo where we knew at first glance).

She told me that Colombian men were the descendants of

Spanish conquistadors who were often freed prisoners. They had no experience of family life and were terrible fathers and all wanted to have several children with several women and that family wasn't the sacred preserve that is was in most Latin American countries. She said that it remained in the psyche from the time of Cortez, when rape and pillage of the indigenous women was common, and somehow, this had just continued. Bram came out to join us, as did Nicholas, and in the end, it turned into something of a little party, but we all agreed, Bogota had big problems. I was, however, the only one getting out of there for good in the morning.

Marcela and I hugged and once again, I felt that I'd arrived as a guest but left as a friend and in the morning, when I saw Bogota fall away below me from the plane, I couldn't help but know, that I would NEVER go back there.

CARTAGENA - COLOMBIA'S FINEST CITY

The coastal city of Cartagena on the Caribbean is surrounded by natural harbours and it was from these that Sir Frances Drake, friend to Queen Elizabeth I, with his fleet of ships , attacked. He and other adventurers plundered the city so often for the gold already pillaged by the Spanish, that they had to build huge fortifications. It took a couple of centuries, but as they still remain today it was worth the effort and not only that, it is those very walls which make the city both remarkable and so beautiful.

I arrived early afternoon. The flight from Bogota had taken me over the mountains and then across a flatter plain which was criss-crossed by brown silt filled rivers flowing towards the sea. Mexico's terrain was barren, inhospitable and inaccessible, but Colombia was green and florid. At the airport to meet me were my new airbnb hosts Alexander and his dad Isaac – a tour guide for the city. Curiously, they didn't just bundle me into a waiting taxi. Instead, they wheeled my bag a couple of hundred metres to the main road, flagged down a cab and took me to their "Big house in Cartagena" – they said that this was half the price of an airport taxi. I liked their thinking.

I've said before that the scale of maps is all a bit disorientating but in truth, I didn't expect to be so far out of town, both culturally and geographically. I was there for four days so I just decided not to be phased by it and to make the most of it. My new neighbourhood was fairly new and seemingly hand built. The land had been parcelled up and sold off in plots and gradually, as and when they could afford it, the houses grew and the infrastructure followed.

In my new home, the veranda and the living room were finished and those were the two highlights of the house and the rooms which were featured in their airbnb ad. Beyond that, it all got a bit haphazard. But it was their home and they showed me, proudly, around. No it wasn't like my house or probably your house, but this was Colombia and NOTHING was the same. It had a kitchen with a massive old rumbling fridge, rough stone work tops, a big old sink and ancient cooker. Nothing was fitted or matched but really, why should it? Opposite was a little bedroom with walls that didn't quite meet the ceiling but will one day (I presume) and a little bathroom with toilet, sink and shower. There were other bedrooms tacked on spreading out into the yard but for me, it was the master bedroom, probably vacated especially that very day. It was enormous, windowless (except for a lattice work air brick that looked out onto the neighbours wall) and boiling hot. Even with a ceiling fan the air was dead, so they brought in another fan plus a little table and chair for me and my laptop. They simply couldn't do enough. And it was enough - a huge double bed, a big mirror and a rack to hang my clothes on. As they pointed out, bedrooms were only for sleeping in and outside was where all the living happened.

Isaac then took me out onto the veranda, sat me in a rocking chair and showed me several "tours" that he could organise for me but all I really wanted to do was relax. They offered lunch but not being sure how many things I wouldn't be able to eat from one to all, I declined and instead Alexander nipped me round the corner on his motorbike to a chicken joint. I'd finally bought myself a Spanish/English dictionary at Bogota airport and feeling invincible and no longer having to mime being a chicken – arms flapping and clucking, I somehow ended up with a plate of rice and chips! Oh well, so much for that.

It was a long way from town, but apparently, all you had to do was raise one finger and flag down a "collectivo" taxi, cram yourself in and get into town for 50p. Even so, it was a bit of a backwater but that's what you get for only paying £7 per night – what could I really have expected? Never mind; a nap and coffee (my little stove top pot was just SO useful), I asked where I could buy a beer. Alexander seemed alarmed that I would walk there on my own – this was only a street away but I was determined to go it alone, so off I went.

There were people everywhere, sitting on their porches and verandas playing or listening to music, men with donkey carts wandering by and boys on bicycles selling that weird "milk" drink of Oaxaca. One man, black as jet, pushing a wheelbarrow saw me coming and I must have looked as weird to him as he did to me and he just said "Wow!" We smiled and I walked on to the shop.

The only thing I know in Spanish, apart from "I love you very much", (it might come in handy...) was dos cervezas por favor and for the first time since I'd been there, I got the chance to say it. Obviously, mistaking me for someone who could actually speak Spanish, he said something back to me and as if my magic (there's that old Marquez seeping into everything), Alexander was by my side, saying that what I wanted, was Colombian beer – of course I did! And all for 75p for two! Things were looking up. So he whisked me back on his motorbike, hair blowing in the wind with no helmets but not before he took me past his grand parents' house and then his uncle's, tooting his horn with everyone waving. I must have seemed like some exotic creature flown south for the winter never seen before in that locale...

So, back out on our veranda, in rocking chairs, I drank my beer, whilst Alexander blasted Salsa music out from his enormous hi fi (also featured in the airbnb photos) and he danced. He was a good looking young man, short cropped curly hair, razor moustache and short goatee style beard, slim and fit and a very good dancer. Then his mum, Esther, came out and joined us. She was a short, round, bubbly woman, proud mother of four sons AND she spoke English – not much, but more that I did Spanish. And so we got talking.

We all agreed that Bogota was awful - miserable people and cold weather, and then we discovered that she loved to dance – dancing was one of my absolute passions and I hadn't done any since arriving on that great continent. I asked her where she went to dance and she said the "disco in town" so I said, "why don't we all go?" And she was thrilled! Suddenly, staying in the boondocks had its merits – I could dance with the locals, eat with the locals, and talk with the locals. Then her son, Andy arrived and events took yet another turn. He was a water sports instructor on the beach and he said anytime I wanted to go, to just let him know.

And so then I had a plan and could stop cursing myself for not paying the extra money to stay in town with other "travellers". I was happy that I'd made the choice to be more independent and had taken a chance. The next day, I would go to the end of the road, raise a finger and take a collectivo into town and walk the streets and take in the sights, Saturday we were all going to the disco and Sunday, we were all going to the beach! Once again, I felt as if I was having an adventure rather than a holiday.

****

Esther sat me down at the big table for a breakfast of fried plantain and sausages for breakfast. I wasn't sure if I could eat it but didn't want to seem disrespectful although I did decline the eggs. Esther's relatives then called in to say hello and see the foreigner and everyone made such an effort to make me feel welcome. It was probably an important venture for the family to make some extra money and reviews on airbnb were all important. They all wanted it to work especially as previously, a group of Chinese students hadn't been impressed. I can't imagine what they would have thought of it – if they were rich enough to travel, they must have been very rich and the house would probably have been a total shock to them.

Even though I'd intended to flag down a collectivo, Esther wouldn't hear of it. All made up and looking gorgeous, she was giving someone a massage in town – that's what she does, and insisted I shared her taxi. The highway into town was the usual concrete conga which followed the Caribbean shoreline. On the other side of the road were hotels and houses that improved in style the nearer we got to the city. It all looked slightly ordinary until the vast centuries old fortress walls came into view. We turned left through an ornate archway and suddenly I was in the wonderland that is the old historic part of Cartagena. Such a difference from the drabness of Bogota.

It was hot, it was beautiful and it was full of colour. Salsa music and the sweet scent of honeysuckle and jasmine carried on the breeze. The city is 500 years old and rumoured to be the most beautiful in South America – and I could believe it. That day, it was packed full of tourists – some rich, some not and the shops and restaurants reflected that. There were ultra expensive boutiques, jewellers selling emeralds and gold in all forms of elaborate design and even an entire road full of material and haberdashery. I couldn't resist taking a look and the fabric was just magnificent! There were brocades and silk of every colour and if I'd had room, I would have bought a couple of metres of everything. I would also had bought the two pairs of sandals but stopped myself – I would after all, be going back that way in a few weeks time.

I had no plan other than to walk every inch of the old city but first, I wanted lunch – it was the most important meal of the day there and so once again, I wandered around looking, but with my new dictionary, I at least had a chance of finding and ordering something that I wanted. I found a little covered passageway which led to a pretty shaded courtyard with tables and overhead fans as big as helicopter blades. It wasn't one of the many glamorous places with expensive linen, cutlery and crockery but was more for the local workers who didn't go out for a sandwich or something fast, but instead, opted for real food.

It had a set lunch menu and so I sat down, and for once, ordered with confidence... First came a cold fruit drink in a metal beaker, then chicken soup and then along came the minced beef, chilli beans, rice and vegetables – I couldn't believe that I got what I expected. Never mind that afterwards, I got lost trying to find the toilet and had to ask a waitress to help me.

Back out on the street and ready to properly explore, I was instantly confronted by a local man who introduced himself as Edwin McCarthy – his grandfather he told me, was Scottish. He said he would teach me to dance Salsa, but first, would I like to go for coffee. Without waiting for my reply, he steered me to the most expensive coffee shop in town and then just loitered. It was immediately obvious that it wasn't him treating me, but vica versa. I'm not gullible; I'm not gullible at all and asked why he had chosen the most expensive coffee bar in town. I didn't mind paying for him, but not at that price so we left in a hurry but still he was persistent – guiding me along with his arm around my waist. Once again, I felt uncomfortable and told him so. He seemed shocked that anyone would rebuff his advances (despite his bad breath), gave me a big slobbery kiss on the cheek and abandoned me – thank god!

Realising that I had almost no money, I went in search of a bank. My trusty Rough Guide listed two, but a helpful girl from Nicaragua took me to a supermarket which had an ATM. I put my card in once, I put my card in twice and NOTHING except a message to contact my bank. Disaster! Did this mean that I had no access to money – ever? I needed coffee and to sit in the shade and think. I walked to the new (ugly) commercial complex, found a man selling coffee from flasks – tiny, hot and sweet and all for about 5p. It was so hard to understand the pricing of **anything** on that continent. Finally, caffeined up, I found a bank and voila! Out coughed the money, so what was all that about? Maybe I just wanted more in one withdrawal than a domestic ATM bargained for. Back in business and obviously delirious, I bought the other thing that I'd been craving – chocolate, in the form of ice cream (forgetting the allergies) and it was sensational! For countries that had cocoa coming out of their ears, it was SO hard to buy any decent chocolate!

Fortified, it was time to walk the city. Compared to the sprawling metropolis of Cartagena proper, the small historic sector within the old walls is tiny and because of its size, it's possible to walk every cobbled inch of it. The streets are narrow with houses lining either side, their balconies overhanging the pavements and all embellished with masses of hanging plants bursting with colour. The walls are all painted vibrant shades of yellow, orange, blue, green and purples so bright you needed sunglasses to withstand the glare. It's so brightly lit by the baking sun as to be dazzling.

On the outskirts, in the area called San Diego, the buildings are so well preserved or renovated it's like walking around a film set or a museum. It's hard to believe people really lived there. And then, just when you needed a rest from the brilliance and the heat, there were little shaded squares everywhere, some with fountains and some with statues of mounted military men – the colonial conquerors, where everyone took the time to ponder and to just sit and relax.

The city has everything and is a living monument to a time long ago when Catholicism and Spain ruled. Cathedrals and churches dotted the city. They're not as important now as they used to be but still their presence and importance is palpable. There's even a statue to Pope John Paul II erected in honour of his visit in 1986 but rather than a spot to be venerated, it had become part of the small enclave where the homeless gathered and smelt accordingly. There were police nearby perpetually trying to move them on but it was pointless – that was where they had chosen and they would always return whether anyone liked it or not. In a centre of such opulence it was curious to even see such squalor but it

91

wasn't the desperation of Bogota, more the everyday tramps of every large city.

When I stopped and took the time to just look at the people, it was totally different to Bogota. Mostly, they were Afro Caribbean, with smooth, shiny milk coffee coloured skin. They were mostly slim, but with the usual flabby ones and once again, no one smoked and apart from beer, no one seemed to drink. And then, similar to Bogota, there were the taller ones with slick black hair who were laden with European sophistication – they could have all been countesses and counts and they carried with them a casual and confident elegance – designer sunglasses and bags to match – and that was just the men. The streets were spotlessly clean although, as usual, there was a traffic problem but with the sea breeze, the fumes didn't linger.

By early evening, I'd walked just about every inch of wonderful, vibrant, Cartagena. Certain parts of it, clearly lost (yet again) I'd walked several times, but what impressed me most was that the buildings had been there for so long – five or six centuries. There was such majesty to it and it had hardly changed at all. Millions must have been spent on the restoration and it showed. The city built for the Conquistadors and immortalised by Gabriel Garcia Marquez was as vivid today as it would had been then. There were still horses and carriages clip clopping over the cobbles ferrying tourists around as they would once have carried the elite, and in amongst its splendour, there were still the myriad of street stalls selling everything from fruit to drinks to jewellery to hats to pastries to bags and to emeralds – what a city! And it exuded vivacity. It was like one big fiesta all day.

As the sun began to fall into the sea, I was about to make my way home when I was bamboozled by dozens of English Language students, desperate to try out their English and was it OK to ask me some questions – of course it was! "What is your name", "what is your telephone number" (?), "what is your job", "do you have children", "what is your address" and their enthusiasm was infectious. We all took photos and they were just so happy!

By then, I was at the formidable wall of the old city. The new city, with all its skyscrapers, straggled south along the coast but I had no idea what that was like and I had barely any curiosity about it. For me, the old city of Cartagena is what I thought Colombia would look like and it is exactly what it **did** look like – a beautiful, happy, colourful, sweet smelling, sweet sounding melange of everything Caribbean but with solid architectural design to compete with, and outstrip, many, if not all, European cities. Cartagena was built to symbolise the sheer sovereignty of the Spanish empire, and that was exactly what it did. I loved Cartagena!

At the sea wall, I flagged down a taxi and headed out of town with a driver who spoke perfect English. He charged me the set fee of 7,000 pesos which sounds a fortune but was less than £2. I kept thinking that everything was expensive because of all the noughts but it simply wasn't. I was delighted that as a tourist, I hadn't been overcharged and when we got back to my end of town, I already recognised enough to direct us home.

But the night didn't stop there. We once again gathered on the veranda in the rocking chairs. When I told Isaac that in England we tend to gather at the back of the house in private he was shocked. He asked why, when all the action took place on the street? Good question. I asked him if the Catholic Church was still as important and he said no. People were realising that with no contraception, families were huge, they couldn't afford to educate them and that that was the very thing that was holding them back. Now, he said, people had smaller families and those who could, paid for education in the hope that the next generation would be more prosperous. And he was so proud that this is what he had done for his sons – put them through school and college, taught them a trade and provided them with a stable home.

It made me feel a bit mean that I could only see it as half built when to him and his family, it was a palace. Then, with Salsa music rocking the house, I drank my wine, they drank beer and whiskey and we all danced as a practice run for the disco and once again, I felt at home with friends, not strangers.

****

In the morning, in an empty house, I was at peace – sometimes you just need your own space. I decided on a day of laundry. Esther, who appeared from nowhere, offered her twin tub washing machine but having no idea how it worked, I declined and washed nearly everything I had in the sink, chatting all the while like a couple of washer women – she was such fun and her sons and husband adored her and I could see why. Next on the agenda was to book my bus from Cartagena to Santa Marta – that's when Alexander introduced me to Google translate – what a revelation!

And so to the evening of dancing. Esther had been working all day so we; Alexander, Isaac and myself, sat on the veranda drinking beer as the street blossomed with kids playing. On all the other verandas, adults talked and ate ice creams and from every doorway, music blared – a different sound from every house including ours - the bass speaker working so hard the floor throbbed. Relatives dropped by to say hello and practice their English and another son Jeffrey appeared. He was a welder and had worked away in the Bahamas but said it was no more than slave labour so he'd come back and worked in the ship yards of Cartagena. Jeffrey had a girlfriend who was a young single mother but after complications, couldn't have any more children – he was desperate for a family of his own but he was also in love. I wondered if he would compromise and become a father to her daughter or would he be driven away by the need for his own?

Finally, Esther was ready. She was all dolled up; her black afro hair straightened, eye shadow and lipstick applied; a pretty white blouse and red trousers and she was ready to party. One other Spanish word I know is "guappa" which I think means good looking woman. I said it to her; she giggled and pointed straight back at me and arm in arm, we crammed into the taxi. We rolled into town, through the city walls by the clock tower and the whole place was heaving. In the entrance stood a slim tall attractive girl with an enormous backside – was it padded? And, shock horror, was she a prostitute? Isaac just shrugged as if to say "of course". She wasn't the first one I saw that night but in a town that oozes sex appeal it just wasn't surprising.

The square was full of people; tourists in casual wear and rich tall, good looking Colombians decked in their finery. It seemed so weird to see such a mélange of people all thrown together; from the raggedy trousered to the utterly sophisticated who just breezed through, or glided past in the little horse drawn carriages, showing off their splendour for all to see and maybe envy.

"Fidel's" was where we were headed – a tiny bar on two floors, shuddering under the thunder of Salsa. The music was via video on enormous screens, showing the most famous Salsa bands of the country and beyond, and the funniest thing was that all the singers and musicians were all over 40 or 50. Maybe like Flamenco for women and Tango for men, Salsa was something you were not respected for doing until you were of a certain age.

First of all, we got a table in the square and ordered our 4,000 peso beers (£1 each) which to them, was expensive. We watched a mime artist lampooning the walks and gestures of passers-by, swapping hats with them and generally drawing attention to their idiosyncrasies. Everyone laughed, even the victims. I thought, if that was England, he'd probably get a punch in the face. But it wasn't England, it was Colombia and people just wanted to have fun. All the time.

Finally, we got a table inside, up the wonky rickety stairs in the over bright little room with its very own dance floor. Couples showed off their steps and without hesitation, Esther was on the floor Salsaing as if she was born to it. Isaac didn't dance and just sat and watched his wife with adoration. People clapped and danced with her and she loved it. Alexander then took her hand and whisked her around and the two of them made such a great team.

Obviously, I was itching to get up there too, but despite doing zumba for two years, I didn't actually know the steps. What I needed was a partner and that partner was Alexander. Next thing, we were dancing as if WE were born to it! He span me here, he span me there, he span me everywhere. I was delighted and so it seemed, was everyone else – the novice did good. At one point I went out to smoke and someone approached me and told me his friend wanted to kiss me – obviously he'd noticed my fancy footwork and this was surely a compliment except that his friend was absolutely plastered and not capable of noticing anything. I declined.

Finally, after about five hours, the place shut, but not before the legendary Fidel was spotted and I have the photo to prove it – he looked a bit jaded – I imagine it's tough being the king of Salsa in the country of Salsa. Esther, however, wasn't ready to go home. She spotted a Mariachi band, whipped out her purse (she's the one who carries the money) and paid them to play us two more songs and so there we were, dancing yet again, in the middle of the square, her effervescence charging the air. I'm not sure if I've met anyone with such a love of life. She was still dancing when we crammed into the taxi and then she sang all the way home. What a woman.

We finally arrived home about 3am and we all fell into our beds - just as the party next door got going and ear plugs or no, when your bed is moving with the beat, there isn't much you can do...

And so to my last day. Everyone was too tired to do anything and the beach plan faded like cloth left too long in the sun. It seemed like an anti climax and in a bid to do anything, I walked to the shop with Jeffrey and his girlfriend. Jeffrey turned out to be one of the sweetest men I have ever met. The only thing I wanted was a small bottle of rum. What they wanted was an entire shopping list – olive oil tied up in little bags, eggs tied up in little bags, rice tied up in little bags – you get the picture. He bought me a beer while we waited – it wasn't a supermarket, but an old fashioned grocer's with personal counter service. And then finally, he bought 30 bottles of beer. I couldn't imagine why on earth he would do that and then it was revealed – they were throwing me a leaving party!

I just couldn't get over their generosity, their warmth and their sheer love of life. I offered to help carry the shopping home but when his girlfriend declined the offer, I insisted and there we were walking along with a heavy handle each and she just looked so happy. We all dressed for the occasion and the little fairy lights joined us in our sparkle.

Jeffrey and Alexander's girlfriends, the latter a dusky, long legged, slim beauty, helped Ester prepare the food. There were chickens, kebabs, sausages and some sort of cheese textured corn (how was that possible) and even though I shouldn't eat it, I simply didn't care. Jeffrey kept the beers coming and Alexander pumped up the sounds. Isaac said that someone had died and the music shouldn't be too loud – I was never sure if he was a bit of a kill joy if he wasn't the centre of attention, but once he'd sat down to translate for us all, the music crept up a few decibels and he didn't seem to mind or notice.

The barbeque was lit and people just dropped by. There was one young girl about 6 months pregnant, slim as a stick from the back but with a huge great baby belly in the front. There were Esther's sisters and their families dropping in and out and half a dozen children including twins. I was having such a good time; I even played with the kids! And then the dancing began. I was made to show off my steps – I'm a show off, I don't mind and when I snuck in a song of my own – George Ezra, "Leaving it up to you", the place erupted and we all spiralled like Whirling Dervishes. And the greatest thing was that you could do whatever you wanted and they really didn't care; they just wanted to have fun and not only that, they wanted me to have fun and that was exactly what we had. What a family. What a city. What a country!

In the morning, I packed and tidied my room, or should I say Esther and Isaac's room. The minibus came to collect me, as planned (even though I doubted it right up to the last minute) and with one last hug, I was gone.   I'd been so welcomed, I didn't leave feeling like a friend, I left feeling like one of the family and it wasn't often you will ever do that after knowing people for only four days.

SANTA MARTA

The road north east from Cartagena to Santa Marta snakes past the shore of the Caribbean for 200 miles. Mostly to the east, it was dry scrub land where nothing much grew interrupted by miles of shanty towns. It reminded me of parts of Africa. Even though the dwellings were only a jumble of rough breeze blocks or wood, with haphazard corrugated iron roofs and open lattice work gates where there should have been doors, for the people there, it was home. In our Mercedes mini-bus, we thundered through, whipping up the dust and all of us on board were glad that we weren't getting off.

We idled through the traffic-choked town of Barranquilla which, apparently, had a carnival to rival Rio, although you just couldn't believe it. And once through, we were on a toll road and picking up speed. This was the land where if a vehicle would start, you could use it. Cars, buses and vans in varying degrees of decay rolled alongside super trucks and coaches – the vehicles, just like the people, reflected a massive discrepancy in wealth.

Finally, the land to the east rose up and turned brown and we began our descent, past a little favela hanging off the hill, dotted with little brightly painted cubes of houses, into the oldest town and port of Colombia – Santa Marta. In the north, along the beach, there were high rise apartment and hotel buildings, built for the tourists from Bogota, whilst on the other side of the road, there was the usual chaos of buildings in varying degrees of construction. I wondered if

99

this was what Spain looked like 50 years ago when the first package holidays flew people to the Costas and Majorca.

I'd reserved a room in the Hostel Miramar for five nights and thought I knew exactly what to expect. I was dropped off outside and entered an airy courtyard. Pedro, the very helpful, tall, Argentinean receptionist showed me to my room. I know it only cost £6 a night but even I was shocked. The window was the size of an A4 piece of paper high up in the wall (to quote Wilde: "that little tent of blue, which prisoners call the sky") and the door looked out onto the brick wall of the kitchen. It wouldn't do. It wouldn't do at all. He knew I was a writer and I think he thought it might be bad for the reputation of the hostel, so he quickly showed me another cell-like room upstairs that opened onto a terrace. It was better. It was much better.

He carried my huge bag up the stairs for me, gave me a toilet roll, a sheet, a towel and a tiny bar of soap and said that it even had its own bathroom! Notwithstanding that the shower and toilet were IN the room at the end of the bed... Never mind; it was mine and I just thanked god that I wasn't sharing. I turned on the ceiling fan which only had one speed – top speed and unpacked. There was nowhere to hang or put anything. All my clothes were lassoed onto a length of ribbon (a trick I'd picked up in India), so I just hauled them out of my bag, hooked the ribbon over the shower pipe (that's all it was, no shower head, just a pipe), draped them over the wall and voila, I was unpacked. With the ceiling fan whirring frantically around, everything in the room was momentarily lifted in one long perpetual Mexican wave.

I went out to explore – about 100 metres away was the black stained beach. I wasn't sure what the black was, but suspected it might have been coal dust rather than volcanic sand – there are no volcanoes. But there was a lot of coal. Kids were swimming happily enough but it was not the crystal waters which apparently, lap ashore nearby. Santa Marta looked a bit like Cartagena except it was shabby and

100

dilapidated. I hadn't seen any buckets and spades as yet, but if they had them, Santa Marta was where they would be. The old "historic" part of town was where the travellers stayed; in hostels and slightly up market hotels, whilst the rich stayed in the new development uptown and I presumed there was no interaction.

I was happy to be in the shabbier part of town – it was chaotic, it was frenzied and there were people everywhere – just what I'd grown to expect. On Carrera 5, the main street, there was the cacophony of street sellers, the smell of food frying on multitudinous stalls, the stink and rumble of traffic, shops selling everything from sweets, to medicine, to shoes (lots of shoes...), crazy brightly coloured clothes, bags, mobile phone covers (they all had one and far more sophisticated than the old banger I had) and hundreds of Colombians doing what they did best – partying.

I'd asked Pedro where I could get a "set menu" meal – I think he misunderstood me and thought I wanted something like a western restaurant and he directed me accordingly. I ignored his advice, and not having eaten all day, to eat, was my priority. I wandered past a doorway that once again, led to an airy courtyard and so in I wandered. A lovely, tall, stylish, blond woman greeted me, spoke English and said that yes, they had a set menu. She was from Medellin, in the centre of the country, which she said was in a valley, had a climate like spring all year and was very beautiful – never mind that in the days of the drug lord Escobar, there were frequent drive-by shootings and a £1000 bounty on every policeman's head. I wished I was going there (things had changed apparently), but I wasn't.

She sat me down under the obligatory ceiling fan and served me possibly, the best meal I'd had in Colombia. As usual, it started with soup, which was like a meal on its own, followed by a plate of steak oozing blood (just the way I like it), crunchy fried plantain, rice and salad washed down with a freezing cold glass of sugar cane water. And once again, everyone was so helpful – showing me how to use the olive oil dispenser when clearly, I had no idea, bringing me a little bowl of super hot chilli and lime dressing (stupendous) and finally, bringing me the bill – more expensive than usual at £2.25 but of course, worth every penny; to sit in such a stylish restaurant and eat from china, drink from a real glass rather than a plastic or metal cup and even to have cutlery that didn't bend when you used it, was priceless.

Replete, I returned to my tiny room to commandeer the communal terrace table, drag it to my doorway and in the light from my room and with the fan whizzing overhead, I sat on my red plastic garden chair and wrote. OK, the Hostel Miramar wasn't the greatest place to stay, but with the whiff of ganga drifting over from the boys from Minnesota, the clink of beers resounding from the Germans and my own slugs of rum, I couldn't image being anywhere else.

I'm never sure how people half my age will see me. In my head, we are the same age but obviously we're not. I've worked and recently studied with younger people and it's never been a problem. Either they don't think I am in my fifties or they simply don't care and we all get along. Once, when my new young university friend introduced me to her parents, it was obvious to them that I was older than they were, even if their daughter hadn't noticed it. It was so funny to see their faces looking from me and then at their daughter, wondering how this could possibly be true. But to Vicky; I and her parents couldn't have been more different. That night, it was the same.

We all got talking; about our travels past present and future and swapped stories and tips as well as a couple of spliffs. Maybe it was more a question of attitude than age that determined how people will perceive you and happily, I was seen as just a fellow traveller rather than some old eccentric woman wandering around on her own. There may also have been a certain admiration for a woman travelling on her own but in any case, we shared a very affable evening. It was only when it was time to sleep that I noticed the lock of my door could be opened by just reaching in through the lattice work metal door covered only by a curtain. I wondered if I was being over cautious as I locked myself in with my own padlock.

****

It was hot. Too hot to sleep, so at 7.30, I wandered down to the deserted kitchen with my trusty stove top coffee pot (god, how I loved it) and made my coffee as the hostel woke up and the little ladies who run the kitchen arrived for work. They came laden with bags of food, unlocked the fridges and cupboards and even supplied me with a cup rather than the plastic beaker I'd been forced to use – they obviously understood the importance of coffee as much as I did.

I wasn't sure where my travels should take me. Santa Marta didn't seem like the sort of place anyone stayed long term, but simply passed through on their way to somewhere more interesting. The boys from Minnesota said that Taganga, where I was already booked for the Easter week (apparently the busiest week of the year and essential to book ahead), was awful and that where I should be going was Palomino. Pedro said no, that you couldn't swim in the sea at Palomino because of the currents and that it was full of mosquitoes. I was beginning to wonder if anyone stayed in one place for long in Latin America or whether they were all on a tour of the continent, which just kept them moving, rather than settling into a community which is what I wanted to do.

What to do? I knew that I didn't want to stay much longer in Santa Marta but where else was there? I had a month to spend which seemed reasonable sitting in my house in a rain sodden and cold London, but in reality, I was struggling to find anywhere that I really wanted to go. What I needed was some of Garcia's magic realism. Failing that, there was the internet.

103

My tiny laptop was my best friend and constant companion – obviously I'd have preferred a real person, but the virtual world seemed omnipresent. I spent ages trying to find information about Taganga and Palomino and also to find a proper map of Santa Marta. My Rough Guide was, in fact, bloody useless. The maps were hopeless and it was ridiculously out of date – and that was the most current edition. In the end, I gave up and in the strong midday heat – only wild dogs and Englishmen, I went out in the sun. I was desperate to swim and change the colour of my skin.

Alongside the beach was a purpose built, palm shaded, promenade and that was where I walked. Little, shiny, milk coffee coloured kids played in the water, beckoning me to join them. What was I to do? I found a woman who was there to take in the rays, asked her in sign language to look after my bag, whipped off my dress and plunged in. The Caribbean didn't have the gargantuan waves that the Pacific had, but the water was cool and clear. I swam on the surface, I swam underwater and I swam with the kids – getting them to put their tiny feet in my hands and flipping them backwards. They couldn't get enough and swam alongside me like little ducklings with big grins on their faces. It was almost impossible to leave them, but leave them I did, to lie in the sun and feel the baking heat trying to permeate my factor 30 and it just felt so good! I hadn't been on a beach since San Agustinillo and I couldn't even remember how long ago that was – Mexico City, Bogota, Cartagena – too long.

Earlier, I'd spotted yet another leafy courtyard and retraced my steps. The streets there were supposed to have numbers but this being Colombia, they didn't. It was just trial and error, all of the time. It should have been simple – you just counted them but then they would sneak in another one – 1a for example, and then their whole grid system went to pot.

Anyway, I was getting the hang of it and found the little courtyard restaurant I'd seen earlier, just as the young waitress was taking in the sign. No matter, if I wanted to eat, they were open – I was the only one in there and once again, there was that language barrier. But not for long – she had a phone (they all had a phone) and she motioned for me to listen to it. It said, "fish or meat." I opted for the latter. The cook must have been standing in the kitchen for hours making enormous vats of everything in a tiny kitchen with no ventilation and then ferried it out to what must really have been her living room.

The surroundings weren't as opulent as the day before and the fork bent when I used it but you know what? If anything, it was better and for half the price. What can I say? The more time I spent there, the more I loved it. They were always so pleased when in my rubbish Spanish, I said "muy bien". They broke into huge smiles as if I had paid them the best compliment, but the funniest thing was that I had – I really meant it. I was full of thanks, all of the time. And just as I was leaving, the cook's daughter came home dressed in her smart school uniform and I just wondered if that was what it was all for – to give her children the education she'd never had so that they wouldn't have to do the same when they grew up. Just as Isaac had said back in Cartagena, the Afro Caribbeans, as second class citizens, had to do it for themselves, little by little.

I finished the evening by putting on some eye makeup thus accentuating the fact that my eyes were blue, to tremendous effect. Suddenly, I was like a VIP. I walked around town like a different person, visiting the local supermarket which just bamboozled me by the things that they had for sale. I bought myself a proper glass and a bottle of 2013 Chilean wine (a mistake – I should have bought the 2014 – it just baked in the bottle – mine was like sherry) and then retired to my terrace to write and drink in the delightful company of three young French boys, who in their turn, guzzled agua diente, which I was told means water of fire, or sex, whichever way you chose to interpret it – this was, after all, Colombia.

Once again, there was no age barrier and we talked until 1pm about our respective travels and their jobs from which they were escaping. They kept slinking off and would return far more animated and I presume they were snorting coke which was everywhere, even though it was supposed to be highly illegal. One of them had a mother who worked for an airline and was determined to travel the world before his under 24 year old concessions ended. I envied him his cheap flights – in my youth it was all long distance coach travel and the very odd short haul flight – it was all we could afford in those days. He also said that he'd worked as a waiter in Paris and how badly he was treated because of his regional accent. We all agreed that Parisians were about the most arrogant people on earth and deserved all the bad press that they got and shouldn't be allowed to live in such a marvellous city.

****

The Parisian couple (oops) were up early, talking to their daughter on loudspeaker and so we were all up early. I presume she overheard our conversation the night before... I decided to explore the beach and walked all the way to the end, past the deserted marina and the swish new development until, finally, the beach ran out and it all began to look abandoned. There were numerous gaudy bronze statues dedicated to the indigenous tribes. I wasn't sure what scale they were working to but they all looked like the Incredible Hulk – both male and female and did them no favours. It almost seemed to suggest that they were some sort of Neanderthals and deserved to be conquered but that they'd honour them anyway and all would be forgiven. My Rough Guide said that tourist money was flooding into the area and that soon, everything would change and improve. All I could see was a tacky casino and the aforementioned luxury developments which all seem fairly forlorn.

The sand, I noticed, glistened in the sun as if it was full of pyrite. I couldn't help but think that pyrite was also known as "fool's gold" and with the empty buildings and marina, I wondered if it was an example of foolish investment. I also noticed two great big blue tubes running across the beach into the sea. They were like giant snakes, with reverse peristalsis, heaving their guts out into the water. They were effluence pipes, but what exactly was it they were disgorging? I couldn't say, but from the stink of them, what else could it be?

I declined to swim there and headed back into town to take in its entire heady cornucopia. Apart from the old city of Cartagena, everything on the coast of Colombia looked half finished with rubble everywhere. Santa Marta was no exception. The air stank of traffic fumes and horns blared all day. It seemed to be Colombia's soundscape. But no matter, you got used to it.

Carrera 5 was the main high street. It had pavements either side which, of course, were all broken and cluttered with make-shift stalls and tables but even so, at the beginning, it had a ramp clearly marked with the universal disabled sign for wheelchairs. How any one in a wheelchair could have got any further than the ramp was beyond me. Both sides of the street were completely jam packed with people who would just stop suddenly; they'd have a chat or look at something, regardless of the blockage they were causing. I wasn't used to it and it seemed rude but no one else seemed even remotely bothered. No one, it seemed, was in a hurry except me and I don't even know why I was. Just something you get used to from living in a Western city I suppose.

The shops were all completely different selling everything from shoddy goods piled high and sold cheaply, to more up-market stores, tiny boutiques full of miniscule sexy clothes (the style of choice), dozens of phone shops and many, many food shops selling fresh (or not so fresh) produce and cooked food both to eat in or take out. In fact, anything that you could possibly need or want, you could get.

What I wanted was salad and that was what I got. A big lollo

107

rosso lettuce you could bury your face in, massive peppers, beetroots and everything else besides and for next to no money. Sometimes, your body tells you what it needs and that's what mine was telling me.

Back at the hostel, once the little ladies had vacated the kitchen (I was afraid I got on their nerves by wandering into their domain, and I probably did, even though they just smiled at me and appreciated that I washed up after myself), I made the biggest salad I've had since leaving England – wonderful!

Satiated I returned to the streets. I'd been searching for two days for a particular hostel which was supposed to be much better than mine and as if by magic, I finally found it – across the street five doors up – how had I missed it? All the websites said that it would be more expensive, but I just thought it would be worth it – there's only so much time you can spend in a tiny room with the whiff of a toilet at the end of your bed.

It looked more like a hotel than a hostel, was the colour of honey and without hesitation, I went in. With my trusty dictionary, I said I wanted a room for two nights (after my Miramar booking lapsed). The proud owner showed me upstairs to a lovely room, with a window and a breeze and a proper bathroom. It had a wonderful rooftop terrace which didn't look like a building site (like the Miramar), a little courtyard and communal kitchen for the use of the guests and when I asked how much, I was completely staggered when it turned out to be exactly the same as what I was paying for a stink hole! I booked for the two nights

Later, I looked once again at Taganga – I still didn't know if it would be the place for me but it supposedly had "long stay communities" and in a moment of hysteria, I'd clicked the reserve button and it seemed that I would be there the following Monday for a week as well as the week I'd already booked. I just hoped that it was what I hoped it would be – a bit like Goa, with like minded people and maybe, just maybe, a new best friend to match Andree from San Agustinilllo... To be honest, I was getting lonely with no one to talk to and was conscious of the fact that just like at home, I was spending far too long on my own.

****

I couldn't stand the suspense. By 10am, I was standing in the middle of the road flagging down the beaten up bus to Taganga. I paid the 35p fare and off we went, passing "houses" that you wouldn't believe existed or even stood up. And then the beautiful horse shoe shaped bay appeared and we rumbled into the village. I wanted to check out my options whilst I still had time to cancel. I thought the streets in Santa Marta were haphazard – in Taganga, they just run out and at best, were rubble strewn thoroughfares. I wandered into the hinterland of half built buildings, creeks with no water, ragged plastic bags strewn from wires and an awful lot of dust.

As if by magic, I found the Hostel Mandela. The photographer who takes all the pictures for Booking.Com, Hostelworld etc, should be given a medal or arrested under the Trades Description Act. It all looked immaculate on-line, but in reality, it was sheer Colombian chaos. No matter; this was where I had booked for £5 a night WITH breakfast (how is that possible?) and she showed me a couple of rooms – the one I'd booked had three beds but which, apparently, were all for me in a bright airy room with a SEPERATE bathroom. I could feel myself morphing into Goldilocks...

My next quest was the airbnb place I'd reserved weeks ago for Easter. By chance, I bumped into a tall, older man wearing a natty straw hat who turned out to be the owner! So we both walked, puffing, up the hill. We passed a tiny clinic, a "beauty parlour", very random shops and then it all just fizzled out. It seemed it wasn't just the road that had come to an end, it was civilization.

Finally, right at the top of the hill he welcomed me to his lovely home "Casa Italia". He poured me a glass of cool, clear, water and proudly showed me the lovely double room. I had to explain that that wasn't my room. For the money I paid, I had been told, by email, rather curtly, that I would be sharing a room with one other girl. Not what I wanted and clearly, not what the owner wanted either. I wondered if providence would work that one out... He walked me back down the hill, introduced me to some of his friends, pointed out a good restaurant and told me that his name was Michelangelo and that he was from Bogota.

Left to myself, I ate in the little restaurant he'd recommended. The tables were outside next to the road and motorbikes constantly pulled up, engines running, stinking the place up whilst they went in for their take outs. I chose to eat meat but it was so tough as to be inedible. I gave it to the dogs and wondered if they make it like that so at least the dogs don't starve. I then wandered the beach front. It wasn't as makeshift as Goa, probably because it didn't have a monsoon and needed to be taken down every year, but the people were vaguely similar in a timeless, "we've got all day" mentality. It had a relaxed feel to it even if it wasn't particularly Colombian. It was definitely more geared to western or at least western orientated travellers than Colombians and I hoped that maybe someone would speak English.

Back in Santa Marta, I thought it just might be too long in Taganga so returned to the hostel of yesterday, booked another two nights with him – he was overjoyed – he called me Deneezzee – I called him Fabio and then I realised, I hadn't seen a sunset in a long time. I went to the beach with my camera, sat and waited, and as it set, the little kids who dived for tourists' pesos just happened to be in my shot – perfect really.

****

110

I finally broke. I couldn't stand the stink and claustrophobia of the room anymore. I whizzed over to check that Fabio had my room ready for me, he beamed yes, he did. I raced back, packed and was out of the door in minutes, crossed the road and entered paradise! (It's not easy to find online so here is the web address http://www.hospederiacasafamiliar.freeservers.com.) The Hostel Miramar was fine if you want little or nothing from a room but why would you? I helped Fabio up the stairs with my bag and he showed me to a better room than he showed me the last time. I was in bliss. I even unpacked! Everything. Suddenly I had a row of shoes – all seven of them! I showered, I napped, I rearranged my belongings and I even watched television that I wasn't interested in, just because I could – I was SO HAPPY! I went up to the roof terrace and could see the hills which enclosed the town – I hadn't even really noticed those before. The view and the air was so refreshing, it felt like a different town.

For the first time in Santa Marta, I was really beginning to enjoy myself. I felt relaxed and happy. It felt more like a hotel than a hostel, had comfortable places to lounge and the kitchen and dining area were an open air treat. We all took it turn to cook and chatted whilst we ate. There was no real need to discover any night life in town – everything I needed was there – good company and good conversation. I talked to two lovely German girls who, of course, spoke perfect English. They'd been to Chile – I had my suspicions about Chile – that Nazis fled there after the Second World War, which explained the military coups and total lack of human rights – never forget, they're the ones who would fling people out of airplanes, just in case they were revolutionaries. But back to the point; the girls had their own little bottle of washing up liquid bought in Chile which they guarded closely. I understood their motive – in Mexico and Colombia, they had tubs of hard green toxic-looking abrasive sludge for washing up and you just wondered what it did to hands, plates and the environment, never mind what it did to grease.

Later, in the sanctity of my room, I was just getting comfortable when my TV broke! Fabio struggled up the stairs with another one but seeing as he needed a spanner, it all became too much and then that word I feel sums up South and Central America was uttered, "Manana"... And the funniest thing was, no one WAS in a hurry. Queues there out queue our queues any day and no one complains or even comments, they just have a chat. In one queue, I was standing behind a woman buying a phone. I stupidly pointed out that it had no wire. She said something to the till man and suddenly I could see me camping out in the same queue for a couple of days until a new delivery arrived. Thankfully, that's not what happened – she went off to find a replacement which meant I was next! (It wasn't until much later I realised that what everyone was doing in these monumental queues was flirting – the longer the queue, the more chances you had – unbelievable but at the same time, so typically Colombian!)

****

Fabio came struggling in under the weight of a new TV. I say "new" - I've thrown away TV's that looked newer and I **never** throw anything away. He unfolded his ladder, got his spanner out, hit the frame to make it bigger and finally got the old one out and the new one in. It was useless. He stood on his ladder for at least 15 minutes trying to tune in a channel – a Spanish channel. I had to point out that I didn't speak Spanish... He tried another few and they were worse. He shrugged as in a "what do you need a TV for?"– never mind that his own one downstairs was the size of a cinema screen! I suggested I change room. That woke him up and he told me to wait. Then he struggled in with an even older TV with knobs that twisted, circa 1970's. It was just fuzz. He shrugged again and that seemed to be an end to it. I later saw him aiming a hair dryer at the first one as if he could blow the dust and sand out and return it to working order and hence my room. I had my doubts.

112

With nothing else to do, I went out for yet another walk which turned into something of a shopping spree (!). I returned with all sorts of hair accessories, a metre of magnificent orange silk (?), ribbon and somehow, another pair of shoes. They were only £5, they sparkled, they were my size and what was a girl to do? In Santa Marta, every pair of shoes was of any size EXCEPT my size. I wondered if the town was like some giant TK Max full of remnants. I also discovered the "market" which had been denied – "market, what market?" as if it didn't exist. It was filthy, it sold everything including MEAT with a few million flies thrown in for free and even **I** didn't want to buy anything.

But what I did buy was yet more rotisserie chicken – I didn't even think they sold it! And as usual, it was great. They even supplied a pair of thin plastic disposable gloves to eat with! I didn't use them of course; I just licked the juice off my fingers. The girl sitting at the next table used hers but the more remarkable thing, was that as she sat eating, her baby was feeding at her breast as if it was the most normal thing in the world and IT IS! It seemed so sad to me that something as natural as mother's milk can be ignored in favour of some manufactured nonsense loaded with calories which can never be as good. At least in Colombia, poverty didn't allow for such an expensive alternative which was possibly why obesity hardly existed. Never mind that next door was the cake shop with kids birthday cakes so brightly coloured, I couldn't even imagine the amount of E numbers they had in them – get them addicted when they're young and you'll have a racket on your hands for life.

But the thing that I noticed about Santa Marta as opposed to Cartagena and Bogota, was that nearly everyone there was dressed to thrill. Tiny denim shorts and sexy tops no matter what shape they were and every body oozed sex appeal. Even the mannequins in the shops had great big breasts and bums. It was as if everyone was on heat and maybe it **was** the heat, but the place was ALIVE. It wasn't overtly sexual in a sleazy way (except at the end of my street, which I thought might well be a brothel...) but more in a celebration of nature's bounteous gifts.

I finished the evening in the company of a young man from Stuttgart. I'm not sure, but I think he was flirting with me. Strange, that when you get to a certain age you don't think young men will be interested in you but if older men were perpetually attracted to younger women, why shouldn't it be the same? Anyway, he not only spoke perfect English, but also had a tremendous grasp of European economic policy and the fiasco therein, so flirting aside, we managed to have a really good conversation about said policies and a lot more besides. He also told me about Medallin, the city in the centre of Colombia.

He said that as usual, there was a mixture of rich and very poor. There was also a cable car so that visitors and locals alike could rise up above the shanty town, look down on it in both senses and not even have to wander through it as they used to have to. Seeing how the other half lived took on a whole new meaning. Germans get a bad press the world over for being too serious and having no sense of humour but I've always found them to be really interesting and aware people. Unlike Basil Fawlty, I just don't mention the war. I also didn't take him up on his advances – he wasn't my type – I'm older, not desperate. Also, it's more a case of quality, not quantity, but if you can get both then you are really laughing - I've done an awful lot of laughing.

****

It was Domingo or Sunday, as we know it, and the streets were very, very, quiet and deserted – apart from the two cable TV men, in sweltering overalls who had come to fix the aerial. It made me laugh to think of Fabio up the ladder with three different TVs when all along the problem must have been the aerial but no matter, they were there fixing it.

I thought perhaps Domingo was a day of rest. I was wrong.

EVERYONE was at the beach! It wasn't the density of Copacabana, but it was close. They were jammed onto the sand in such bright clothes I wasn't not sure if they were day-glo or just looked it because of the brightness of the sun. There were hundreds of little kids with their parents and even salesmen wandering along, selling not only buckets and spades (!) but little bright orange or yellow plastic inflatable life jackets. Big black inner tubes were for hire and the water was abob with all of it. The ice cream sellers cycled along the promenade ringing their bells; the coffee men with their flasks wandered the sand, along with the churros, sunglasses, jewellery, fruit and giant cheesy wot-sits sellers. Stands were set up everywhere selling ice cold orange or lime juice or just fizzy drinks in varying lurid colours sweet enough to dissolve your teeth. There were even girls selling the set lunch menu food from giant saucepans on street barrows. And most of them were blaring out music from salsa to reggae.

Some people hired little tent affairs like mini gazebos only big enough to fit two plastic garden chairs, and others, mostly, just sat on the beach whilst the picnic came to them. And they shared. They shared everything, even with strangers. One tiny boy, his little bum sticking out of his little yellow trunks, stood next to a family watching them eat and they just handed him a sandwich the size of his head. Everyone seemed really happy, gregarious and vivacious. They seemed to take life as it came and made the best of it, day by day and, not for the first time, I admired their simplicity.

It was so hot, I could actually watch my skin change colour (I'd abandoned the factor 30 for something less impervious...) and feeling a couple of shades darker as well as looking it, I retired for lunch. The usual place was shut (shock horror) so I tried a new place. After the usual mime and sign language, my soup and then main course arrived just as a beggar turned up at the window behind me. On my plate was something unidentifiable – it could have been the weird pressed corn stuff I'd seen before or maybe it was just a lump of boiled starch but in any case, I didn't want it so wrapped it in a napkin and gave it to him hoping he'd go away.

But he didn't. He just stood there eyeing the rest of my food and my bottle of bright red fizzy drink. One of the waitresses approached him, said something to him and I thought that maybe he would move along and let me eat in peace. Again, what I expected wasn't what happened. She brought him a cup of water and when two men at the next table finished their lunch, they poured him the remainder of their giant bottle of coke. That's what I mean. They were generous, good people and I so admired them. Sometimes I wonder if we in the so called sophisticated West have forgotten what charity means in our self centred material world.

Back at Casa Familiar, aka Fabio's place, my TV was indeed working! I'd planned on a nap but it turned out that the big covered construction on the roof wasn't a hot tub or a Jacuzzi, it was a mini swimming pool for Fabio's grandchildren and there they all were, splashing about right opposite my window, waving and shouting hola. Obviously, a nap was out of the question – for quite a few hours, but who needed a nap when I had a TV. I tuned into the English movie channel and settled down for some idle time with John Cusack except that despite having Spanish subtitles, it was also dubbed into Spanish. Only in Colombia.

****

Breaking news in Colombia; there was a hail storm in Bogota and part of the city had collapsed! There were clips of crushed cars, broken houses and people shovelling up piles of hail the size of snow drifts. It was such a country of contrasts in every conceivable way. I saw that on the TV news whilst baking from the heat in my lunch time café.

Usually, the other customers didn't pay me much attention, they just showed mild curiosity. That day however, there were three young women dressed in next to nothing, a huge

116

cleavage at both front and rear and giving me really hostile looks. They even jostled me on the way out and from their appearance I would guess that my suspicions were correct. I was in the Red Light District of town but what did their looks mean – surely they didn't think that I was hustling on their turf? In my flowery frocks, I hardly looked like a threat – or did I? I'd probably be regarded as skinny beside the buxom local women. Just think, it's not a question of "does my bum look big in this?" it's "does my bum look big **enough** in this?" Oh, the irony.

The town was once more deserted – it was a fiesta day. For a moment, it felt like "Groundhog Day" and I was worried I would be caught in an ongoing loop of deserted streets and busy beaches. At my end of the beach, lots of little stalls were being erected so I went out later to investigate and there were still lots of little stalls being erected – things took a little longer in Colombia. I was just sitting on a wall, watching another perfect sunset when I noticed an older man sitting nearby who looked European and might, just might, speak English. I approached and asked him. Yes, he did!

His name was Franz, he was from Belgium (thought to be uninteresting but never forget it has some of the best beer, chocolate, mussels and doughnuts in the world – how can that be bad?), he'd been travelling through South America on and off for 40 years and he spoke Spanish – two for the price of one. We got talking and I told him the story of why I was there – basically, Gabriel Garcia Marquez and he said he was going to Aracataca the next day which was the real town of "Macondo", immortalised in *One Hundred Years of Solitude* and asked did I want to go. It was a 50 mile bus journey which, in Colombia, was nothing and so I said yes. I meant to pack and buy provisions for Taganga but hell, nothing ventured and all that...

****

I'd set my alarm for 7am but was woken at 5.45am by the man in the next room's TV. If I had one little complaint about

Colombians, it was their lack of consideration. I don't know why it was, it might even have something to do with the legacy of slavery, but it was slightly annoying. They NEVER gave way in their cars and if there was a narrow confluence, they would barge right through. I'm used to saying "after you" and the reply being, "no, after you". But not there, they just crashed right through and so, with the man in the next room who thought it was totally acceptable to put his TV on LOUD before dawn, I too was awake before dawn. Never mind. I was going to see the birthplace of Gabriel Garcia Marquez, my literary hero.

At 8.30 Fabio knocked on my door and slightly disgruntled, told me there was a man to see me. I felt as if I was cheating on him – never mind that he had a wife and family. Franz had no idea of the friction he had caused and just sat there in cool sunglasses, shorts and a T shirt, his grey hair tied back in a pony tail and his rucksack on the floor between his sandaled feet and long legs. Once upon a time, I could see that he would have been very good looking. He wasn't bad looking now but he wasn't my type, whatever that was.

Finding the bus stop for the terminus, when they all seem to stop anywhere they liked, wasn't easy, but soon we were heading that way and I suddenly realised just how big Santa Marta was. I'd only seen the tourist district and a tiny bit beyond, but it was a city and it spread for miles. Some of it was new and clean but the old bits were a complete shambles. Junk of all sorts was piled up on the streets to be repaired or sold and it all had a slightly desperate air about it. Again, I was reminded of India. Colombia isn't really deemed to be a Third World country but there in Santa Marta and all along the coast, the poverty was visible and grim.

We arrived at the terminus and someone corralled us onto a dilapidated bus for Aracataca for a mere £5 each and off we went with just three of us on board. It didn't seem very cost effective and in no time, we were pulled over by the police (in heavy uniforms and guns and yet not a bead of sweat – how

118

did they do that?). We couldn't really understand why but presumed that it was exactly because it wasn't cost effective, so we returned to the depot and picked up more people until we were packed as tight as fruit in a Christmas cake.

One of the only bonuses of being in a land where no one speaks English is that you can talk about anything you like without being understood and so I asked Franz about his life. Before he retired, he said, he'd been an engineer and responsible for modernizing the port of Antwerp. I presume he'd been paid a fortune. It always strikes me as odd that when I go out, I take all the money that I will need, whereas men will take all that they had. His wallet was bulging and I'm sure that he was prepared to spend it all.

He also told me about his turbulent love life – married firstly to a Belgian woman with whom he'd had two children but little passion and then he'd married a Chilean woman who was the opposite. He said that the sex had been astronomical and that even now, he couldn't go for more than two weeks without it or he became completely grumpy. I agreed that sex was one of the most important elements of life and that thank god, it was mostly free. Free or not, he said, when necessary he paid for it. I wondered if that's why he was staying in the "red light" district of town (as was I for no reason other than it's locality) and I also wondered if he was thinking that he and I would have sex for no other reason than that we could, like the two consenting adults that we were. I was sure that he would have been a great lover but thankfully, I'm no longer ruled by it in the way that I once was. I changed the subject and was glad that, unlike the local girls, I wasn't dressed to thrill, just in case he got the wrong idea.

We rolled along the seashore; the hills of the Sierra Madre de Santa Marta to our left, coal termini ports to the right until finally, we turned inland. The country opened out onto banana plantations as far as you could see, with mango trees growing wild along the road, dropping its fruit for all to eat.

119

Cows and horses grazed and little trees dotted the land. The grass was brown – sometimes it didn't rain all year and I just wondered how anything grew let alone flourished and yielded.

After a couple of hours, we stopped at the tiny town of Aracataca where we got off. The streets were no more than dust, the houses all one storey, short stumpy trees lined the streets, the odd bougainvillea brightened the landscape and suddenly, there was a cycle taxi before us. It was baking hot so we climbed aboard and for 50p, he cycled us the very short distance to the museum. This was the house where "Gabo" as he was known (by everyone) in Colombia lived with his grandparents and it was a shrine to Colombia's, if not the world's, greatest writer. There was a guard at the entrance (there was a guard at the entrance to everything), he asked us to sign in and the shrine was ours.

It was a simple wooden framed house, with small rooms either side of a long corridor and with apparently, the original furniture. The sitting room had rocking chairs, little wooden tables and an old gramophone of the wind–up kind and an accordion. The bedrooms had wooden or metal framed beds with porcelain wash had basins and jugs. The kitchen had a big old table and what looked like a slate tile which would be heated by a fire beneath for cooking on. The dining room was set with table and chairs covered in a white linen tablecloth and candle stick holders and the study had a roll top desk and chair. It wasn't big and it wasn't grand and it wasn't like the grand old palatial houses he described in his books. But nevertheless, that was where he created those fabulous characters and narratives and I was simply in awe at the imagination of the man.

On the walls, printed onto big boards in Spanish and English, were pieces of text and I remembered why he meant so much to me. It was sublime, awesome, beautiful and breathtaking. The prose of that man was enough to give me goose bumps and even, at times, made me cry, and there I was, in his house. When no one was looking, I even sat on his bed and held his cup to my lips. Simply outstanding.

We wanted to imagine what the town would have been like in his day, so sat and drank beer in an old cafe with wonky wooden tables and chairs and looked out onto the tree crowded square. The very few people who were about, were either in the cafes or sitting quietly in the shade. I could imagine it with no motorbikes, no amplified music and just a man with an imagination surrounded by people who all had a story to tell and even if they didn't, he would invent one for them. Aracataca – it even sounded onomatopoeic.

Walking back towards the bus stop, we crossed the train tracks. You couldn't even imagine a train going through that tiny town which would have been long forgotten if it weren't for Gabo, but through it came. It took ten minutes to pass – full of coal on its way to the port. Whilst I waited I noticed a mute woman smiling at me and with absolutely no language of any kind, we had a conversation – I seemed to be able to communicate with no words better than I could in Spanish!

And so replete, we began our journey home – this time, by chance, on an air-conditioned bus and then a taxi in the 4pm rush hour of Santa Marta to our street. We agreed to meet later for cocktails – it would be my first since leaving Mexico and this being my last night in Santa Marta, it seemed appropriate.

By 8pm I was dressed up. I wore mascara and my new sparkly shoes and Franz and I went out on the town. Santa Marta wasn't remotely bustling with night life but there were little pockets of glamour and that was where we went. Young (affluent) Colombians crowded into leafy squares or the pedestrian part that crossed the old town and sat at tables outside, whilst Bob Marley or Salsa boomed on the breeze. We drank Margueritas and talked of where we would go next – me to Taganga and Franz to who knew where. But one thing I was sure of; Colombia was a beautiful country and the next day would be another day in another part of it and I

121

couldn't wait! Adios Santa Marta.

TAGANGA – VILLA MANDELA

I left the lovely Casa Familiar after a weird trip into town. My reading glasses had gone awry and needed fixing. I thought it was just a case of tightening a screw but no. It was more serious. The man on the street directed me to a proper opticians. Miraculously, I found it. He looked at my glasses, moved the arm alarmingly and spoke to me in Spanish. The dictionary came out – it wouldn't take long and it would cost 10,000 pesos (£2.50). I handed him my very expensive glasses and took a seat. Shortly afterwards, I saw him holding the broken arm, unattached to the glasses and feared the worst. Minutes later, he returned them to me completely repaired! Bravo!

I then went to an ATM to withdraw cash. In those private booths, you got mere moments to complete your transactions, obviously to default fraud but as a foreigner, it just wasn't enough time. I thought I'd requested £150's worth but instead, only £75 came out. I thought of going into the bank to question the amount but what would I say - "I speak no Spanish but..." I decided to leave it to providence and went to another bank which just spat the money out, no problem. I then went to the supermarket to stock up – Taganga, my next stop had nothing in the way of anything as far as I could make out on my recce a few days ago. I bought coffee, lactose free milk and a big bottle of rum to go with the three bottles of wine I already had – well I was going to be there for maybe two weeks.

I packed my bag, stashing the booze, a kilo of brown sugar

(?), nearly a kilo of coffee (I drink a lot), fruit and salad –
even I questioned my sanity and when it came time to check
out, even the maids were alarmed at the apparent weight of
my bag and offered to help me down the stairs with it. I
thought that if we dropped it, what with all the rum and wine,
it would look like a blood bath and smell like a drunk.

Fabio rang a taxi for me, we took photos and he mimed
crying. I mimed it too – for nearly a week, we'd been miming
everything and it had been such a laugh and a treat. He had
been such a memorable host. The taxi arrived and it took
two of us to carry the bag to the car. It took up the whole of
the back seat – I had to sit in the front, and when we finally
pulled away, waving as we went, the car could barely move
under the weight. The taxi driver assured me he knew where
Villa Mandela was but even so, at the first corner, he called to
Fabio's son for directions. I said, in a language he didn't
understand, that I knew the way – I'd already been there and
as a motorbike courier in London for four years, if I couldn't
remember the way, no one could.

We set off, listing on the corners what with the bag, and
retraced the route (for me) of a few days ago. Once again
the beautiful horse shoe shape bay came into view and then
the descent into the tiny village that was Taganga. We pulled
in and he asked again for directions. Off to the left he was
told. No, it was to the right I mimed. Somehow, he trusted
me and within minutes, we pulled up outside Villa Mandela
Casa Mojito. We BOTH carried my bag in, I explained to a
young girl who had no idea what I was talking about, that I
had a reservation and after a few minutes, she passed her
mobile phone to me. The proprietor, Chico, was on his way!

On arrival, he showed me a pokey room and told me that that
was what was available for the price I'd reserved – here we
go again, I thought. He then showed me the room that his
wife had shown me and which we'd agreed a price on only
last week. Except suddenly, it was more expensive... I opted
for the cheaper room except on reflection, it had no real light

124

and the bathroom was the size of a very small closet. I pulled myself together, got the girl to ring him back and told him I'd take the more expensive room with a double bed, air conditioning, TV, windows and LIGHT.

He was so obliging, he told me that he'd take the bunk beds out so giving me more room which he did – well he didn't but a lovely young man called Oscar, who's involved in extreme sports, and who speaks English, did. I asked if I could possibly have the big old wooden table and chair from the other room as well, on account of being a writer and they didn't even raise an eyebrow. I offered to help, having once worked as an antiques removal person with my wonderful ex boyfriend Sean. He accepted my offer. We got it out of the other room but short of sawing the legs down, which I was all for, (they thought I was kidding but I wasn't), we couldn't get it in. We had to give up and instead, I was given a plastic chair - not quite the same, but what could I do - we couldn't even get a plastic table through the door.

Never mind; I had a huge double bed, a TV that on closer inspection didn't work at all, massive windows (with security bars – slightly alarming) that didn't really lock (even more alarming) and as it turned out, a room that didn't lock either. Security was just not a concern there. Out in the "reception" all the computers were left out and personal belongings were scattered everywhere. All the walls ended before they met the roof, the rooms ended at the garden/courtyard where there were no walls, simply open lattice metal frames, much like a garden gate at home and no one seemed to ever lock the door – at least not during the day. I felt a bit weird being so security conscious as if I was staying in some kind of crime centre but everyone had warned me that Taganga was full of thieves. In the end, my door just needed a really good (noisy) slam and I was out into the street with no street lights...

There were two things moving in the shadows right in front of me – were they muggers??? No, they were a couple of donkeys – there can't be a person on earth who doesn't like donkeys. I turned the corner – not forgetting that people had also told me Taganga was full of drug addicts, only to find a floodlit football pitch with a load of little boys playing on one pitch and a load of girls and women playing on another and not a thief in sight!

It just seemed to get better and better and as I wandered into town, there were people everywhere, just hanging out, having a drink, having dinner; locals and tourists alike and I just thought, I like it! And as for the whole place reeking of ganga, it simply didn't – in London, I smelt it absolutely everywhere – I knew what it smelt like and it wasn't what it smelt like there! Notwithstanding that there were police everywhere. They all looked about 16 years old and I doubt they shaved yet – they scooted about on bright lime green motorbikes but to be honest, they looked as if they were having more of a holiday than we were.

When I finally went back to my room, I unpacked and made it my own. Then I attended to the bathroom – if I was going to stay in that room, for a week, I might as well invest in it. The shower head was blocked with calcium so I got the little sewing kit I'd bought in Oaxaca, took out a needle and simply freed them up. I then adjusted the ball cock in the toilet cistern so that it stopped overflowing onto the bathroom floor, gave it all a good mopping and a good clean, opened a bottle of wine, tuned my little radio into a local station, directed the AC unit directly at me and sat there researching on my laptop whether it was worth moving any time soon to another part of Colombia's coast when suddenly, all the lights went out, the air con stopped, my laptop went on to battery mode and apart from my radio, all went quiet and no one seemed bothered. They just went to bed and in the end, so did I. This was Colombia!

****

There were two little boys living in the house and just like

126

most little boys, they get up early and make a racket, so I got up early too. The power was back on and strong coffee (just the way I like it) was on the go. Coffee and filtered water was free, something that I'd forgotten when lugging a kilo of the stuff with me... Eggs and toast were also complimentary but as I could eat neither, it was immaterial. It was however great to just wander around the kitchen, as free as the ants that inhabited everything, helping myself, whilst people came and went. I didn't know who actually lived there and who was related to whom, but it went on all day.

I meant to make an early start and walk over to the other (apparently better) beach and back before the midday heat. But that's not what happened. I don't why I bothered planning anything in that part of the world. Suddenly, there was a knock at the door. Oscar was there with the plastic table from yesterday, now dismantled. He carried it in, assembled it in the corner by the window and then my room really was perfect!

Obviously, the table was filthy from being in the garden for god knows how long so I asked the cleaning girl if I could borrow her stuff. She gave me a baffled look – but that might have just been because she hadn't understood a word I'd said, or was it because she couldn't see any need to clean it – never mind that it was covered in dirt and home to a hundred dead and living spiders. In moments, it was sparkling and wasting no opportunity, I quickly cleaned the sink and the soap dish that looked as if it hadn't ever been cleaned. Cleanliness didn't seem to matter there. Even when I washed up the plates later, there were bits of food stuck hard that must had been there for weeks. I wondered if we were too obsessed with cleanliness in the West but even so, some things really needed to be clean – or do they?

By then, it was too late to make it to the further beach and back, so I walked to the town beach instead. It wasn't tidal there for some reason, so the beach never got a good clean and it showed. It looked a bit like builders sand mixed with

127

gravel, dog ends, dog poo and other jetsam. No one seemed to mind, so like them, I lay down and took in some rays. My factor 30 was too much and my factor 8 not enough, so I mixed the two together – in the shop it's either factor 70 which I didn't even know existed or factor 3. And slowly, I turned colour.

It's too hot and too boring to sunbathe for long so once I felt my blood boiling, I went for a swim. The water was clear and blue and very very calm. There wasn't a wave or current in sight so I swam out to the buoy and just bobbed about. Looking back at the town, I could almost imagine what it must have looked like a few years back when the first travellers arrived. Probably like a little piece of heaven – some brightly coloured fishing boats on the shore, a few tiny houses dotted up the hill – the Sierra Nevada de Santa Marta hemming it all in, save for a little palm fronted beach. Today, those cliffs had little houses on them that almost defied gravity and away up the hill to the south west was the little road to Santa Marta with little blue buses rolling to and fro.

In a way, it was like San Agustinillo in Mexico – heavenly and alluring but once all the city folk arrived to buy up and take over, the original lustre vanished. The original folk must look around their town and wonder what happened. Once upon a time, it was theirs and now it was full of strangers, hostels, hotels, dive centres, second homes and to them, weird looking people. I just hoped they got a piece of the pie rather than just the crust.

It was also not dissimilar to Arambol in India where I stayed not so long ago. There were people who had made it their home, if only for the "season", usually the winter of the West, and those people tended to lord it over everyone else, forgetting that they too, were once the new boys in town. So it was with some satisfaction that I returned to the simple café that Michelangelo had told me about last week and sat down as their first customer of the day. When the be-hatted, irregular, regulars arrived, they regarded me with a certain curiosity – how did **I** know about the place – I'd only just arrived... I ate my menu del dia with smug aplomb, paid up all of 6000 pesos and wandered off as if I knew exactly where I was going. Of course I got lost, but they didn't know that...

And so back to Villa Mandela for a lengthy shower and general clean up and once I'd rubbed coconut oil in my hair and dried it in the sun, it actually looked like real hair again rather than a salt hardened coarse blanket. The afternoons were too hot to do anything - for me, although there were builders swarming over the house not even breaking a sweat. I retired to my bed, popped the air con on, fell asleep and woke hot and drenched – another power cut. I wondered if that was a daily occurrence and a warning to get all my writing done when the sun shone. I just thanked god I packed a torch! I asked Chico, the Italian owner (he came to Colombia working for an NGO, fell in love and stayed) if I could stay on for Easter but he said no – the room was booked out for three times what I was paying.   It looked like I would be moving further up the hill the next Wednesday to Casa Italia – for good or bad.

****

I was up early with the boys and the cleaning girl who just seemed to sweep all day. She swept the dust out and the very strong wind just blew it straight back in again. Gale or not, it was early enough for me to get to Playa Grande. It was already hot at 9am although bearable.   I walked to the end of the town beach and then followed the path up past a new hotel. The steps, in the beginning, were made of old car tyres with cement in the middle – quite clever, I thought and climbed up. When the path wasn't so steep, it was back to rock, dust, baked earth, dead or dying trees and huge cactus rising like gnarled fingers into the sky.

After about 10 minutes, the track branched in two. One led up and over the cliff and the other, less daunting, which I

129

took, led down to the sea. I'd read that for some reason, Playa Grande was underused. Looking at what was before me, I wasn't surprised. I was also mystified as to how anyone could even call it a "beach". There was a shabby shaded area covered with torn and tatty gauze and lounging beneath it were 13 men and one woman. They eyed me with suspicion and I eyed them with alarm. I didn't want them to sense my fear and prey on me like a pack of dogs, so I just said "buenos dias", walked past them and on to the end of the very short beach pretending to take an interest in the rubbish bins – I was desperate – I even took a photo.

Suddenly, a shout went up from the snorkeler out at sea and they all jumped up and began heaving on two enormous ropes. They weren't vagabonds, they were fishermen! They hauled and they hauled and as their net closed in, fish leapt up and thrashed about but they weren't going anywhere except ashore. They even invited me to take photos and when finally the haul was in, there must have been 20 big sea bass like fish and hundreds of tiny ones which they just returned to the sea. They threw the big fish into a plastic crate and congratulated one another on a good catch. How many times a day they land a haul, I really didn't know but I couldn't help but think that with the price of fish – ludicrously cheap, for all that work, they'd just earnt about £2 each, if that. And European fishermen think they've got it bad.

Excitement over, we adiosed and I climbed back up the path and pushed on to where I didn't want to go – over the cliff. But it was worth it. Far below me, I could see a kind of mini Taganga, or at least what it once was – a tiny bay, with bright boats and little palapas restaurants all lined up on the beach. I walked down the path and was astonished to see, climbing up the cliff, an eco lodge "Jaba Nibu". It was an architectural masterpiece – it gripped the cliff like barnacles, had open thatched cabana style cabins with palm leaf roofs and balconies and you could only reach it by boat. Imagine the logistics of even getting food and supplies delivered. I Googled it and it cost over £100 a night which was astronomical for Colombia but for once, I could see why.

I was early and the little beach had hardly woken up. Rows of deck chairs sat beneath the shade of small leafy trees and behind, were the row of restaurants. I say restaurants, but again, nothing had a wall, just a foundation and a roof and a kitchen somewhere out the back. I found a spot free of chairs, laid out my sarong, took off my dress and settled down in ray mode wondering why such a lovely beach was so underused – I was one of the only people on it. But not for long...

Boats began pouring in, ferrying people from either Taganga or Santa Marta. They just cut their engines, drifted to shore and the people clambered out. Some of them had food in huge polystyrene cold boxes, some had pushchairs and tiny babies, some were old and infirm and needed a certain amount of navigation and pulling and pushing to get them ashore, some brought their own folding chairs and all were Colombian. And with each boat, the noise, colour and activity increased.

Within an hour, the beach was filling up and gearing up. From somewhere came the massive inflatable called "Super Mable" – it was like a giant armchair towed at top speed around the bay by a speed boat. Similarly, there was the "Hot Dog" which people sat astride and lastly there was the round "Doughnut" which you just had to grip onto with white knuckled fists. And people just queued up for a ride. They couldn't get enough. At one point, Super Mable had a family with two very young kids on board – when they got off, the youngest seemed in a stupor – I doubted he'd been so terrified in his life. Amazingly, they all wore life jackets but apart from old Mable, the whole point of the other rides, was simply to turn the thing over so that you ended up in the sea and had to swim to shore. Health and Safety – what's that again?

So what does the archetypal Colombian beach dweller look

like? Body image was just not a priority and it was so refreshing. Old, young, fat and slim wore the tiniest bikinis for that all over indispensable tan. Or they wore sheer leggings over their bikini bottoms and they all looked fantastic. Just think of Sophia Loren throughout her lifetime in all her gorgeousness and that was what those women looked like. The men, similarly, weren't bothered, but then again, they seldom are. They were families at play, with children, parents and grandparents, all paddling, swimming or going on death defying rides. Until lunch time that was.

As the sun climbed into the sky, there was no shade. The beach faced west, the big ball of fire gradually glowed right overhead and that was when it was time to hit the shade. Suddenly, the beach emptied and the women restaurateurs carried around trays of fish so fresh, the gills were still flapping. You selected what you wanted and sometime later, it arrived on a plate with rice, fried plantain and salad and was cooked to such perfection that you wouldn't want to waste a speck. How did I know this? Because even I had one. I meant to just shelter from the sun in what I thought was an abandoned abode but it wasn't. I was just the first one there. The bare tables weren't laid nor had anything fancy about them. You just sat and ate and that was exactly what I did. It was three times what I normally paid for lunch but hey, I was on the beach, everything came in by boat and it was fantastic!

There was just one problem. I presumed it worked out very well for the business folk, but the boats ferrying people to and fro, suddenly vanished. I'd probably peaked too early in the food stakes. I was ready to go home but with no watch on I had no idea of the time. I thought it was about 3pm but it was only 1.30. All the boats back to town were gone and there was only one thing for it. And not for the first time, there I was, like a mad dog or an Englishman, out in the midday sun.

I slathered on Factor 30, pulled my sarong over my head like

(I presumed, but was probably wrong) Benazir Bhutto in her heyday (obviously before she was gunned down...) and defying any sensible logic, began the almighty climb back up the cliff, heart banging away in my chest, with barely any water, panting like a parched dog and the only shade that I could see, was my own minuscule shadow. Fat lot of good that was! I imagined myself staggering into town, foaming at the mouth, lifeless with heat exhaustion and possibly being pronounced dead on arrival. Why did I do those stupid things? Because I could? Because I wanted to? Or was it just a constant test of my resolve and survival instinct? I thought about all of those things as I stumbled home and when I finally staggered up to Villa Mandela, sweat pouring in rivulets down my face and body, one of the little boys actually looked at me in alarm. Truth comes from the mouths of babes...

****

A strong wind gusted through blowing everything everywhere. Chico said it was unusual to have wind at that time of year and called it Viento del Loco – you can guess what that means. It seemed like a good day to replenish food supplies. Some of the little older shops had resisted change and still had goods stocked on shelves behind a counter. A couple of enterprising souls more geared up for tourists, had gone upmarket and opened bright new shops on the front with a more self service feel – except the booze that was, which was stashed firmly away. With drink, it was the same everywhere – it was all locked away and yet I didn't see anyone drinking illicitly – maybe it was because it **was** all locked away. Anyway, I selected a pineapple as big as a baby, carrots that looked as if they'd been grown in the ground rather than on a production line and many other things besides. It filled an enormous bag I had a job to carry and then he told me the price – 8000 pesos. How much!? I mentally gasped, thinking I'd been massively overcharged but then realised it was only £2 – I kept forgetting to knock off three noughts and divide by four. Once you did that, everything was nothing.

133

Chico also owned a restaurant – a pizzeria – he was Italian after all and it was the opening night. I wasn't sure if it had been closed for refurbishment or whether it had just newly opened, but there was a little party and everyone in the house was invited, including me. I think I was the only "guest" but I simply didn't know for sure. Pizza to me was anathema but dying for a night out, I went along anyway. I even dressed up.

Once again, I had to explain my "alergia" to a disbelieving crowd who were simply not having it. An enormous slice of pizza was proffered my way – it looked and smelt so GOOD. My mouth salivated – I think I may have drooled. What was I to do? Sod it, I thought, what's the worst that can happen and quite frankly, I was sick of constantly yielding to it. I greedily and ravenously accepted it and ate my first pizza for over 15 years and it was just magnificent! The melted, creamy cheese caressed the roof of my mouth, the chorizo exuded oily paprika, a meaty tang tantalized my taste buds and the crispy bread base just seemed to dissolve like shortbread . I couldn't even think or see. I could only taste and make strange noises closely associated with love.

The damage was done. What could I do but have another slice – in for a penny and all that, and then another and then another. I was momentarily so satiated that when I washed it down with cold Colombian beer from the bottle, I felt like a Roman emperor or even Bacchus himself. If that was the beginning of a downward path in the epicurean stakes, then saddle me up and let's get going!

****

"I told you so", I felt like saying when everyone gasped at my golf ball eyes in the morning. "This is what happens when I eat wheat, never mind when I eat wheat AND cheese". But you know what, I really didn't care, it was worth it and besides, I wasn't exactly there on the pull, so to speak. Thinking about it, I hadn't seen one attractive man the whole

134

time I'd been there apart from the jet black man who drummed up custom for the Super Mable, but I wouldn't say he was from those parts – not with those sculpted cheek bones and body of hewn ebony. But I digress...

Despite the visible disability, I once again headed for the beach, sunglasses firmly in place. That day, I thought, would be a good day to invest in a snorkel so I could at least keep my face out of other people's and for long periods of time, in the water. It was great! I could just swim. Snorkelling gives swimming a whole new purpose. Even when there was nothing to look at, and there wasn't, the sound of your own breathing was so relaxing. I swam over to the rocks on one side and then swam across the bay to the rocks on the other side. When I finally took the mask off, the pressure was so intense, I thought my eyes were going to pop out and end up dangling on my chest like in a Cormac McCarthy novel. I thought, in some weird way, it had also reduced the swelling or was that just in my imagination?

Back at Villa Mandela, there was a gorgeous young girl, not unlike Hale Berry, swinging in a hammock. Imagine my surprise when she turned out to be from Boston and spoke ENGLISH!!!!!! I was beside myself. I hadn't spoken in my native tongue to anyone who also spoke it since Mexico City. Even Andree in San Agustinillo was a native French speaking Canadian. Her name was Allannah and she was there teaching English on a government programme. The Colombians had finally realised that if no one there spoke English, it would impede their progress in the wider world. That seems unfair, but it was, however, true. The amount of times I'd tried to explain to people that if they could speak English, they could speak to the world, was multitudinous.

She was on a placement in the dire town called Barranquilla that we'd sped through on the way to Santa Marta, thanking god that none of us had to get off. She agreed that it was a stink hole and unfortunately, she was there for a year. But in any case, I was so happy that, at last, there was someone

135

who spoke my language! With her was a young American man who seemed to have an inexhaustible budget. He was telling me about Palomino being full of hostels and you could just turn up and check in for eye watering amounts of money. I presumed he had rich parents but Allannah said no, he'd just sold all his belongings and headed for Colombia in search of music and salsa. We seemed to spend all day just talking and hanging around, and in that heat, that wasn't such a bad thing to do. Cold beer and good conversation – what more could you need?

****

Imagine my shock when I got up the following morning and found two other newcomers – one from New York and one from Bogota chatting in English! They asked if I missed anything from home – yes, CONVERSATION! So I got their life stories in a couple of hours. Like Allannah, the New Yorker was teaching English, but in Bogota. When I mentioned my horror at all the desperate people there, once again, it was received with bewilderment – "what desperate people?" How could they not see them, they were everywhere.

Thinking of Bogota and the difference in so many ways between there and the coast, my intuition told me that the original European settlers had abandoned the heat and chaos of the coast and headed inland to cooler climes, thus leaving the Caribs to dance and party and, to an extent, get left behind in the development stakes. But if it meant that they had time to pause for a little dance whenever they liked – and they did it all the time, who, I wondered, was having the better time? Allannah agreed with me and said that in Barranquilla, despite the poverty, there was always a party atmosphere.

Somehow, it was cloudy (which I didn't expect – ever) and stocks were running low, so I decided to head back to Santa Marta to shop. I flagged down a really knackered old van,

136

squashed aboard and 10 minutes later, I was further away than when I began. There was no route, no timetable and no reason. We finally rumbled off when the bus was full and rolled out of one town and into the other. I decided to try another restaurant for lunch which I hadn't noticed before even though it was within throwing distance of Casa Familiar and who should be there but Fabio. He greeted me like a lost lover and I think I managed to explain that I would be back there for a night before returning to Cartagena – at least I hope that's what he thought I said... I have a friend, Ray, in England who is fluent in Spanish, translating things for me so that when I did finally show up, I could flash my laptop at Fabio and all would be understood...

Other than that, there wasn't much to report except to say that when the sun didn't shine, the whole place seemed so much calmer. It could also have been the calm before the storm both in the weather and as the whole place geared up for Easter. They were even giving Villa Mandela a good clean (apart from my room of course...), although the newcomers complained of ants in their beds. They asked if I had them too – I didn't have the heart to tell them I had air con and I didn't even have flies, let alone ants.

****

My last day at Villa Mandela and I decided to, once again, walk over to Playa Grande. The Colombian girl who worked there, thinking I hadn't been before gave me three warnings: never to walk there alone, to take at least two litres of water and NEVER be caught out by the midday sun – all of which I'd done the last time...

I wanted to try out my new snorkel, having been told that there was so much more to see. And there was. Near the shore, there were lots of tiny fish and over near the rocks, a bigger one that would look totally at home in a tropical fish tank and then I saw absolutely shoals of the lesser spotted peeled off beer bottle labels lurking in the shallows. They

137

were everywhere! I doubted this was what everyone was raving about, but that's all I could see and god knows I tried. I diced with death to outmanoeuvre the boats going to and fro and swam the width of the bay. I passed other snorkelers equally surprised – I could have stuck my face in the aquarium back at the hostel and seen more, but never mind, it was a good swim. I was told that at Tairona National Park, nearby, there was coral and all sorts and as I was so close, I intended to go despite the hour trek to get there but then I often intend to do things but don't – apart from casting myself off alone half way around the world...

I treated myself to a boat ride back. It only cost 5000 pesos (£1.25) and I was the only passenger aboard. I could see the path I'd walked and it looked treacherous. I did try to get the anchor man to take a photo of me but when I checked, there were just my feet – how does that happen?

Lunch beckoned and whilst woofing down another super meal, I got talking to a French Canadian man who'd been spending the winter there for seven years and confirmed my thoughts – when he first went, there was one bar, one baker, one coffee shop, a few rooms to rent and no litter. How times change. He said that although he didn't drink, he could recommend the cartons of wine. By the look of him, I'd say he did nothing but drink and after minor cajoling, he admitted that he and several others met at the beach at sunset and had a little private party and did I want to join them. I thought about it but it sort of smacked of desperation and I could see myself turning into Lana Turner in "Madame X" discovering a love of absinth and going down the pan...

In the evening, back at Villa Mandela, there were more people coming and going and even more little boys than usual all sitting around the PC where they sit for hours playing computer games. I once again talked to Allannah. I asked what she did in the day – lays in the hammock mostly. I suggested we walk to Playa Grande together and she was all for it. So, as usual, I had made a friend just as I was leaving

138

but at least I wasn't leaving for another city, just another hostel. She drank a few "Aguilla" beers which means "eagle" (suddenly the bonkers Werner Herzog film "Aguilla, Wrath of God" made sense with the little wings on his helmet) and I drank wine, trying not to look like a total wino, but I don't know why I worry because no one there cared what you did. Funnily enough, Allannah said that I was the least judgemental person she'd ever met. Who is anyone to judge?

Much later, I returned to my cool room and packed to the tunes from my radio. For all the chaos there at Villa Mandela, my room had been a total luxurious joy and I had to say that I was not looking forward to sharing a room way up the hill at Casa Italia for a whole week – god have mercy on her – I couldn't even share a room with a boyfriend for a week without both of us wanting to kill one another!

TAGANGA – CASA ITALIA

What was the all night ruckus? It sounded as if they were rehearsing Ionesco's *The Chairs*. I got up to discover Villa Mandela had been totally re-arranged to make it look more like a hostel than a total free for all. They must have been expecting a deluge of people for Easter, but as for me and Allannah, we were both checking out. She was off to another hostel to sleep in a hammock, whilst I got into a taxi and headed up the hill to Casa Italia; my new home for a week. It was so far up the hill, I thought the taxi driver was going to refuse to take me – it was just rubble for road up there. BUT with more room, the houses were bigger, newer and more luxurious. There was even a rumour that a senator and a football player had houses there. I presumed this was how Los Angeles got going.

Maria was of Italian descent and it showed. She was well groomed, good looking, blonde and robust and for some inexplicable reason, she greeted me with a big long lost type of hug but also instant confusion and once again the language barrier was immense. I think she was hoping that threatening me with having to share a room, she would have put me off going there (so why the hug?). Obviously, being Easter, she was expecting to be packed with every bed full rather than with me, on a cut price rate I'd negotiated a month ago, taking up a whole room which was what I had booked. And so began our tiny war of words albeit via Google translate.

I showed her my confirmation email stipulating a double room – not mentioning that she'd already told me that I would have to share. Thankfully, she had somehow forgotten that and she apologised for the over booking and said that if I would share until Sunday, I would then have a room to myself and in the meantime, I could have free meals! Well, I think that's what she meant – Google translate wasn't perfect – she might had been saying that for that price, I'd have to do all the cooking but what did I know? I felt a Cinderella moment coming on.

Further confusion was avoided when a young boy, about 12 years old, who spoke fluent English, appeared. He'd lived in the USA for a year and was a guest at the "hotel". I asked how long he was there for and he said he was just leaving. DAMN! But he did manage to explain to her that I'd been there a week already and knew about the fab cafe down the hill to which I was repairing for lunch.

Sitting at the cafe with a plate of unidentifiable food, I looked at the phrases in my Rough Guide and despaired. I knew that not being able to speak Spanish, my travels would be problematic but I never imagined that it would be that much of a problem. Of course it was that old arrogance of the English speaker that we think everyone will be able to speak our language and usually, that was not that far from the truth. In Colombia it simply wasn't true and I was more aware than ever that without even Allannah, I was looking at a few days with no conversation whatsoever.

When I returned to Casa Italia, so did the confusion. The sink and toilet in my pristine bathroom weren't working and whilst they waited for the plumber, I was given a glass of very cold, teeth melting, sweet, fizzy drink and led up to the terrace and invited to relax in a hammock with a view all the way down the hill. It was spectacular - the whole bay spread out before me and I could see all the little boats speeding about in the distance. There wasn't that much behind us apart from a few more lonely looking buildings all newly constructed and dirt roads linking them to the town.

Finally, I was let into the room which had two bunk beds and two double beds but curiously, nowhere to hang anything. Maria was trying to shove my gargantuan bag under a bed which was like trying to shove an elephant into a telephone box – it took up half of the available floor space. But at least the room was clean and airy and I began to settle in.

Casa Italia was new and lovely. It was set over many levels, all the floors were tiled, there was an open air mezzanine floor, a huge roof terrace with hammocks, there was light and air and right at the top, a self contained apartment which I presumed belonged to Michelangelo. I wasn't sure if Maria was his wife, but the way she bossed him about all day, she probably was.

The distance from the beach was a bit daunting, but a terrific breeze from the mountains meant that it was cooler and cleaner than the town. It also gave me lots of space and rather being confined to my room, I could sit at one of the many open air tables within the hotel and watch the tiny world around me – Maria cooking or washing and the clean laundry billowing on the lines strung across the open space in the middle of the building. The strangest thing though was that after the palaver of earlier, as I sat there awaiting the crowds and my roommate to arrive, nobody appeared. I presumed that Maria was simply preparing for the holiday influx which for that day at least, didn't arrive.

A few idiosyncrasies: I now had my very own five litre BAG of water in the fridge. Everything came in a bag but how I was meant to pour from it was beyond me. On my first attempt, more went on the floor than in the glass. Secondly, the little gas cooker with two burners, was almost directly underneath the fan so it was like trying to cook on a camping gas stove in the middle of a field in a high wind. It took me five minutes to make coffee as they all stood watching my little pot do it's stuff – it was a complete mystery to all of the people all of the time. How could they not have seen one before?

143

But it did feel good to be outside with the stars right above me, the moon rising and all the little street and house lights of Taganga flickering below and yet still be in the sanctity of a clean and spacious house. The light and space seemed to conjure a new clarity from the chaos. I was wondering what to do once my time there was up after Easter, the following week. Selection being a process of elimination, with a clearer mind, I set to Googling my options.

I again considered the rugged beach and rivers of Palomino. That was until I discovered recent news that as well as the mosquitoes, there were also bugs as big as budgies that carried a new disease with no cure. Considering that I got bitten by deforming bugs in England, it just seemed a risk too drastic to take. I could just hear the bug bongos banging - "she's coming – dinner time!" Whereas, Minca, my other option, was high in the lush, verdant hills of the Sierra Nevada and was full of waterfalls only a short trek away. It had an abundance of wild birds and monkeys and views to die for. But you know what – sod the wildlife and views – it had something far more important. Real CHOCOLATE – and that was worth all the birds in paradise. What choice was there to make? I booked the Hostel Calibri and salivated at the thought of it!

****

Despite the early hour, Casa Italia and Taganga were already heaving with people – it was finally the Easter weekend. Police had closed the "roads" to the beach and people were pouring out of buses at the crossroads in the same manner that they poured out of the boats in Playa Grande. They carried whatever they might possibly need for a day at the seaside – everything! I was going the other way into Santa Marta and could hardly believe the traffic jam. There was even a temporary ambulance along the road parked up in the viewing spot. The place was also awash with people selling souvenirs.

My mission was to explain to Fabio at Casa Familiar, that I wanted to leave my bag with him for three days whilst I went to Minca, stay with him for one night on my return and then leave the following day on the bus for Cartagena and would he be so good as to book me a bus ticket. I would NEVER have been able to do this without my friend Ray's translation and with the additional services of Google translate, my mission was accomplished! I was never sure if they really understand me and I was always shocked when it all went right – like when the bus, as promised, turned up at Alexander's house in Cartagena to take me to Santa Marta, which now seemed like months ago.

For some reason, my left thigh was aching as if I'd pulled a muscle. I was usually completely fit and couldn't understand how this had happened. (It turned out to be my new Mexican bag continuously banging against my leg). But it did make me feel vulnerable. Being physically strong obviously gave me a visible advantage and confidence – the sort of savvy that allowed me to barge in amongst a gaggle of men at a street stall and such like. But suddenly, for the first time in my life, I felt like prey – animals always hunt the weakest and heading for the bank, I felt uneasy. Colombia was not the sort of country that you wanted to show or feel unease in. I didn't know if it showed or if it was just my imagination, but all of a sudden, I felt as if people were looking at me and sizing me up. I was even questioning the sense of using an ATM booth at all. I didn't like this new feeling of fear. I didn't like the feeling at all. But what was I to do?

In the end, I conjured up an imaginary force field, tried not to limp and dodged into the ATM. For once, thank god, it was without fault and feeling braver, I popped into the supermarket to see if they'd replenished the wine I was growing rather fond of – well, the price of it at least. The shelf was bare but on closer inspection, I found lots hidden away in the wrong place. I thanked Colombian inefficiency, loaded up and headed back. I don't know if it was the bargain wine, but I felt a lot happier and somehow safer. It

145

might also had been that the streets were busier and I wasn't so obvious.

The crush to board the bus was worse than normal but once we were all squashed on things got really funny. The driver had seen a girl on a bus next to us and he just blatantly chatted her up, keeping level with her bus, despite people trying to get on or off and despite the fact that she was clearly not interested. He was beeping, leering and calling to her and all the while, people were trying to pay him, attract his attention or simply get off. He was having none of it – flirting seemed to be a national past time and everyone just accepted it. Things only returned to "normal" when the other bus turned off and bus stops were again attended to.

And that's when the kid wearing a great big bright pink dinosaur shaped rubber ring climbed aboard. The bus was packed and he was completely oblivious, pushing past everyone while the rubber ring squeaked and puckered to the point where I thought it would surely pop. Why didn't he just wait and blow it up at the beach? But that just wasn't the way they did things there. Thank god he didn't have a Lilo as well.

I stopped for lunch at the cafe on the hill yet again and perusing my phrase pages in my Rough Guide, I suddenly realised where I'd been going wrong all that time – I was "speaking" Portuguese. Oh how I laughed. Finally, I got some meat – pork, which wasn't indigestible and feeling so happy, I even left a huge tip – well, huge for me...

Back at Casa Italia, Maria was SO excited! I staggered through the door, hot and exhausted and headed for my room only to have Maria whip my bag from me and lead me up the stairs to my NEW ROOM!!! It was all mine and it was all pink and pretty with its own pretty bathroom and all my things were already in there! She threw open the cupboard doors, she showed me the "TV", she turned both fans on – ceiling and floor and then the weirdest thing happened – I HUGGED

146

her! We were almost crying we were both so happy. There was nothing like having your own room where you can do exactly what you want. After living on my own for nearly 20 years, the idea of sharing even with someone I loved seemed a compromise too far, let alone with a stranger.

Wanting to take full advantage of it, I unpacked and hung my clothes on hangers rather than stringing them up on ribbon – it felt like home and I hadn't been so happy with a room since the lovely Posada Paloma in Mexico which also seemed like a totally distant memory. Suddenly the six days I had left there in that house and in Taganga, didn't feel like an ordeal, they felt like a pleasure. Never mind that the TV didn't do anything except connect to the internet – there was nothing on it anyway and I simply didn't care. And then, as if by magic, I found a little Barbie doll in my cupboard, sat her up on the pillows, (which were as coquettishly coloured as her dress), and took photos. You could barely see her, she blended in so well.

And then, with my invaluable English/Spanish dictionary I headed to the nearest shop for food supplies. On the outside, it didn't look as if it would sell anything, but on the inside, it was a cornucopian labyrinth and the loveliest thing about it was that the two girls thought it was really funny, rather than pathetic, that I spoke no Spanish – at least I was trying and it wasn't easy. For example, I picked up a carrot and asked for the name in Spanish. "Zanahoria", they said and asked me what it was called in English – "carrot" I said. They laughed out loud at what a stupid ugly sounding word it was compared to their word and they were right! "Susurrar", meaning to whisper was another example almost onomatopoeic in its subtlety. I wondered how many other Spanish words would outstrip English in their beauty.

Back at the Barbie Bedroom, still with no one to talk to, I felt as if I was morphing into a Gabriel Garcia Marquez novel – *No One Writes to the Colonel* or *One Hundred Years of Solitude* sprang to mind. Sometimes, travelling could be so lonely,

147

especially in a land in which I simply couldn't communicate with anything other than smiles and hand signals.

GOOD FRIDAY

It suddenly occurred to me, that Casa Italia, was in fact, a very up market guest house which could accommodate 30 people. Backpackers didn't arrive at the door in a pool of sweat, like they did at the other hostels I'd stayed in. They didn't arrive at all. Instead, the people who did arrive came in a convoy of super swanky cars or 4 wheel drive monstrosities (at least, with those roads, they served a purpose) and it was obvious that they weren't from the coast, but from the inland cities. They were very middle class Colombian families on their Easter vacation which was a continent apart from middle class English families. Sitting at the little table on the mezzanine floor, I got to see it all: had it been a cartoon film and speeded up, it would have been similar to a human swarm of locusts.

Everyone piled out of the cars into the house, up the stairs and without pause, threw open the fridge, loaded it with Aguilla Lite beer and they drink it ALL day. And I mean everyone. Teenagers, mums and dads. They were as uninterested in water as they were in one's personal space. It was party time Colombian style. Michelangelo kept out of the way whilst Maria tried to take control without much success. They commandeered the roof terrace, turned their music on full blast and, well, partied. I didn't mind, I just sat there saying "no huebla Espanole" and smiled beatifically and with a look of pity, they left me alone. Never mind that my Barbie room was right off the kitchen and with cardboard thin walls, it sounded as if they were **in** my room rather than on the other side of it.

So, being Good Friday, I wandered into town to the little church to see if Catholicism still had any influence. The doors were shut – apparently not. Once again, road blocks were in

148

place and it was outside the church that people were being turfed off the bus. I thought the town had been packed the day before, but that day, it was completely heaving but not with the usual Western tourists. That weekend, Taganga belonged to Colombia and there were no rules.

Usually, if you wanted to find shade on the beach, it was in front of a restaurant and for that privilege, you had to buy something. Not that day you didn't. Every inch of shade was taken with people packed in as tight as pomegranate seeds and they were all eating their own food and drinking their own beers stashed in tent sized polystyrene boxes and no one was saying anything to them. There were more street food sellers than normal too. They'd just set up in the shade at the entrance to the beach and what they had was enormous aluminium pots full of some kind of risotto which they piled into polystyrene containers for next to nothing.

And the sea was absolutely packed with people too. They didn't swim; they just stood there keeping cool in their super trendy bright day-glo outfits in varying degrees of decency. The noise was MAD. Everyone had their own devices and they all blasted out, oblivious of what was playing next to them and everyone was doing some sort of soft sand shuffle, thighs brushing and bumping while little kids hollered and screamed and splashed about. One little boy was sitting inside a massive blow up shark which also doubled as a rubber ring – I wondered if he too had worn it on the bus.

All the little palapas restaurants on the front were rammed and the only vehicles that were allowed through the road block were the Coca Cola, water and beer delivery trucks with gangs of men ferrying crates to every single shop and bar. The fridges must have been cranked to maximum to keep all that stuff cool and there was a definite hum in the air and a rumble in the street. One white Rasta man, replete with machete in his trouser waist band (?) was gyrating with such abandon, I worried he'd just keel over and kill himself.

Imagine; when I was a kid, Good Friday was a trip to the church to wander blankly along the Ways of the Cross in sombre procession and the only high light of the entire weekend, was a new outfit and enough chocolate in over elaborate boxes to satiate any craving (I had a vivid memory of the Milky Bar Kid in his own wild west saloon replete with swing doors – they don't make them like that anymore). I wondered if inland, they still had elaborate religious processions, but there on the Caribbean coast there was only one way to do anything – with extreme hedonism!

But hedonism was the only common denominator. Once I'd swum out to sea and glanced back at the beach, I noticed that there were two distinct tribes. There were the usual Caribs but there were also the more affluent types who were checking into Casa Italia and the difference was obvious. The latter were the ones with the money and it showed. They looked different; they had a style that set them apart. I supposed that's what a good education, access to money and generations of European sophistication had done for them. They were all wearing designer clothes with accessories to match and they all had the confidence and arrogance of the rich. I wondered who was having more fun though. The posers or the peasants.

Back at Casa Italia, it was no different. Another horde of well dressed revellers arrived and that evening, once again, they were up on the terrace having a party. The teenagers were sneaking vodka and all sorts past me on their way up the stairs whilst I just sat there having my own personal party, listening to their music and drinking wine. And then at 9pm, dressed to the nines, all smiling or posing and taking selfies, they headed into town for dinner and dancing leaving Maria to clean up the piles of empty plastic cups, cans and bottles, sighing as she did so and giving me looks of happy exhaustion. I supposed she was making a fortune and it was worth it but even Maria seemed peeved when they all returned after midnight and carried on where they'd left off. Thank god for ear plugs.

EASTER SATURDAY

As quickly as they'd arrived, half of the house emptied. From what I could understand, they were on their way to the wild east of Riohacha on some kind of road trip. Phewf, I thought and wandered up to the deserted terrace to sunbathe and then, the most amazing thing happened. A man appeared and greeted me in Spanish. I asked, perhaps in desperation, in Spanish if he spoke English? He said, "sorry?" obviously not understanding me, but with that one word, I knew I was in business. Yes, he did speak English and he understood every word I said! He was a biologist working on his MA and naturally, he said, most research papers were written in English and so he, like every other advanced student, could speak it. When I told him that I'd worked at the Natural History Museum in London and had held Darwin's finches (from which he'd formulated his evolution of species theory) in my very own hands, he was flabbergasted. And so I'd made a new friend.

I had so many questions about his homeland that we talked for hours. We discussed the diversity of Colombia, the politics (about which I am passionate) the people, the culture and the war that had been raging for 60 years and how that was now trying to be resolved so that the country could finally move on and stop spending 60% of its GDP on its military and only 0.6% on education. He also told me that the Pacific Coast was where many of the ex-slaves had completely retreated to and was so underdeveloped and impoverished that children were blinded from lack of vitamin A and that it was all but abandoned by the government.

It was the most insightful conversation I'd had about Colombia since talking with the Dutch NGO, Bram in Bogota and I was thrilled. It was like exercising a muscle I worried I was losing the use of. It was also fantastic to be hearing my words out loud rather than in my head where they usually

151

lived. Again, I was reminded of how important conversation was to me and how little of it I was getting – so much for my quest to abandon my lonely home in London.

And if that wasn't exciting enough, he invited me to join him and an Australian girl (he'd met whilst trekking) for the evening – if I didn't have any other plans – I had NO plans! I even got changed and put on make-up. We met Emma on the corner of the beach at 7pm by which time it was getting dark and even then, the beach was still partially full. The plan was to eat, so we walked around but I was so busy talking, restaurants weren't even on my radar. We circumnavigated the town, finally arriving back to where we started and a Creperie, that on my own, I wouldn't even consider (what with the allergies and the sheer opulence of the place). We looked at the menu – I was aghast – it represented almost a week's lunch at any of my ordinary Colombian restaurants but they thought it looked "reasonable" and so we went in. I still can't equate pesos with pounds and even if something costs 24,000 it was still only £6 but like in India, you get used to living on nothing.

The fish was sublime and Emma, it turned out, was the most interesting Australian I had ever met. She'd simply sold up and was travelling the world. Money was no object and she spoke of places that on my budget, I could only dream of. We again talked politics (how I missed it) and many more things beside. She said that Murdoch and the conservatives had Australia sewn up and even though it could generate all of its power from solar, the subsidy had been cut to allow fracking to take place. It was polluting the vast subterranean water supplies so that in the future, all flora and fauna would be affected.

And why were they doing that? Because they could make more money. I told them about my dad's theory - that the rich didn't care what sort of planet they left behind for their children because they didn't care about their children. They sent them away to school and they didn't even know them

152

and the only thing that they did care about was simply amassing a fortune. They both thought this to be profound, as did I and it went someway in explaining the basic concept of human greed. And there endeth the lesson.

We then bought beers from a supermarket and sat on the beach wall and talked some more. Emma planned to establish an on-line news agency in Australia much the way Huffington Post exists elsewhere, beyond the influence of Murdoch's machinations. I was so happy to be having such interesting conversations! Unfortunately, as was so often the case, they were both leaving the next day. And as the town thinned out and all of the little beach bars closed, Emma took a taxi to her hostel and Diego and I tramped back up the rocky road to home only to find yet another group of Colombians had arrived – they came and went with astonishing pace. He went to bed and being too early and far too noisy for me, I coaxed a beer out of Michelangelo, found an almost quiet retreat on the terrace and took in the night. The clouds, what there were of them, were so low and the wind so ferocious, that specks of rain were rinsed from the sky like wet laundry blowing in the breeze. Kind of perfect.

EASTER SUNDAY

I exchanged Facebook details with Diego and then everyone, including him, vanished as swiftly as they arrived. Left to the silence and myself and with nothing much to did, I turned myself another shade darker on the terrace and waited until hunger sent me down the hill for dinner.

I didn't know if it was the constant battering of the wind lately or just the baking heat, but everyone seemed to be slightly mad, including me. Impatience was default mood; ear drum bursting music boomed out from everywhere, almost in defiance of the elements and on my way into town, there was even a fracas to which the police had to attend, keeping their motorcycle helmets firmly on. Even I, with my now recovered leg, striding confidently, was menaced by a motorbike. I felt like pushing him off, getting on it myself and wheelying off down the road which believe me, I could have done had I wanted to. I meant to go further to sample more fish, but just gave up and went into the closest restaurant I could find. It was a bit of a dump and yet the prices were the same as the opulent establishment of last night! Instead of fish, I opted for steak. Whilst I waited, I was treated to a complimentary papaya juice – how can something which smells like baby sick, taste so good?

When the "steak" came, it was practically inedible – why did I bother? Too irritable to even wander around town, I was back up the hill determined to get the TV working. I knew there was nothing to watch but with no one to talk to, I was reminded of what my dad once said to me, "there was nothing lonelier than just four walls for company". First I asked Michelangelo who called Maria. In she came with a set top box (the missing equipment) wired it up and NOTHING. We just stood there looking at it whilst she twiddled and fiddled. Then Hector, the handyman arrived, and was also enlisted. Four of us in my room was BOILING. The floor fan was turned to maximum as was the overhead fan. Tempers (well, mine) were beginning to fray. Finally, Maria fetched a little TV, Hector wired it up and she put it up high on the wardrobe so that all I could see was a picture very much like an old negative photo. Never mind; I thanked them all, they left and I moved it to the little table at eye level.

And then it hit me – every room in the place had a TV which worked except mine. Was that her way of exacting revenge for how much I'd paid for the room? There was of course nothing to watch, but I watched it anyway and relived the same fiasco of an English language film with subtitles but dubbed into Spanish. All I wanted to do was dash off an angry email of complaint to Colombian TV - how was anyone supposed to learn English if they never got to even listen to it. And then I realised that no one would be able to read my email.

I'd noticed a bottle of the fabled Agua Diente in the fridge and as everyone had checked out and I knew Michelangelo would never be allowed to drink it, I gave it a try. It tasted like Pernod – one of my old favourites, so I had another and then another – I don't know what came over me but when I went to bed, I felt a whole lot better!

EASTER MONDAY

A gale in the night had left the village looking more windswept than normal. Everywhere, corrugated iron panels lay battered and bent and where they used to be, were holes like empty eye sockets. It all looked a bit sad and it seeped into the psyche. It was if the party was over.

At Maria's suggestion, I dropped my washing in at the laundry house. I don't know if she was hinting that she didn't want me to do my washing at the house (the water supply arrives in a tanker, not a pipe), or whether she was hinting that I stank, but I got the message. I had to explain to Olga, the laundress, that one dress, though it looked ragged, was one of my favourites and to be gentle with it. I'd had to give the same with the washer women in India who wondered why I didn't just throw it away then and that was eight years ago! Olga seemed equally baffled but agreed to go easy on it, weighed all the items and said that it would be ready in five hours and all for less than £2! That was half of my clothes AND a bag – unbelievable.

Then into town for lunch and I bumped into Canadian Simon so we sat and chatted. He was the one who'd been going there for seven years. He said that it hadn't rained there for 18 months and water was becoming a bigger and bigger problem. He also said that the mountains used to be covered in trees but they had cut them all down, the soil had eroded and that now everything was dead or dying. It was such an old and familiar story. It was completely ridiculous that no

155

one heeded the warnings. What did they think would happen?

After lunch, we wandered down into town. It was empty. The beach was empty and the constant flow of little boats to Playa Grande had all but stopped. He again invited me to meet him and friends for a drink at sunset but somehow, I knew I wouldn't make it. I returned to the house to find someone I hadn't yet seen – a huge white Russian who could quite possibly be the owner of the hooch in the fridge I'd all but finished – oops. He spoke a little abrupt English as if he was barking orders and I turned the conversation to vodka and asked was he partial. I thought he would explode – vodka, he screeched, was ruining Russia, the men of Russia, the women of Russia – you get the picture, and that no, he never drank and never would. Later that night, I snuck back to the fridge and finished the rest of the bottle.

****

I thought I was dreaming when I woke in the morning and could hear a female voice speaking English. I wrapped a sarong around me and raced out before she could vanish. Her name was Elizabeth, she was a friend of Maria's, she'd learnt English in school, had worked in hostels and hotels and now taught English. Simple. So why couldn't anyone else learn the language? (More importantly, why couldn't I?) We had a wonderful chat and she translated for Maria who said how frustrated she'd been not being able to talk to me. She suggested she make coffee and that we should sit down and enjoy ourselves and that's what we did.

Basically, we covered everything that she had wanted to ask me about since I'd arrived and the three of us had a week's conversation in an hour about men, men and men. Apparently, they were not as macho as they used to be – according to Elizabeth, although Maria still had her doubts, and they even helped with the children. It was quite funny to be able to talk to her at last and she wanted to know all about

156

me; what I was doing on my own when I was so attractive (!), what I was doing on my own in such a dangerous country and where, on my own, would I be going next. She simply couldn't believe that I was just travelling around where ever I liked without a care (or a man) and for no reason, she hugged me (again) as if that was somehow a talisman and would keep me safe.

She then hit me with the bill which was 20,000 pesos a night more than what I'd already paid up front for the week. Once again it was a Google translate war of words. I showed her my receipt from airbnb which had been paid in full and in advance and although she feigned understanding and managed a smile, she wasn't happy. She was a business woman; I got it, but come on. She then talked me into waiting in for the big Russian to get back (where was his key?) and headed down to the town for lunch – I bet she never ate in the small cafe (where I ate every day) in her life.

Once the Russian was home, I too went down the hill to eat, dumped the empty hooch bottle in case she charged me for that too and went for a last swim. The sky was overcast – something I hadn't seen for months and it all just seemed a little bit sad and forlorn. It felt like time to leave and as luck would have it, that was exactly what I was doing. It had been an experience there at Taganga, watching Colombians do what they did best – enjoy themselves, but the party really was over. Next stop Minca, up in the hills where the rivers roar, the multitude of birds soar, the monkeys paw and the aroma of organic coffee and cocoa filled the air and real CHOCOLATE would replenish my soul!

MIGHTY MOUNTANOUS MINCA

Leaving Taganga and arriving at Minca was possibly the most bonkers day of my life. Maria's handyman Hector arrived in his big 4 wheel drive truckette to take me to Santa Marta. Maria hitched a lift and told me that he'd take me to Minca for 50,000 pesos – all of £12.50. I'd read that I could get there for 5,000 so declined the offer. We dropped Maria off at the market clutching an enormous rolled up orange thing which might had been a single mattress, but this was Colombia, so who knew what it was. Maria and I hugged and kissed, as I knew we would. I thought of taking a photo but somehow, the moment just got lost and Hector took me to Casa Familiar and the lovely Fabio, who once again embraced me like a lost lover.

He took my enormous bag from me and locked it away; I reassured him that I would be back on Saturday and I presumed, although I couldn't know for sure, that he understood. First I went to the ATM - twice – it was so difficult to just get what you wanted vis a vis money withdrawals and I knew that there was nothing where I was going (except chocolate). And then to the supermarket to stock up on rum (well, what else was I going to do for three days in the mountains).

All ready, I headed for the place where I was assured, I could get a collectivo taxi to Minca. "Minca" they told me, was all I had to say and as if by magic, it would all become real. I said Minca here, I said Minca there, I said Minca everywhere and no one had a clue. One kid hanging out of a bus beckoned me to get on and in no time at all, beckoned me to get off – I

159

didn't even have to pay but where was I? And NO ONE spoke English. Finally, a bus stopped, I said "Minca" and he waved me on.

Well, we drove around Santa Marta to parts I had never seen before. We went near to the bus terminal, where I was convinced he would drop me off, except we didn't even stop at the terminal. The next thing, we were driving around a new housing estate which looked like a prison; absolutely bloody awful with guards on the gate and then there was only me left on the bus. I said, once again, "Minca" and he slapped his head with a gesture which meant that he had totally forgotten. By that time, we weren't even on what we would call a "road"; it was just dust and gravel.

Never mind; he was on a mission to get me to where I needed to go. He drove past what passes as bus stops, not even bothering to stop, just gesticulating that there would be another bus along in a minute. And then finally, on a sand road, to what seemed like nowhere, he told me to get off because that was where I needed to be. I got off and all I could see was one shop and a few motorbikes. The driver gestured to the motorbikes and drove off. "Minca", I said again, not believing that I would ever get there and a kid on a motorbike said "Si" and gunned his motorbike into action.

"You've got to be joking" I said to no one who could speak English except me. I had been told that the road to Minca was too dreadful for even a bus or an ordinary car to make it through and there was this kid, on a motorbike suggesting that he would take me there. All I had on was a little top, a little skirt and a pair of moccasins with a shoulder bag containing almost everything of any value to me – laptop, camera, credit card, passport, plus a bag with some clothes and toiletries. I told him I needed to smoke (and seriously think about it).

So I sat there in the baking midday heat and thought about it. But what else was I going to do? What else could I do? I

160

couldn't even get back. So I slathered factor 30 sun cream on my bare arms and legs, put on the pathetic toy helmet he offered, climbed onto his bald tyred bike, wedged my bags between him and me and off we went. Notwithstanding that I've been riding bikes for most of my life and I hardly ever trust ANYONE on two wheels because usually, they are useless and I am better, and off we went.

I was reminded of my despatch riding days and being on the back of "Mad Mick" - appropriately named, who used to race around everywhere as if he had right of way against oncoming traffic, with me on the back. On one occasion, I was so terrified, I thought I was going to be sick in my own helmet. The ride to Minca wasn't dissimilar. To call the thing we were on a "road" was a massive exaggeration. Mostly, it was worse than a path that donkeys would falter on. It was a steep, winding, mountainous track full of pot holes, craters and sand, which with bald tyres, you don't grip, you just slip, and there was I, sitting astride this beast with bare legs and arms, just waiting for the bike to skid over and for my skin to shred like coleslaw.

I felt sick with fear. I even wondered if my insurance would cover it or would it just be considered an act of lunacy and void my policy. The sand was so treacherous, the bike kept sliding as if on ice At one point, we were even racing another bike – I wanted to shout "SLOW DOWN - IT'S NOT A RACE" but with no Spanish I just gripped on with my hands and legs until my entire body ached. I couldn't even look at the road or over the edge at the sheer drop in case it was strew with broken vehicles and people. All that I knew for sure was that we were climbing really high because my ears kept popping – or was that my brain?

Somehow, we made it to Minca intact. We finally rolled over a metal makeshift bridge into town and suddenly I was aware of the mountains, so close I could touch them. There was snow on the top and clouds on the ridge. They say that the rise in altitude from Santa Marta to Minca is one of the most

161

extreme in the world – just 15 miles and you were from sea level to mountains and I'd experienced every inch. He finally dropped me at the base of a track that led up to my hostel, I gave him back his helmet and 7,000 pesos – less than £2 and I was so relieved to have made it and to have had such a stark raving mad journey, once again, I was hugging a complete stranger. Colombia!

I walked up the very steep path with beer bottles half buried in the soil to act as steps (just imagine) and almost by accident, found Hostel Colibri which rather quaintly, means "hummingbird". The communal area decked with tables, chairs and hammocks was all open plan and open air. It had no windows and just a corrugated iron roof to keep it waterproof. It stood on stilts leaning on the hill and as described, was surrounded by nature.

There was a man sitting at a table who I thought might be the English, French and Spanish speaking owner, but he wasn't. He was a Dutch guest who, like all Dutch people, spoke English. He told me that there was a power cut and I told him about my crazy journey. He and his wife had been travelling through South America for six months but I think, even he, found my account alarming. At some point, someone who also wasn't the owner, turned up and showed me to my room replete with a mini bust of Simon Bolivar, the liberator of South America. It had a double bed draped in a mosquito net, a window which looked out onto the forest and cushions and curtains decorated with all things parrot. For some reason it also had a painting of the Eiffel Tower. I dumped my bag and headed back into town.

"Town" was perhaps too grand a word for Minca. It was tiny. One little church, two streets and that was about it. I wondered why people even bothered to go there except that there were millions of birds, a river, waterfalls, a coffee plantation and, the reason why I was there, CHOCOLATE! The mountains dwarf the town – it was like a miniscule oasis of flatness where people could settle and build something that they could live in. There were a few bars and restaurants, which I presumed used to be houses (before the tourists arrived) and not much more.

I wandered around looking for a restaurant for later. I found one up the hill and went in during their afternoon break.
 "Menu?" I asked. They looked at me as if I'd recently arrived from Mars.
"Menu?" they repeated rubbing their chins and looking at one another. They just didn't have a clue. Finally, one of them said,
"Ah, bano," meaning toilet/bathroom. "Non, non bano," he said. I paused trying to remain patient – never forget that I'd had weeks of no one understanding me and it really was wearing me out.
"Non, non bano." I repeated with as much calmness as I could muster but really wanting to just clobber them – all of them. "Menu". Again, there was complete bafflement and more chin rubbing. I was in a restaurant, surely they would make a connection. After a few more minutes where it was turning into some kind of banal comedy sketch, one of them finally got it.
"Ah, menoo!" he said – they all congratulated him.
"Si, menoo," I replied, ready to just lie down and cry. I just couldn't make out why they could never make the mental leap and try an educated guess – menyoo, menoo were not that dissimilar, particularly when I was standing in a restaurant. Somehow, the idea of eating there had suddenly become pointless. Somehow, the whole idea of Colombia was becoming pointless. I knew it was my fault for being stupid enough to visit a country where no one spoke English but I really couldn't get over it and walked back down the hill repeating loudly to myself, "ah menoo".

Finally, I found a map with one word of interest to me – and I don't mean to keep going on about it but I am addicted, and that word was simply CHOCOLATE. I followed the sign and back across the bridge, found a little stall, all on its own, with a sign saying "Kakaw". Somehow, I seem to know the name

163

for the thing that I love in every language. The stall lady told me that in one hour, the chocolate would arrive – I had nothing to do and nowhere to go so just sat down to wait.

In the meantime, two of the fabled Kogi tribe, synonymous with the Tairona people who'd retreated to perfect isolation in the hills five centuries ago, appeared like an apparition. They were dressed in white cotton fabric much like a toga, had brown lined skin much like leather and long black matted hair much like a blanket. They didn't look very happy, as if being forced to come to town for anything was deeply distressing and unpleasant. I can hardly imagine what they were there for unless it was to deliver produce rather than buy it. I was tempted to take a photo but didn't. It just didn't seem appropriate – they're not birds of paradise although I hoped they were still people of paradise.

I returned my gaze up the hill where a laden donkey stood and sure enough, after awhile, down the hill, came a woman in a hair net with a bag FULL of little heart shaped jewels of such extreme delight I think I lost my mind. 2,000 pesos for three – 50p! I bought three. I didn't want the ones with fruit, I just wanted the ones with cocoa. I just sat there and ate them, letting them dissolve in their pure goodness of thick, dark, bitter perfection. For the second time in one day, I questioned my sanity and then bought three more. This was chocolate that I'd never tasted before. It made even the finest chocolate seem like junk. So I bought another three. The only thing that might have come close, was the chocolates that my nearly god daughter Tess made me for Christmas.

I was so satiated, I saw no reason to move and eventually, the man who seemed to be in charge, invited me to stay for the chocolate making "tour". So I just sat there. They gave me a little cup of organic coffee to sustain me, raw cocoa beans to suck, dried beans to peel and chew and finally, a course in how to make the perfect chocolate – they even let me caress and press the mixture into the little heart shaped moulds. I was staggered to discover that the only ingredients they used were just organic roasted and ground cocoa, coconut oil to bind it, panille which was the juice wrung out of the sugar cane without the bulk of the sugar, and that was it. No milk, no cocoa butter, no cream, no nothing. So I bought another three, hoping that they would somehow last till later.

Probably delirious, I staggered back to the hostel and the "Bolivar Suite" as my room was very grandly named, took a shower to rinse the dust of the journey from my body and then there was yet another power cut. I knew wi fi was almost non-existent up there, but to have no electricity meant that I couldn't even use my lap top to write. I suppose I could have bought paper but the idea of finding somewhere to buy it and then trying to ask for it was just too much to even think about.

By then, the tri-lingual owner Romario had arrived so I asked him what I was supposed to do? He gave me a candle for my room, invited me to join him and the other guests sitting in the candle lit lounge and we talked! Mostly I spoke to the Dutch man from earlier about his travels and all things Dutch – I was curious as to what Holland creates and sustains itself from – hi-tech micro chip machinery for one, and once he'd gone, I talked to Romario who was, of course, supremely interesting – why else would he be there, high in the mountains with a Colombian wife, a precocious funny pretty little daughter, a hostel and a loaf of bread in the oven which he baked every day.

We talked about how perma-culture ruins the soil, his time living in Hammersmith (where I used to live), Paris where he was from (and where I also used to live and was married) and many other things, and I thought; I only went there for the chocolate, but in one day, I'd had, perhaps, the most interesting day I'd had in my entire time in Colombia. What a difference conversation made. And not only that, up there, nature was SO noisy. In Taganga, there was just the wail of the wind. In Minca, the land was alive; probably with things

165

that would eat me alive. But with my 100% deet insect repellent, I was prepared to risk it...

****

I'd paid extra to have breakfast and Romario promised me fruit in abundance and coffee with non-lactose milk. I waited until 8.30 when the Dutch couple gave up and left and then the Colombian kid from yesterday arrived. I expected him to be buckling under the weight of a tray, possibly balanced on his head, covered in a vast array of tropical fruit for me to gorge on. But no. He had nothing edible whatsoever. He opened the kitchen to a swarm of tiny fruit flies and then he opened the fridge. All I could see was the fibrous end of a pineapple and 3 half mouldy strawberries which tasted more like carrots – I ate them anyway. I even risked a slice of his homemade bread – I was starving. I looked around for the coffee – the kid pointed at the cold coffee left over from yesterday. "Caliente" I said meaning "hot", so he poured it into the kettle and boiled it up for me. Only in Colombia. I was then left on my own – everyone else had checked out and I was seriously wondering if I could stay up there for two more nights, with absolutely no company and probably sitting in the dark. I was reminded of the film *The Shining* when Jack Nicholson heads up to the deserted hotel at the top of the mountain to write, and goes stark raving mad. Did I really want to risk it?

I couldn't. I found myself on automatic pilot, packing my things. I paid the kid for one night and he had the cheek to mention breakfast. I actually lost my temper and delivered a terrifying diatribe and even though he spoke no English, even he understood EXACTLY what I meant. I picked my way, goat-like, down the track to the road and walked into town. I just had to say "Santa Marta" and was led to a meeting point where the Dutch couple and an elderly man were already waiting. That made us four and we were ready to go.

We climbed aboard an old worn out Land Rover and with a

bang and a cloud of smoke, we creaked out of town. Without being scared out of my wits, I noticed just how beautiful the route up or down the mountain really was. The vegetation was so lush and verdant. The river could be seen rolling over boulders, racing down to the sea and the air was charged with positivity – just what I needed. I wouldn't say that Minca had been great but it had been eventful, and not only that , it had given me the best chocolate of my life and that, after all, was the only reason I had gone there. I was thankful and grateful.

When we finally approached Santa Marta, we didn't head along the bus route; instead we took a new super duper ring road which I had never seen before. There was word that the road would continue to Minca and why would they do that? Because the Colombian government had legalised the use of marijuana for medical use and guess where they were going to grow it? Yep, up in them there hills. I asked if it meant land clearance but no one could tell me – I supposed that meant yes. And the most ridiculous thing was that the fare in the Land Rover was the same as the motorbike – just 7,000 pesos – less that £2. What a country of contradictions.

Back in the relative sanity of Santa Marta (and I never thought I would say that), it was back to Casa Familiar, yet again. Because I'd returned earlier than expected, my old room was occupied so they took me up to another room with no real window, no natural light and it just wouldn't do. Google Translate was loaded up and I told Fabio I'd have to find somewhere else. We both feigned crying again and in the end, for a little bit more, he gave me a double room with a view of the mountains – it was perfect and would do for the three nights I had left.

What else I was going to do was a mystery. I'd walked nearly every inch that was worth walking, so I bought a book from the "library", plonked myself on the big clean double bed and just got on with it. Later, I did wander out for snacks and my theory that it was a red light district, was confirmed. Half clad girls languished everywhere and one club, belting out music, boasted of girls for all tastes. I did get a few calls of "hola Chica", but I don't think anyone was under the impression that I was for sale. For one thing, I wasn't 16 and for another, most of my bum wasn't hanging out of a tiny pair of shorts. Of course, had I known, I could have bought a pair...

IN MEMORIAM

I learnt, by email, that my brother-in-law, who had been gravely ill, had died six days short of his 60th birthday. I knew his illness was terminal, but I still expected him to be there when I returned to England in May. Nothing prepares you for that news and it was the loneliest thing I had ever experienced. There was no one to talk to about it, no one to hug, no one to raise a sympathetic eyebrow to me; no one to do anything with me. Travelling alone is a test of everything that you possess; your fortitude to deal with difficult situations, to make decisions for better or worse, to get used to only having yourself for company, to overcoming fear of both the known and the unknown, developing your instincts to keep you safe, being an attractive personality so that others will want to engage with you and getting used to talking aloud to yourself when you are, inevitably, all on your own. But to grieve and mourn on your own is the loneliest thing you can do and there was no respite.

Travelling isn't all about having fun experiences and it is important to consider how you will deal with bad news. I considered not mentioning it here because it isn't entertaining but that would ignore the fact that when you do travel, things beyond your control will always happen and if you think that they won't, then you are wrong. You have to be prepared for everything. It's not just one long raucous hullaballoo and when you are in communal places, like the kitchen, and others are talking about how awesome Nicaragua was and all you want to do is cry, you have to disguise it so that you don't look like a depressive nut case, and then you have to go and sit on your own, because that is the only place that you can bear to be.

I knew that he wouldn't want to cause me any despair and in that knowledge, I drowned my sorrows in the only way I knew how and then tried to celebrate the many happy memories that I had of his life, rather than mourn his passing. He was a remarkable man; my sister Colleen's wonderful husband and father to their two fantastic sons, Ryan and Mark – I will miss him.

Mick Waters, please rest in peace.

GETSEMANI

It was something of a relief to leave Santa Marta behind, as if by boarding a bus, I could resume my travels with a lighter heart. I retraced my earlier journey of a month ago, but this time in reverse, back to Cartagena. Weirdly, I had a feeling of returning home to civilisation, and away from the chaos and the cacophony and the constant concussion of the senses that was the Carib coast of Colombia, where the human body was not just something to hang clothes on, but was a protagonist all of its own. I say that meaning that everyone on the coast seemed to ooze sex appeal without even trying. Whether fat or thin, tall or short, young or old; the way they dressed was so provocative it was as if the human body had a mind of its own, like an unconscious extension of the person that they were unaware of. It was almost like being possessed by a sex maniac who wouldn't sit still or shut up. And there is nothing wrong with that. I wished that more people were as unrepressed as they were but at the same time, for someone coming from the West, it was a shock for everything to be so blatant. May it last forever!

As we rolled into the outskirts of Cartagena, buildings and bridges became familiar to me. We passed the district that I'd stayed in before and sped into the old town and out the other side to Getsemani. This part of town was outside the walled city of Cartagena but it shared the same beautiful architecture and colour. The only real difference was that the streets were narrower and the people weren't as well heeled. It was, I supposed, the poorer part of town, like Hackney and Shoreditch were once to London. It made me wonder about London – with the poor being priced out, was Crossrail simply

171

a plan to be able to transport them all back into London to do all the so called menial jobs?

My home in Getsemani was another airbnb, but it was truly spectacular and special. It was more expensive than anywhere else I'd stayed, but I just couldn't resist it and also thought I deserved a treat. The house was 400 years old, was bought as a wreck 20 years ago and after an awful lot of love and hard work, it was perhaps one of the most remarkable houses I had ever been in. It was like a little piece of Andalusia; Moorish (aka Islamist) arches and air ways, rough hewn bare bricks, a jungle of hanging plants, original art work on all of the walls, cinema posters, both old and new, (there was even a poster celebrating Irish writers!) big wooden cupboards and book shelves, elaborately tiled floors, a tiny open patio within the house, old shuttered windows, hand-made customised stained glass windows doors and lights and a little galley kitchen.

I had my own bijou bedroom and bathroom and it was right next door to where Gabriel Garcia Marquez lived! At that, I was flabbergasted! Considering he was precisely why I was there, it had all come full circle in the most extraordinary and satisfying of ways. And not only that, it was owned by an American (Todd), who was a writer and a teacher and barely was I through the front door than I started to talk and ask questions, which was what I like to do more than almost anything, and I talked so much, by the end of the afternoon, I was literally hoarse. I had the feeling that anyone who lived in such a fantastic house would have to be fantastic in his own right and I was absolutely correct!

And even weirder, he'd lived in London and shared my love of Richmond Park, he'd met his fiancée on a boat in St Katherine's dock where a friend of mine lived and for both of us, our favourite pub in Brighton was the Lion and Lobster! All these thousands of miles away and we were talking like old friends and it felt so good. People moaned at me that I should have learnt some Spanish but to have the

172

conversations that I wanted, I'd have to be fluent – or just chosen another country or, indeed, another continent.

Before it got too late, I wanted to see what that side of the city walls looked like. It was Sunday, and whilst that made no difference further south, it did there. Most of the shops were shut, the traffic was non-existent and so I walked off, hoping my homing instincts would work and headed over the bridge to parts previously unknown. There was a massive marina full of very expensive yachts, then there was the new high rise development shredding the skyline in the distance and just nearby, a new neighbourhood which could be anywhere in the world. Kids rode their bikes or played Frisbee, ice cream parlours melted in the sunshine and all was washed white. Cartagena, Todd told me, was being flooded by new money, a lot of it laundered drug money, and it was taking on the persona of a jet set city and it showed.

I headed back over the bridge to my seedier side of town and just wandered around. Everyone had decamped to the street for the hot, humid heat of late afternoon – lounging on the pavement or at tables and chairs playing dominoes and such or just talking. There was a comfortable laziness of music and people, but there, I noticed, it had an edge. Not necessarily of hostility but more, "this is our town and it's not for sale". But, with money pouring in, just as it is in any other city in the world, I hoped that their pride was bigger than the amount of pesos in other peoples' wallets. I just passed them by, showed respect, said an "hola" here and a "buenos" there and then noticed a club with a sign on the door which said "NO WEAPONS". I didn't stop for a drink...

And then my glasses broke – again. I'm not blind without them but reading was impossible so I returned to my new home. Once through the front door, the hall, crowded with bicycles, led into the lounge and from there, a brick archway housing a big old wooden door led to my room. Through the door and to the left was a big old wooden bed and beyond that a royal blue wooden shuttered window. The top of the

173

window had no glass, just bars so that the breeze could drift in. On the right hand side was a floor to ceiling dark polished wooden cabinet with bookshelves filled with books. I scanned them and simply couldn't believe that so many of my books at home were duplicated – from McCarthy to Pynchon! No one read Pynchon! Opposite the window there was a little writing desk. It was as if the room had been especially made for me and without hesitation, I set up my laptop and got to work. I couldn't have been happier. Even when Gabo's old house next door began throbbing with music, I really didn't care – it was good music and I was replete.

****

In the morning, by the time I woke, Todd had gone to work and it was just bliss to sit in his gorgeous living room with a breeze blowing in from the open roof top adjacent. In the two months of the year when it did rain, the water falls straight down to where the open air shower was and simply drains away. The house was so at one with nature it was a joy. I drank coffee in peace and quiet, almost an oxymoron in Colombia, and a total first. At the start of my travels a friend in England had put me in touch with his friend in Costa Rica who although was a total stranger, had invited me to stay with him at his ranch. We'd finalized plans for me to stay on the day I would arrive in Costa Rica and it was his email that I sat and read – the plan was coming together and it felt that just by being there in that house had righted every wrong. I was so happy!

If I could take that house and put it somewhere liveable, I would never move again. It was almost a struggle to even go out and I may well not have done except I had to get my glasses fixed. So back to sight-seeing mode, first I walked to the end of the road and the Plaza del Trinidad – the place where in 1811 the revolution to shake off Spanish colonial rule began. I was expecting a huge great square which would have held thousands of angry people but instead, I found just a small sleepy space amidst a confluence of streets with a few

174

bronze statues dedicated to the people of the revolution. It obviously didn't take much for a revolution to kick off in Colombia (or anywhere else in Latin America).

I then found an optician, handed her my glasses and winced every time she hit them with her tiny hammer but it seemed to work and she only charged me the equivalent of 50p! Unbelievable. I wandered into the old city of Cartagena and it was all so familiar. Once again, I had a feeling of coming home. I even wondered if I could live in a city like that, but as the clouds closed in and the humidity rose and sweat washed off me, I decided that I couldn't. It was about 90 degrees and it got much, much hotter. The rains arrive in October by which time I would be exhausted, depressed and withered. It was so humid I didn't even want to wander and get lost in the streets of the old town again – plus I was afraid that if I did, I'd buy yet another pair of shoes...

Instead, I roamed Getsemani. Part of it was all new characterless buildings and malls selling junk. One stall was just selling mouse traps and alongside were a couple of bricks – I wondered if the bricks were the inhumane way of getting rid of them – simply flatten them. It was obvious that this was the poorer part of town probably built to house the workers and the other side, where I am, was the older, up and coming bit and it showed. Whether the idea was to regenerate the whole of Getsemani or ethnically cleanse it was debatable. There was an enormous new concrete conference centre and also swanky restaurants and up-market bars (weapons definitely not allowed) and you just knew, that bit by bit, the swank would spread.

But it was lunch time and as always, Colombians emptied the streets and filled up every restaurant available. It was to be my last menu del dia and I wanted it to be a good one. I roamed up and down until I found one full of locals; it had chicken, it had a table beneath a fan and so I sat down. Unfortunately, the waitress was absolutely useless. The whole place was a riot; sending things back, demanding this and demanding that and when my main course finally arrived, I hadn't even had any soup. In simple terms, I pointed this out and much later, half way through my lunch, she slapped it on the table, spilling half of it. Thank god the food was good. I didn't leave a tip. So much for my last lunch.

I wandered home – after all, I was only back in Cartagena to stay in that magnificent house – I'd already seen just about everything that there was to see of the city and I didn't intend to waste house time. I took Todd's advice and had an open air shower – bliss – the sun shining down, the water pouring down and it was about the cleanest and freshest I'd felt for over two months! No clammy, grubby shower curtain, no grime anywhere and proper huge fluffy bath towels – heaven really.

Todd returned from school later in the afternoon and said he'd down-loaded a movie we could watch and we discussed music. Turned out we were both late arrivals to The Smiths and Radiohead - as well as everything else we had in common – it was so weird to feel so akin with a complete stranger! And with all things ready and packed, I wandered out to the booze shop which apparently sold wine that came from the liners which docked there and was sort of duty free or black market. I didn't ask any questions, I just went and bought myself a bottle and it was like being in a proper off licence – well maybe I could live there... But before you speculate – Todd had a girlfriend who I also think I would have got on really well with, but she wasn't there – she had to return to Europe for visa reasons.

So movie time – Todd had downloaded a Swedish Cannes Film Festival winner and so we settled down, wine glasses in hand and watched it. I'm not a fan of Swedish films – they're more out to shock than to entertain. (Think Festen and Dogma in general) and before long, we'd abandoned the film and were talking about anything and everything. It turned out we were both Leos, we both liked Iranian cinema (how was that possible – I didn't know ANYONE who liked Iranian

176

cinema) and we had a truly amazing, interesting, stimulating evening:

We discussed Murdoch and his insidious monopoly of the press, American day light robbery medical insurance, Dick Cheney and how much money he'd made from the Iraq war, the American national anthem which I'd realized recently was all about bombing and killing people (!), how Rome after World War Two was just broken bricks and broken people. You get the idea. It was not an ordinary conversation, it was not an ordinary night and it was not an ordinary house.

I just couldn't get over it. And despite having to get up early in the morning to travel on, we stayed up far too late but I just didn't care. What a totally SUPER night – the most interesting I'd had since Andree the French speaking Canadian lady all those weeks ago in Mexico, and maybe longer. I am so glad that I took the risk, spent the money and chose the house that was magically beckoning me to stay. Right up until the end, Gabo's magical realism was still at work!

****

In the morning, I locked the house, loaded up a taxi and left for the airport. I checked in with the usual palaver, didn't have to pay the departure tax (?) and watched my bag disappear onto the conveyor belt wondering if I'd ever see it again – after all, it was Colombia. A short flight later, I was back in cold miserable Bogota but thankfully, only for a stopover and then onto another flight bound for San Jose. I settled into my window seat and as I watched Colombia disappear beneath me I thought of all the ridiculous, exciting, colourful, rhythmic, musical and utterly bewildering and magical things I'd encountered there. And with a smile, I waved goodbye. Adios Colombia, hola Costa Rica!

COSTA RICA

THE RANCH

After many hours, it was with incredulity that I watched my bag shoot out onto the console at San Jose airport like a torpedo from a submarine. I was so sure that if you could lose your luggage in Europe, you could lose it anywhere (especially in South America and especially with a connecting flight), that I'd stashed emergency supplies of everything, including tobacco, into my carry-on luggage. Some things I could do without, but tobacco wasn't one of them. I really didn't expect to see my bag for days, if ever.

I'd already flown along the coast of Costa Rica (which literally means Rich Coast) from Mexico to Colombia but this time I'd flown over it. From the air, the country was a mass of green with brooding volcanoes poised to erupt. It was bordered to the north by Nicaragua and to the south by Panama. On the map, Central America was the shape of a lobster with Costa Rica being part of its tail. It was tiny – only 76 miles wide at its narrowest and 172 at its widest and less than 300 miles in length.

It apparently does Eco Tourism better than anywhere else on earth, has more species of plants and insects than anywhere else on earth and was so committed to tourism, that it could cater for any type of trip you would ever care for, be it an ecological pilgrimage, sheer spa luxury or extreme sports. It had it all. Not that I wanted any of those. My plan was to see the beaches of both the Pacific and Caribbean and hopefully find some people like me. That's all I ever want to do. On this trip, I'd only met two; Andree and Todd – not good odds but I was, as ever, optimistic and when the fasten

181

seat belt sign came on, I buckled up and prepared for the landing which, like a child, still fills me with excitement.

San Jose, from the sky looked like one enormous caravan park – colourful, ordered, clean and constructed; unlike most everywhere else I'd seen so far. It was hot but not debilitatingly so and it was cloudy. It was green and pleasant and clean and lovely. I'd intended to take a bus into town, another one to the coach station and then another to Cuidad Colon where Paul from the ranch would meet me. It seemed an enormous time consuming palaver and I wasn't looking forward to it, especially as I wasn't really expecting anyone to speak English.

As soon as I was through customs, a man holding a taxi sign asked if I needed help. I always needed help but didn't tell him that. Instead, I said I was looking for the bus station. In English (!) he confirmed my fears that it would take forever, laughed when he saw the size of my bag and said that for the equivalent of £20 he would take me all the way there. I'd obviously lost my mind from the day's travelling, because somehow that seemed like a bargain and the next thing, we were leaving the airport – him wheeling my bag whilst I trotted along behind.

He spoke fluent English and said that lots of people in Costa Rica also did. So far, so good/excellent. Deranged as I clearly was, I was surprised that most of the cars around were Japanese – I expected them to be American as the USA has such a presence there, so much so that a lot of money in circulation are dollars and the new bus terminal is called the Coca Cola Terminal – no mistaking that one then.

When we pulled into the small town of Ciudad Colon, we drove around looking for a bank so that I could pay him. The ATM threw out five brightly coloured, parrot faced notes worth £25 each and he just rolled his eyes when I gave him one. He had no change. No one had any change, even the shops didn't have any change so in the end, I gave him the parrot note and he gave me back $10 complaining that he'd lost money. It felt like a small triumph for mankind.

I sat myself down on a bench next to a basketball pitch where teenagers, who looked like any other teenagers, were playing the game. I got out my old joke of a phone which I hadn't used for two months and dialled a number. Ten minutes later, Paul, who looked uncannily exactly like Tony Soprano, arrived in his huge four-wheel-drive necessity to meet me. Even though we had never met, we both had an overwhelming urge to hug one another and that was exactly what we did. Sometimes it just feels right. He loaded me up and off we went to The Ranch, deep inside the tropical rainforest of Costa Rica. When I mentioned his doppelganger, he said that he milked it whenever he could to queue jump but since Gandolfini died it didn't really work anymore.

The ranch was huge and lush and modern. It looked like a regular hacienda except the attention to detail – like mosaic walls, swimming pool, palapas roofs, guest house bigger than my house, every fixture and fitting, in fact every single thing in and on that ranch, made it a place of wonder and intense natural beauty in total empathy with the wonder and intense natural beauty that is Costa Rica. Paul introduced me to Dunia, his petite, pretty, Costa Rican girlfriend, who was as welcoming and lovely as he was. They had never met me, knew nothing about me but as Paul said, if I was a friend of Daniel's then that was good enough for them. Thank you Daniel!

Paul showed me around and asked where I'd like to sleep – in the huge Artists' House in the garden or in the bedroom in the house with its own palatial bathroom. I was after company, not isolation – I opted for the bedroom in the house. I'd brought a bottle of Colombian rum for them and they opened a bottle of French wine for me – he had a Swiss friend who imported wine! It was the first decent wine I'd had since England – it hadn't been in a shop window in direct sunshine for god knows how long and it showed.

183

Paul liked to cook and in a kitchen that size, so would I. It was of course, fully equipped with a fridge the size of a cupboard and a range the size of, well a range. It had an indoor barbecue, a griddle and gas rings – everything you could ever need. He cooked a mountain of meat and a big bowl of salad and we sat down to dinner. Bearing in mind the meat in Colombia was almost indigestible and only fit for dogs, I ate more in that sitting than I'd eaten in a month. And yet despite a monumental appetite, I still managed to talk the entire time. In fact, we hadn't stopped talking since our initial hug. He was a very interesting entrepreneur which was why he lived outside the USA and in Costa Rica. Sometimes, I wondered if all the interesting North Americans had all left home in search of something with a bit more freedom – the same reason that Europeans left for America all those centuries ago.

Paul was an early to bed early to rise type of man, so he retired early. Dunia and I then talked girls stuff – relationships mostly. She'd started working for Paul but they soon fell in love. She'd been married before when she was young but said that like many Costa Rican men, her husband was immature and it hadn't worked out. I could see what she saw in Paul, a rock of a man who you could even feel safe falling overboard with. Security had a lot to offer.

When it was time for sleep, Dunia showed me to my room, turned my enormous TV on, handed me the remote and the A/C control and left me to it. For the first time in a very long time, I managed to watch a film that wasn't just silhouettes in a fog, speaking Spanish. No matter that it was Tom Cruise - I would have watched anything and not a sub-title in sight. Bliss really.

****

On the terrace, by the pool, overlooking the Rainforest, drinking coffee was the way I started my day. Paul's ranch (what a great word to be able to use) was up on a ridge with

184

views to San Jose 30 miles away. The mountains in the distance were wrapped in clouds like white candy floss. Everything was green in different shades and birds of every colour swooped by. Hundreds of different butterflies flitted around the flowers all of which, in nature's way, were saying "come and taste me". It was alive with nature and its sound was one of animals communicating on the breeze.

Paul came out to join me with his iphone and ipad and seemed aghast that not only did I have neither, but that I was also travelling with neither. Yes, it would be easier, but it would be like giving in to technology and consumerism and I just couldn't do it. He told me that in his youth, he'd worked on a kibbutz for three years and I wondered if that was where his phenomenal ability to share had come from. We both wandered what had happened to them – at one time half of Europe's youth seemed to be working on a kibbutz and then they just vanished. I Googled it – individual fulfilment had taken over...

He and Dunia had to go into Cuidad Colon on business so I went along for the ride. I mentioned that I'd like to buy some wine and he looked puzzled – why did I want to when he had plenty? His generosity was beyond boundaries. We bumped into his Tico (Costa Rican) friend Victor who was driving around with a car full of straw bales (?) and so we all went for lunch. It was a little local cafe which does the best ceviche in town. I'd heard about this delicacy, but had never tasted it. We sat on high stools at a high table and what arrived was a big bowl of raw Tilapia fish marinated in lime and mint. It was so soft, it was the texture of the freshest cooked squid and it was sublime.

We drank bottles of beer, and whilst Dunia engrossed herself in the Spanish football derby, Victor and I talked. He wanted to know what team I supported (I don't), and about my travels. He too had been to Colombia and Mexico and I think he was slightly in awe that I was travelling solo in such apparently dangerous places. By the end of lunch, we were

185

nudging one another like old friends and he suggested I go to the Finca Cabello Loco – The Crazy Horse Ranch the next day and he'd take me riding. It was five years since I'd been on a horse – a short trek in the Dominican Republic and many more years since I really rode. That was back in Cairo when I galloped through the desert on a beast which I thought would never stop. I didn't tell Victor that though. I offered a contribution to lunch – Paul just laughed.

Back at the ranch, I went to explore. It was massive. There were little pathways leading to hanging bridges, follies in the trees, an actual tree house, huge aviaries full of toucans and parrots and there were workers everywhere tending to everything. Even in the house, there was a troupe of maids constantly cleaning and dusting – they even had a Dyson vacuum cleaner which must be something of a miracle or an expensive import. And all to keep the dust out which must have been a bit like King Canute trying to turn back the tide. And they all worked so diligently. There was even a house for any of the workers who needed it though mostly, they lived in town but in any case, they all looked so happy – and why wouldn't they?

But the ranch was for pleasure not profit. Paul also had a fresh water trout farm and another which grew hydrangeas – diversity in the extreme. But primarily, he was a business man and Dunia was the company lawyer and they seemed to make a great team which must, in fact, be quite difficult – mixing work and pleasure doesn't always work so well.

After the inevitable siesta, Paul opened another bottle of wine – an outstanding Argentinean Gran Reserve and cooked up another mound of meat – steak this time marinated in mustard and Worcestershire sauce and once again, seemingly from nothing, a feast arrived. They said they were going to San Jose in the morning and they'd take me to look around but I'd already promised Victor to go horse riding and didn't want to let him down. I suppose that Costa Rica was so relaxed that I could have cancelled for another day but you know what we British are like – a man is his word and all that. In hindsight, I wondered if that was a signal for me to leave but feeling so at home and oblivious to everything, it didn't manifest itself to thought or action. After so long of slumming it with no one to talk to, it was as if I was being lulled by luxury and all ideas of adventure had popped like a bubble.

****

So it was with some surprise, when I arrived at Finca Cabello del Loco to find no sign of Victor or anyone; just six snarling, fang baring dogs. There were horses in the field and even a tiny foal, but people there were not. I walked back up the hill to the two enormous electric gates of the ranch. There was a rope connected to a big bell so I gave it a tentative pull. Nothing. I used a little more force. Nothing. In the end, I was swinging on the rope like a crazed campanologist – or Quasi Modo if you prefer, and still nothing. I wondered if I should just sleep in the shade like a Mexican until someone turned up except I didn't have a sombrero and then I noticed the intercom. Oh, I see, you simply pushed the electronic bell...

With nothing else to do, I decided to swim. I couldn't remember the last time I was actually immersed in water, but when I dived in, it was wonderful and not only was it revitalising, I had the whole thing to myself! I swam and sunbathed and sunbathed and swam until the maid came out and told me there was a telephone call for me. For me? Yes. If I wanted to go riding – be there at 2pm.

I was there at 2pm and so was Victor and so was Krisia, a Canadian woman with green eyes, white blonde hair, a cowboy hat and boots and a swagger that would match John Wayne's. I thought it would be just be me and Victor going for a bit of a ride but Krisia meant business. She'd been around horses for so long, she was horse. She asked if I wanted to ride English or Western style. I had no idea what

187

she was talking about and just looked vague. She said in Western style, you held the reins together as if you were holding the stem of a wine glass – that sounded very familiar so I opted for that one.

She kitted me out with a straw hat – I declined the offer of a helmet and signed a waiver saying so, even though I realised it was madness, especially with one brain injury to my name already (a long story – a party five years ago, hoisted onto someone's shoulders, being dropped, concrete floor – you get the picture). I then mounted my trusty steed "Habibi". Krisia adjusted the stirrups and asked if they felt comfortable – how should I know – I looked confident in the saddle but that meant nothing. I just smiled and off we clattered, up the cobbled track, out onto the road and then onto the mountainous forest path. We clopped over brooks and rivers, we climbed over boulders and we went up and down, always under the canopy of the Rainforest.

Krisia led the way and almost rode side saddle so that she could talk to me. We talked the whole way and as usual, I asked hundreds of questions. I'd say she was from serious money - she went to boarding school in Yorkshire, studied in Manchester and was an architect. She'd gone to Costa Rica with her husband (and children) to build gated communities and just never went back. I wondered why, in the safety of Costa Rica, anyone would want to live in a gated community rather than in amongst the people. She had divorced and Victor was her new partner and companion and they seemed perfectly matched. She said that she'd taught him to ride and unlike most men, he didn't presume to know how to do it, he just followed her lead and learnt like a natural...

I don't even know how long we were out for but it seemed like hours. We mostly just wandered through the forest. Sitting way up high in just my straw hat, I did worry at times when Habibi seemed to lose his footing on the bigger boulders and I shot perilously forwards. It always surprised me how horses could be so sure footed when they had such big hard feet, surely made worse by having a great big metal shoe attached to it. But he was safe enough and when Krisia suggested a gallop he was keen to follow. It reminded me of a time in Killarney in Ireland with my dad, when he rented a horse for me on a racetrack and there I was, all of nine years old, hacking round at full pace like a little jockey. I think I was better at it then and felt quite relieved when Habibi slowed back to a walk.

When I asked Krisia about the other ex pats, she told me that unlike in the past when Costa Rica was cheap and they came in droves, it was now expensive and only the rich could afford it and rather than buying a house, they bought land but that they didn't farm it, they just let it go back to nature. I wasn't sure how I felt about that one when agriculture was a big part of the country's economy, but I supposed like elsewhere in the world, technological manufacture was taking over and with the right companies, it could make the government more money than farming ever could.

Finally, when we trekked back into the stable, it seemed over too soon – I could have talked to them all day. Paul had told me that at Cabello Loco, they liked to drink beer and thankfully, he was absolutely right and that was our next treat. After we'd desaddled the horses or whatever it is you do with them, we walked to a kind of open air saloon built around and within the trees. It was like a giant tree house. We settled down and Victor brought the beers in iced glasses. He'd taken lots of photos and I said not to bother showing me because I wasn't photogenic. Krisia took the iPhone from him, had a look and said "oh yes you are – you even look cute!" And I did! How does that happen? Sheer enjoyment?

And so we got talking some more and I just thought that with good company, you could live just about anywhere and need nothing other than each other and a common goal. And that was what they had. Krisia had bought the land some years ago and from nothing, had created the ranch, much the same as Paul had done with his. It seemed like a very obliging country, but only if you had pots of money or a successful business. The north Americans who used to retire there were now having to opt for cheaper places like Panama, or Belize (where they spoke English) – maybe it was better that way and stopped Costa Rica from losing any more of its heritage and identity.

After many, many, many beers and a good few hours gassing, they walked me back up the hill with the eight dogs. Victor suggested I used the Interbus service which was reliable and inexpensive to take me to Montezuma; my next destination. He even rang them for me but it was too late for the following day. We hugged with gusto, bade farewell and the maid let me in to an empty house. I made a snack and retired to the garden to smoke and caught Paul and Dunia's return through the closed doors. They seemed exhausted and fraught and vanished to bed. I was beginning to feel in the way and prepared myself for leaving. I wondered if it would be my last night, so retired to my lavish room, rummed it up and goggled at the TV - *Taxi Driver* for the umpteenth time but is it possible to tire of it?

****

Both Paul and Dunia were gone when I got up at 7am. I was determined to get going to where I should be going so as not to outstay my welcome, if I hadn't already. By email, I requested a place on the shuttle, but when it came to confirm it, the internet wasn't working. What a time for it to go wrong and by the time it was working, the bus was full. Dunia was hosting a birthday party for her nephew which meant the entire family would be arriving the following day. I really didn't want to intrude.

Paul had been to a funeral but on his return, we tackled the problem together. We found another company but nothing was straight forward. I couldn't believe that in the third world that was Colombia, I could call a number, make a reservation and the bus just turned up, on time and took me exactly where I wanted to go but in civilised Costa Rica, I couldn't. We had to download a form, fill it in with credit card details, photograph it and email it back to them – ridiculous and it seemed to take forever and even then, there was no confirmation.

In celebration of what would, theoretically, be my last night, Paul took us out to dinner to a Peruvian restaurant in San Jose. It was my first real glimpse of the capital and it looked pretty unremarkable. Dunia had shown me a book on San Jose in the 1920's but since then, many of the colonial buildings had been knocked down and replaced with parking lots – the Joni Mitchell song *They paved paradise and put up a parking lot,* came to mind. It was very functional but totally ordinary. In my mind, I likened it to new towns in England – it did it an extreme injustice, but I couldn't help thinking of Milton Keynes...

I'd never eaten Peruvian food before and when it arrived and I'd scraped off the cheese sauce and batter, I was still slightly ambivalent. The conversation on the other hand, was excellent – how often does Napoleonic law come up? But it did with Paul and Dunia and what with me and my law A level, I was engrossed. I was amazed I could still remember it all – torts, precedents and my old favourite, Res Ipsa Loquiter. I offered to contribute to the bill – Paul just looked at me in his comically mystified way and said "you are our guest" - I think I was beginning to form a bit of a crush. It just seemed so unusual in this dreary day and age, that there were still men who wouldn't even dream of allowing a woman to pay for herself – and damned right too! Call me old fashioned, but I didn't even know I was SUPPOSED to pay for anything. When I was younger, if I went on a date, I didn't even take money out with me – what would I possibly need it for?

✶✶✶✶✶✶✶✶✶✶✶✶✶✶✶✶

There was no word from Montezuma Expeditions as to whether I was booked or not and people were already arriving

191

for the party. I felt like the proverbial elephant in the room.
Finally, Paul got on the phone and explained to them in a very
forceful way, that we were tired of waiting, we were tired of
their antiquated systems and what they needed to do right
away, was accept a booking over the phone. Miraculously, he
handed the phone to me, they accepted my credit card details
and in minutes, I was booked on the 2pm from Santa Ana –
what a difference a firm hand makes.

Paul insisted that I join the party although I sat there like a
ventriloquist's dummy, turning my head back and forth as if I
had any idea what anyone was saying. The kids spoke
English and even French but they were all busy dive bombing
one another in the pool. Not to be too much of a burden –
after all, it was a huge loving family affair, from grandparents
to chicos, I took an interest in the cook and his food. In one
enormous cauldron he was deep frying half a pig and in
another, he was frying plantain to make patacones. I was
under the illusion that patacones were fried once and then
coated in batter and refried making them fluffy and
exceedingly good. Not true. They were fried once and then
they were flattened in a metal device which was the shape
and size of two ping pong bats tied together and once flat,
were refried and then, as if by magic, they puffed up on their
own – and there was I, all that time, afraid to eat them what
with the allergies and all. He even let me flatten some and
for the first time in days, I actually felt useful.

And then it was time to go so that Paul could get back to the
party in earnest. A friend of his had just arrived so he came
with us as we rolled out of The Ranch; me for possibly the
last time. Paul said to come back again before I left for home
but who knew where I would be but if I didn't, I hoped that it
wouldn't be the last time that I'd see him. Something told
me that it wouldn't be. He dropped me at the hotel pick up
point and we had such an almighty hug. His friend took a
photo which didn't come out so I had dozens of his ranch but
not one of him. I know I keep saying it but I have to say it
just one more time - Paul was one of the kindest, most

192

generous men I had ever met. He didn't know me, he'd never met me and yet he'd made me so very welcome and had begun my Costa Rican adventure for me with an experience I would never forget. Thank you Paul and thank you Daniel for bringing us together – you are both stars to me!

MONTEZUMA

The minibus finally arrived nearly an hour late but considering I didn't really expect it to arrive at all, it was as remarkable as the Second Coming. I climbed aboard and off we went. My four companions were a young Canadian couple also heading for Montezuma and two American girls off to do a yoga and surf retreat in Santa Teresa, just along the coast. We instantly bonded and were so busy talking, we barely noticed that we were ascending into the clouds until it began to absolutely pour. Torrential. Rain. It was the first downpour I'd seen for months but within ten minutes, it stopped. A mirage of evaporation rose from the parched earth, the air sweetened and the verdure, if anything, grew brighter. It was Tropical Rain Forest in all of its ethereal beauty.

The yoga girls were both well travelled – Amy from Indianapolis had done a volunteering stint in what she thought was a suburb of London called Ipswich. She was doing a Post Grad in psychology at Columbia University (I presume an achievement in itself) and somehow drew the short straw and rather than being seconded to actual London, Ipswich was where she ended up. Luckily, she could laugh about it. She was a good looking, stylish savvy entrepreneur who owned two yoga studios and used to work in advertising on Madison Avenue, New York.

The other girl Jen, was pretty, vivacious and very well travelled. She'd spent time studying biodiversity in Costa Rica in the past, spoke fluent Spanish and she'd studied yoga and meditation in an Ashram in Rishikesh in India which, not funnily enough, was the only place in India that I really didn't

195

like. She told me about Vedic mediation which, she said, you could pick up in a few days and it emptied your mind and body of all the stress of today, yesterday and the future and hence, filled you with energy and positivity – I intended to try it.

The Canadian couple were the opposite. John, a chemistry major, in his twenties, had never been on a plane before and was on the journey of a life time and it showed – he just couldn't believe everything that he was seeing. He said that working as a chemist was a very negative practice because he was always dealing with failure when an experiment to prove a point proved futile. He said that was why many scientists were drunks. It made me think of my time at the Natural History Museum and the Friday night booze ups, originally hosted by the science department, which were rampant with drunks – the nights only ceased when somehow, someone pulled down half the ceiling... Alice was better travelled and as coincidence would have it, as well as also being of a science background, was a Pilates teacher. All of them were really interesting and delightful. One last little point, Jen, the meditation teacher, worked in a winery in California where they had perfected the art of wine in cans and just to prove it, she unzipped her massive bag and pulled out eight giant cans – and I thought I was weird lugging rum and wine everywhere with me! (We also snuck a quick illegal smoke on the ferry – those yoga teachers, you just don't know what they will do next).

Montezuma was on the south eastern coast of the Nicoyan Peninsula which itself, was on the western Pacific coast and to reach it we had to cross the Gulf of Nicoya from the little port town of Puntarenas to which we arrived at about 4.30pm. There were bicycles everywhere – something I hadn't seen before and rather than piles of garbage on the side of the road redolent of Colombia, there were brightly coloured rocks acting as a kind of kerb. We stocked up in the almost bare supermarket, unloaded our bags (I thought my bag was big – you should have seen theirs and they were only there for two weeks!) and wheeled them onto the car ferry.

I have always loved boats. Our one was way smaller than a cross channel ferry but that wasn't the only way it differed. There was a little cafe selling hot dogs and beer and right there, next to it, were two enormous speakers blasting out Salsa and Calypso music. The locals treated it as a party and danced the whole way there. What a sight. We set sail, with frigate birds and pelicans accompanying us on our journey. The sun slowly sank towards the sea and the colour of the sky turned from blue to purple to vivid pink and then burst into flaming orange as the sun vanished through a flimsy curtain of fine twilight haze behind a little hilly island into the black sea of the west. At last, I was seeing the Costa Rica of my dreams.

We found our new driver – grumpy Barnaby and minibus at the port of Paquera and off we sped in the dark. Costa Rica was so civilised, it even had cats eyes in the road although, off the road, it was just lumpy gravel that you wouldn't want to drive over in anything other than a tank. We reached the little town of Cobano where I and the Canadian couple transferred to a "taxi" and bumped down into Montezuma. Their destination proved hard to find so I was dropped at my hostel – Pura Vida ("Good Life") which I had booked three months before in January. I had changed my arrival dates a couple of times which they had always been happy to do for me, but the email I'd sent the day before, saying I'd be a day late, but to hold the room and I'd pay for it, had never arrived. This wasn't their fault. This was Booking.com's fault for not forwarding the email. But regardless of whose fault it was, I was homeless and livid. Not the best way to arrive in paradise.

It was irreconcilable – there was no room at the inn. The very lovely Rossetti like Madonna of a pregnant woman, recommended somewhere very nearby; I left my bag with her and wandered back down the path into town.

"Downtown" hostel was dark, dingy, dirty, dishevelled and dilapidated. It did however have a room with no window to speak of (the one it did have opened onto a tiny corridor), no fresh air, nowhere to put anything, in fact no nothing except a bed. The walls were so grubby I didn't even want to hang my clothes on the hook and it was twice the price of the Pura Vida. How was that possible? In truth, I think that when people see me, all of the bloody time, they for some god unknown reason, presume that I am loaded so just think of a price, double it and then add a bit more. I had no option but to take it so I paid up, collected my bag and bought some wine – well what else was I going to do? And dashed off an email to Booking.com telling them that they'd ruined my holiday etc etc etc and what did they intend to do to make reparations? I was furious.

****

At 7am I was up. The fan I'd kept on all night just for air, was driving me mad. The hostel did have one thing in its favour though – lashings of strong coffee albeit with no milk. Miraculously, Booking.com had already responded to my email. They blamed it on Pura Vide for over booking, trying to exonerate themselves, but offered to refund me any additional expense I should incur. Quite a result. I raced back up to Pura Vide to see if they had the vacancy for a double room they were advertising but I seemed to be in their bad books and even though I explained that Booking.com had more or less accepted blame for the catastrophe, they were still upset by all the fuss. They were upset – what did they think I was??? She recommended somewhere else and we tried to part as friends.

Hotel Lucy, her second recommendation, was along the road facing the ocean. I walked that way and found the first receptionist so far who spoke no English – typical. Nonetheless, she showed me an expensive double room (here we go again I thought) with lots of light and space, but facing the road. With no other option, I took it. There was a

198

possibility of a better room the next day and my fingers were crossed. Back to the other hostel for my bags and not even attempting to walk the lot up the hill, I took a taxi and finally settled in, no matter how briefly, and went out on the veranda to look at the ocean. I was back on the Pacific and it was magnificent.

Just like in Mexico, the waves thundered in, the roar was cacophonous, the beach was clean and it was so close – when the tide was high, it came right up to the wall and the danger was palpable. The air was clean and clear and positively charged and I loved it! I was supposed to go over to the Caribbean coast but I just didn't think that I wanted to anymore. There's only so much soft shoe shuffling I could cope with and I felt that I'd coped with as much as I wanted to. There just seemed to be so much more energy and the ocean, rather than being a gentle lapping plaything, was like a wild animal – unpredictable and exciting. The way I preferred my men.

They say that there are more species of animals and plants in Costa Rica than anywhere else on earth and it seemed that half of the insect population was in my room. One crafty little creature scurried across the floor and when it sensed me, it rolled into a little, almost, imperceptible ball and stood perfectly still, hoping I wouldn't notice it. Insects that can and will bite me, I flatten outright, but that crafty little trickster I simply batted gently out of the room like a cricket ball.

Not having eaten for over a day, I walked into town for lunch. I was told the "sodas" were the local places to look for and I stopped at the first one I found – Soda El Balcon del Mer. The owner, Carlos, recognised me from the night before – apparently he'd said hello to me – I had no recollection – obviously my mind was on other things. Anyway, he sat me down, gave me a menu and a map and I ordered more or less, exactly what I ate everyday in Colombia. The difference though was that there was more of it, it seemed better quality and he let me drown the whole lot in olive oil and balsamic vinegar. It was more than twice the price but this was Costa Rica and that's just the way it was and I really didn't care.

Almost refreshed, I walked into town. Montezuma had a reputation of being full of hippies smoking dope – it sounded like Arambol in India where I'd spent four glorious months a few years ago and that was really why I was there. Not to smoke tons of dope, but because I felt the people would be interesting, like they were in Arambol. But it wasn't like that anymore. I doubt the hippies could afford it these days and they'd probably left for Guatemala or some such poverty stricken backwater where you could still live on nothing.

These days, it seemed to be full of young Americans or Canadians on a "spring break" as they call it, doing very sensible things like studying Spanish or learning to surf and they didn't even smoke cigarettes, let alone spliffs. There were also groups of well-heeled English girls on either a gap year or a trip. They were all nice enough but somehow, they all smacked of superficiality.   I wondered if it was just too much TV and seeing endless wannabees trying to seem interesting. I admired their giddy excitement and enthusiasm but they weren't really my people. But who was? I was beginning to think that ex-boyfriend Sean was right – I should just go and live in Ireland and be with my tribe - generations of writers and poets ...

But nonetheless, I liked it. I loved the ocean, I loved the pace of life i.e. that of snails, it was very beautiful – the forest stopped at the beach and for some reason, everyone was super friendly to me, especially the men. Odd. In Colombia I was invisible but then, as I've mentioned, unless half of your bum was hanging out of a pair of microdot shorts, everyone was invisible.

Later, back at Hotel Lucy, when the tide had gone out, a million tiny things began to move. The whole beach was

200

heaving and as darkness fell, the whole sky was heaving. As I sat there on the verandah, under a bright light, shrouded in blackness, I had to drench myself in super deet insect repellent in the hope that they would fly close, get a whiff and recoil in horror. It seemed to work. So far, on the insect front, so good.

I decided to catch up on my writing so transferred my diary to my laptop. That was the first time I'd written in public and it certainly attracted interest. Some thought my tiny writing was shorthand, others wanted to know what I was writing about. One Canadian man sat down to chat whilst his voluptuous Mexican wife lolled in a hammock. We got talking about politics and he was delighted with the conversation. His wife just swung and sulked. I thought about the way people choose a mate. Men might go for what they think was the easy option of an attractive wife with no opinions but then all they craved was interesting conversation to the chagrin of their mate who probably had opinions aplenty, just not the ones that he agreed with or wanted to hear.

I could sense a frisson between them which seemed to get wider as the tide and the roar of the ocean crept closer. By the time they retreated to their room, the Hotel Lucy looked more like a houseboat adrift in the water than a building on the edge of it, waves swirling up to and around the veranda. Made only of wood held together with nails and topped with corrugated iron, it felt so temporary that you just couldn't imagine it withstanding anything in the way of a storm and yet there, at its very edge, was the mighty Pacific. Maybe with a big Spring tide, the Ocean would huff and it would puff, just like the wolf in the Three Little Pigs, and blow that house down.

****

Traffic began to roll past early and my room had all the sound insulation of a tent. I might as well have been sleeping on the side of the road. Thank god, once again, for free coffee.

I'd even found soya milk and even though it was wildly expensive, I bought some – there's only so much puffiness I could tolerate and quite frankly, I'd had enough of trying to tolerate milk, lactose free or not.

I waited patiently by the reception as people checked out, hoping beyond hope, that I would finally get a room that I wanted. The young girl from yesterday was gone replaced by an older lady, possibly the owner, sitting in her place. She couldn't speak English either so we waited for help to present itself which it did – a Tico guest offered to translate and suddenly I was in business. I told him that (all) I wanted was a room with an ocean view which had wi fi and he translated. Without hesitating, she led me up the stairs and showed me the best room in the house. Perhaps the best room in any house. It had a big double bed, windows across two walls; one window opened out onto the ocean with not even a veranda between us. I could see the sea, I could smell the sea and I could hear the sea. There was no mosquito net – with elements that powerful, flying insects simply didn't stand a chance. She even negotiated a price for me which was less than the room on the road. I couldn't believe it, I was ready to pay what she originally asked but as I had the same name as her mum, her heart softened as did mine, and she reduced the rate even further! I was absolutely dumbfounded – for once, I wasn't being heartlessly ripped off; I was being treated fairly and I could have hugged her.

She helped me up the stairs with my bag and I was so happy that I just thought to myself as I unpacked properly – I wasn't going anywhere else for quite some time. Who cared if there was no electrical socket in my room – there was one on the upstairs veranda and if the wi fi was intermittent in my room, I could be sociable and actually sit on the veranda, which was probably a good thing anyway. For the first time in three days, I could relax and start to enjoy myself and relish what Costa Rica had to offer. I was more than happy. I was totally euphoric.

Lunch was the first stop and it was the same place as the day before and as chance would have it, John and Alice were there with the two friends they were staying with. John seemed keen to see me but the others weren't. I didn't interrupt them, but I did eavesdrop. I don't think, even as a child, I was ever that naïve but in a way, what would the world be like without it? It was almost refreshing to hear the uncynical, uncluttered, unknowing, optimism of youth.

When I'd finished yet another bountiful plate of fresh local produce, I went to pay and chatted again to Carlos and he actually asked me out! He said that he closed at 10pm and if I wanted to drink some beers with him it would be his pleasure and that he'd escort me back up the hill to home. See what I mean? I said not today – I had some serious writing to catch up on, but definitely tomorrow. I said "muchas gracias" he said "mucho gusto" and I said "huesta luego" - thank god he spoke perfect English or that's all we would ever be saying. He wasn't my type but it was only a drink – at least that's all it was to me.

Legend had it that there were waterfalls nearby and that they were magnificent. I set off to find them. Almost at the next bend in the road, I found the path. A young green eyed Tico also named Carlos, pointed the way and said to make sure that I saw all three. I set off in my moccasins – the most sensible shoes I had, and noticed with both shock and horror that they were falling apart. I'd only worn them nearly every day for five years, so how did that happen? Of course I knew it would, but also knew they were good for a few more weeks yet.

I picked my path like an all knowing, fleet of foot Apache (I'm sure I was one in a previous life) and sped past people in far more suitable footwear than mine. The only surprising thing though was the complete lack of courtesy. No one except me gave way and I wondered if that was what the world had come to – kill or be killed. No one gave an inch and considering that all the people there would have had to have

203

been successful to have the money to be there in the first place, I wondered if that was how they got their money – by riding rough shod over everyone else. A very depressing thought – me, I'm on a minimal budget and doubt I've ever ridden over anyone, rough shod or not and nor would I. If I had, I'd probably be able to afford an awful lot more than I could.

But never mind. I passed one mini waterfall, past a second mini waterfall and then finally, approached the third by way of a precarious length of rope secured to the cliff face. Water cascaded down the steep rocks and as promised, there was a big pool of water where I, and many others, could swim. I stripped down to my bikini and cursed myself for not wearing the durable yet totally alluring swimsuit that I also had with me, because there were treacherous high rocks to dive off.

I love to dive and even used to dive for the school aged 10, but in a bikini, usually what happened, was that as soon as you hit the water from any height, you and your bikini parted company and with so many people watching, that was not the spectacle I wanted to leave them with. So instead, I just plunged in and swam to the cliff face, found a slippery perch and just sat there, under the falls and it was like one almighty shower. I looked at my legs in the water and thought the water must be brown with some sort of oxide and then realised that was just the colour of my legs. I'd gotten a tan without even noticing – great.

I didn't linger long – the sun was vanishing behind the cliff and I had no insect repellent, plus I didn't want to pick my way back in the dusk. I bumped into Carlos the guide again and he admonished me for not going to the third waterfall. But I did, I said and even showed him the photo. "That was the first one", he said. At the third one, much higher up, there were ropes that you could swing on like Tarzan and really launch yourself into the pool. He said that if I wanted, the next time I came, like tomorrow morning, he'd be my guide. It reminded me of the waterfalls in Koh Samui,

Thailand when once again, I thought I'd gotten to the top only to be told by a local man that there was much more to see, much higher up and that if I liked, he'd take me. I went with him, half man half goat and wearing just a pair of plastic jelly shoes, I climbed right on up there with him, to the very top and surveyed the whole of the island in all of its glorious splendour. Nothing ventured nothing gained. I hoped to be up there with Carlos sometime soon, moccasins and inclination permitting.

Carlos at the soda bar had told me about Cabaya which was full of Italians which I thought was nearby so I took a detour to have a look. It was much further than I expected and out of my reach that late in the day, but I walked for a mile or so anyway and found an alternative way of living. People had just set up tarpaulins – Ticos and Europeans alike and were just living on the beach as people must have done for generations. I wasn't sure if I'd be welcomed or just seen as an intruder and was reluctant to go further but when they saw me, they beckoned me over. They were probably frowned upon, but they seemed totally happy and content to me. I wondered how many more of these make shift camps existed along the coast where they could fish for food and live a simple easy life, living on what they could forage in a land where mangos, avocados and coconuts literally fell from the trees and belonged to no one. It seemed like utopia; kids playing on the beach, sleeping in the open, eating together in a communal fashion but with America and Coca Cola closing in, I wondered for how much longer the largely empty coastline would be home to anyone, unless, of course, they could afford it. Sad really.

I whiled away the evening out on the veranda sitting at a little table coming up to date with my writing and once I'd finished, it was with some excitement, that I returned to my room to see just what it would be like at night. All of the windows were open, as were the curtains and the ocean was so LOUD and near it was quite frankly, frightening. But at the same time, the power was mesmerising. I just lay there,

205

listening as wave after wave pounded the beach beneath me and then withdrew, dragging the shingle remorselessly screeching like gargantuan metal chains. The force was so fierce that the sail-like curtains were sucked in and blown out like huge bellows. It was so exhilarating and yet hypnotic in its rhythm, I was asleep in minutes.

****

I woke with the dawn as the sun rose out of the water behind a row of perpendicular clouds that looked like steam puffing out of a locomotive. The sea was a placid grey blue and the tide was out. It had left behind it hundreds of little rock pools and grander lagoons where the water, I was told, was as warm as a bath. I was shocked to realise that I hadn't even swam in it yet. I decided to try out the little inlet and tiny beach lying at the side of the hotel. I took my snorkel just in case and waded in. It was so WARM. I had no idea that the Pacific could be that warm anywhere.

As I did whenever I was snorkelling, I just put my face in the water and swam out between the rocks, spotting little fish but not a lot more. I looked up to see where I was and was shocked to see that I was out at sea. How had that happened so quickly? I was right back in Mombasa when I was nearly washed out to sea with no one to help and no air/sea rescue. And just like then, I had no option but to just put my face in the water and front crawl towards shore as hard as I could. Luckily the tide was coming in but there must have been an undertow to take me out in the first place. Maybe we all need to be reminded now and again that we were mortal and not infallible. I had been warned...

For safety's sake, I walked round to the town beach. The first cove was fairly unremarkable with boats moored up after fishing or the daily tours they run to neighbouring beaches or across the peninsula to Jaco. At the end of the cove is where the town started. It was, in fact, tiny, no more than a village but it was full of life. On the edge of the beach was a bar and

206

then I was up onto the "road" which was at most, 200 metres long. There were a couple of yoga studios, a tattooist (of course) tour shops, a mini market, boutiques, an ATM which astonishingly always had money in it, an ice cream parlour, a bakery and a couple of "soda" cafés. Half way along was a left hand turn and a little road that ran up to the "main" road in and out of town. It was almost identical except that it had a bigger super market. The main road had a few restaurants and that, my amigos, was that. You wouldn't think anything would happen there and probably, it didn't, but there did seem to be some interesting people and as we all know, it was the people that made it happen.

I walked to the further beach which was soft yellow sand, edged by the jungle, gently curved with a steep drop to the water. It was the first decent beach I'd been on since Mexico so inevitably, I layed down and soaked up some rays. I was brown enough by then to have more or less cooked the top layer of my skin to a permanent degree so I didn't have to hang around for long – plus it was deadly boring and the waves beckoned. Because the beach was so steep, the waves broke in deeper water and rather than being able to body surf on the top of the wave, they just knocked me over like a ten pin and rushed me to the shore and threw me up, bikini bottoms full of sand and bikini top askew and then as I tried to find a hold, it just dragged me back out and the whole process started again. At one point, it felt like I was in an automatic washing machine on a spin cycle.

There were only three of us in the water and when I abandoned it and returned to the dry, a dark haired, tattooed and pierced Amazonian German girl warned me about the undertow – there was that word again... We got talking. She was a personal fitness trainer without an ounce of fat and her muscles seemed cleaved from teak. Her name was Simone; she came from Hanover and had been visiting Montezuma for years, several times a year. She had friends there and was established. That was the beauty of it – small towns attracted people who just kept going back because it was a

207

community rather than a resort. I asked her if there were any other towns worth going to and she just looked at me. No, she said, that was the best place on the whole peninsula and I was happy to agree with her.

Back at Hotel Lucy, there was a new man on the veranda, talking and whooping to himself with a great big laptop and a great big attitude. He had very blue eyes, a waft of blonde curls beneath a bald head and reminded me of the Leprechaun doll my dad had bought me as a child from Ireland. Naturally we got talking. He was a landscape gardener, working on Mel Gibson's new pad nearby and he showed me his work – unbelievable. His name was Dominic Champagne, he was from Quebec and what he did with wood, stone and water was unique. We made friends on Facebook and he offered me a commission if I could find him any work. I told him I didn't know any super rich people and he laughed out loud, said neither did he, and we shook on it. It was his last day and he invited me out for a farewell dinner. I would love to have gone but of course, I had a date and I am a woman of my word.

And then three other people checked in and they were very remarkable looking indeed. The man was Japanese and the two Italian girls; one blonde, one brunette, were stunning. They didn't look like regular people and when I asked, it turned out I was right. They were circus performers and their forte was flaming torches. I told them that one of my ex boyfriends did the same and was also a fire breather and suddenly we were all the best of friends. It seemed extraordinary that in that tiny hotel and just around the one veranda, there we all were, alternative travellers of the world. I was so happy that Hostel Pura Vida had no room because I just knew that I was in the best place in town – funny how things worked out.

And so, to the date. I didn't want Carlos to be overcome with desire, bend me over backwards in some lurid Tango position and start snogging me and believe me, that has happened.

So I didn't make much of an effort but enough so that he would be happy. He was happy. I thought he owned the place but he didn't, he managed it for a mean money obsessed Italian who made him work like a dog and treated him like one. Carlos said that he used to own all of the surrounding land but he'd sold it (at the wrong time) to build houses for himself and his mother and that now he was forced to work for someone else. He wasn't cross about his present situation; he just accepted it and got on with it which was a truly admirable way to be. He gave me an ice cold beer to drink whilst he closed up the restaurant.

I have a saying – "red on beer, have no fear, beer on red, you're better off dead". Despite knowing this to be fool proof, I'd had a couple of glasses of red back on the veranda with Dominic, as a farewell celebration. I didn't even like beer but as wine was so expensive, it seemed churlish to expect Carlos to splash out. So it was to a night of beer that I abandoned myself. I drank another bottle before we were ready to go at 10.30. I was expecting to go to an elegant bar, if indeed, there was such a place, but that wasn't what Carlos had in mind. Totally unphased, he went into the supermarket, bought more cold beers and a bottle of rum and led me to a wall by the beach as if this what everyone did on a "date". Not what I had in mind, but then most things that happened since I'd been travelling were not what I had in mind. So we just sat down and got drinking and talking.

He told me about his life; growing up in Montezuma, having hardly any education because his dad had died young and he had become the bread winner and how much the place had changed. He said that the first western tourists to come were Italians and once word spread, there were hippies walking naked on the beach and his life changed forever, particularly as he left for Switzerland with one of them. It didn't work out so he returned home, became a professional footballer (with his waist length hair) and lived the high life until he was 30. He then fell in love with and married a 14 year old girl (!), had a child very quickly and to support his new family, went to New York for work. He had a huge adventure, she had an affair and a love child and that was that. He'd been single for years and just in case he had his sights on me, which I think he did, I told him I was practically married. When he asked me about the mystery man, I just described my last boyfriend to keep it real – it was just easier on their ego and I used the excuse all the time.

So there we were, sitting on the wall swapping life stories but as Carlos knew everyone and everyone knew Carlos, any one passing just sat down and joined us. At the end, there was the security guard from the expensive hotel who also ferried more beers and ice for the rum from the hotel kitchen, another man who had simply pulled up in his car (music blaring), a random friend and there we all were, by the beach, dancing and drinking the night away. It was the first time I'd been out late and finally, before I was too plastered and in danger of losing the use of my legs, Carlos walked me back up the hill to Hotel Lucy and I barely remembered going to bed.

****

By morning, I **had** lost the use of my legs - and the rest of my body and woke with something I haven't had for absolutely years – a hangover! There was nothing for it except to just give in and do nothing. When I did manage to rouse myself, I found Dominic out on the veranda trying to pack his bag – and I thought mine was big. He even had a huge set of bongos squashed in. He didn't even attempt to carry his though – he'd ordered a taxi and between them they hefted it in, we hugged and off he went with a whoop and a smile. Lovely. I then noticed another lady tapping away on her lap top and we too got talking. Her name was Aurelia; she was French and translated films into French. She travelled to where ever she liked, working when she liked and her only three commitments were the Cannes, Dubai and Toronto film festivals. What a life and what a woman.

I was then back into town to Costa's for food (he wasn't there – maybe he was in a similar sorry state) and got talking to a girl from England, Lisa, who was a travel writer. She'd been away for nearly a year, worked for an English language journal in Medellin, Colombia, had a web site called Girl About the Globe and she was interesting! She was staying at Pura Vide, paying a fortune and said it was OK if you liked listening to people talk non-stop about surfing. I was so glad I wasn't there. She intended to visit other places nearby and stay a couple of days here and there and seemed intrigued when I said that I intended to visit those places too, but by bus, as day trips. I showed her my hotel to give her a more civilised option. We sat on the veranda and talked about what we missed the most. She said "friends", I said "interesting conversation" and thankfully we were to become and have both.

****

Well what a strange day! I was at the bus terminal i.e. the patch of gravel where the bus turned round at 9.45am. A man asked where I was going – ultimately Santa Teresa and he said he would take me for $5 and it would only take 30 minutes rather than two hours. It seemed like a good deal so five of us got into his clapped out people carrier and off we went. I sat in the front and as often as he could, he put his hand on my knee, told me what a byoodiful woman I was and proceeded to give me something of a guided tour. We seemed to be on a dry river bed full of great big boulders and I just hoped he was also keeping his eye on the road.

Ultimately it was the deer that did us undone – he was so busy patting my knee and pointing them out that we hit a boulder and came to a stop. Nothing to worry about, apparently. He got out, pretended to fiddle with the engine, got in, tried to start it and again, nothing. This went on for five times and all the while, we could hear monkeys howling mean and menacing all around us. I suggested we push start

211

it – there were five of us after all. He poo pooed my suggestion but when two men came by on their quad bikes, he asked them to help push... So there we were, me and three men pushing it back over the boulder whilst the man in our company just stood and smoked. Thanks. So then we pushed it forwards and with a bit of a backfire and a cloud of black smoke, we were back on our way. He patted my knee again and thanked me. Just keep your eye on the road, I felt like saying.

We eventually rolled into Santa Teresa. He pointed out the soda café, the bank and the bakery and dropped us off. I couldn't believe that this was the place with all the boutique hotels and the fancy restaurants where the two yoga girls from the boat were headed. It looked like, and was, a one street town with, well, a bank and a bakery. I sat down at the café and had the usual plate of rice, beans, salad, meat and vegetables and was surprised that it was cheaper than in Montezuma. I then headed through the trees to the beach. It was enormous. Almost as long as Zicatela in Mexico and with almost no one on it. The tide was on the way out but there was still some surf so I found someone to look after my bag (just in case). His name was Chase and he was from Colorado. He said to leave my bag right next to him because there were thieves. His bag was tied to his foot and he also had a knuckle duster! I was all ready to just leave my bag anywhere and take my usual chance.

I still couldn't get over just how remarkably warm the Pacific was. It was as warm as the Indian Ocean and that was just not the way it was supposed to be – I wasn't complaining – it was wonderful, I was just very surprised. I crashed through a few waves and body surfed some more until it was ray soaking time. Chase's friend Spencer was back with the surf board so we got talking. They worked the Colorado ski season in the winter and the white water rafting in the summer and had money to burn. They'd toyed with Mexico but, as I suspected of Americans, they'd thought it was too dangerous so had flown to Costa Rica for next to nothing and were staying with an uncle who'd set up a dental practice so that gringos could fly south, get their teeth fixed for a whole lot less than back home and he too, was making a fortune. They'd been bungee jumping, abseiling and paragliding – if it was an outdoor activity, they'd done it. They said they'd just come from Montezuma and that they were really enjoying Santa Teresa because there was so much more to did. I couldn't see that there was **anything** to do and wondered what they were talking about.

Desperate to find out, I walked over the little concrete bridge out of town and when I saw nothing, I turned back. I had a chocolate ice cream (allergies or no) and then I had coffee back at the soda cafe where I'd started, wondering what on earth to do – give up and catch a bus back or wait for the clapped out people carrier to turn up (or not) in two hours. Suddenly, a big good-looking black man breezed in, caught my eye and came over to talk. His name was Eddy; he was half Jamaican, half Colombian and had lived in Costa Rica since he was a child. He told me that he had a guest house in Santa Teresa and if I was looking for somewhere to stay, he would give me a very good price and if I had the time, we could take the bus and he'd show me. "What do you mean, take the bus, this is Santa Teresa." I said. "No", he said, "this is Playa Carmen" - the town was two kilometres further along – oh, so that's why it looked so dull.

He paid for my coffee, bundled me up and yanked me onto the bus and whether I wanted to or not, I was going to Casa Eddy. Santa Teresa was the last stop for the bus and it just turned around and headed back after a half hour rest anyway, so we did have time and Eddy wasn't going to miss the chance to show me around. He said that no one was allowed to build between the beach and the road anymore, so all the hotels etc. grew up the hill through the jungle of trees.

His, thankfully, was right on the road and it seemed jolly nice. I didn't really have any intention of moving from my stupendous room at Hotel Lucy but suddenly I thought, I

213

don't know, all that time in one place when the whole of Costa Rica was waiting for me to see. The room was big and white and blue and beautiful. It had its own kitchen and bathroom and Eddy promised me full use of his bicycle, his surf boards (I suppose I could learn) and as he twirled me around, he promised to teach me to dance salsa, merengue and another one I couldn't even pronounce. He also told me that he loved blondes with green eyes (mine are blue...) and that at the age of 14 he'd fathered a child with a much older German woman. I used the same fib about having a boyfriend but I didn't know if he chose to hear me. Unfazed, he whizzed me across the road and down the path to the beach and it was big and it was blissful and not quite as deserted as Playa Carmen. He said there were parties on the beach and of course, he knew everyone. He spent the whole time high fiving people, calling to them or them calling to him and I just thought that it could be another whole adventure!

And as easily as that, my mind was changed. I said I'd see him on Monday and he just beamed at me and said that as soon as he'd seen me sitting in the café, looking so byoodiful (there's that word again) he just knew that we would have a connection and it seemed that we did. He even paid my bus fare back to the main town. And then even more serendipitously, when I got back to Hotel Lucy, Lisa "Girl About the Globe" had checked into the room next to mine.

So there we sat, on the verandah, drinking wine together and had a proper conversation about life, men and the universe long into the evening. And just to make it even more enjoyable, she came from the south east of England so we had more in common than we could ever have imagined. It was just so great to be able to discuss everything as if we were life-long friends. That was one of the joys of travelling. When and if you do meet someone, the moment has to be seized and you can perhaps confide in a stranger more than you would ever do, even to your best friend.

When I was finally back in the boom of my room I was so

excited by the day. I'd almost begun to think that doing absolutely nothing wasn't so bad without realising what a waste of time it was. I was back on the adventure trail and just lay there thinking; if I hadn't decided to even go to Santa Teresa, if I hadn't gone in that particular vehicle, if it hadn't conked out and I hadn't been dropped off directly opposite the soda café, I would never have met Eddy and hence be contemplating a new destination. Funny how things turned out – I wondered how this one would? But one thing was for sure – nothing ventured, nothing gained!

****

It was my mum's birthday so we skyped – what a great invention. I'm not sure my mum understands it, but we can talk and that's the main thing. Talking to home puts being away into perspective. My sister-in-law Jackie asked what was a typical day. My answer - there was no typical day and often, it was more about relaxing and doing what you wanted with no stress and no anxiety. That was the beauty of it. No wonder Ticos lived well into their 100's; good food from good soil, good weather, an ocean and rivers full of food and not a care in the world. That was a typical day.

Aurelia checked out which left just Lisa and I - in fact we were the only guests there. She hadn't been to the waterfalls so, me leading the way, we trekked once again over the boulders and through the jungle but this time, I had someone to talk to. She too was leaving the next day for Nicaragua and not wishing to waste time, we talked non-stop, almost oblivious of the terrain over which we climbed. When you are at home, you take conversation for granted. When you are away, you cherish every second of it. In retrospect, I spent almost the whole five weeks in Colombia without a truly decent conversation (apart from Todd in Getsemani). Yes, I had interesting ones but the ones that you really wanted were the ones where your visuals were familiar and you didn't have to keep elaborating on and explaining everything.

When we reached the waterfall, it was empty and without hesitation, I did what I didn't get to do before – I launched myself off the perilous rocks. I hit the water with such force, I was lucky to find my bikini bottoms at all. Invigorating in the extreme. We picked our way back across the boulders and then carried on into town. I even treated us to beers – not in a bar of course, and we sat on the wall like locals, drinking from cans and talked some more. We even carried on our conversation back at the hotel whilst we both sat there, on the veranda with our laptops open, writing our missives. It was almost as if we didn't want to waste time writing when we could be talking and yet there we were, unable to stop ourselves tapping out our messages like birds on a wire. Does communication ever stop?

****

After a huge hug, Lisa left with a heavy bag and a heavy heart. She hadn't been home for months and didn't plan to return for quite some time and even then, only if she had to. Part of me wondered why she kept pushing herself. It can be so unbearably lonely when you travel solo and sometimes, it was the knowing that you **were** going home that sustained you. She planned to work on her book and website and grow her online presence in the hope of being invited to write travel reviews until she could return to her beloved Medellin on a new visa and finally unpack her bag once more and reunite with friends. I admired her enormously for her stamina and the way that she was following her dream, no matter how hard and possibly lonely that was. I'm a Celt and it's in my DNA to travel but as we all know, it was the journey home that was often the most exciting and emotional.

After Lisa had gone, I just walked into town to find the market which was supposed to bring everyone together and people were supposed to arrive laden with home grown organic fare, jewellery, handicrafts and whatever people can think of making, in order to sustain themselves in paradise. A man called Forest, who I'd met with Dominic on the balcony of Hotel Lucy a couple of nights before, had told me about it. He said that his mum had started the organic movement in Costa Rica 35 years ago and was still a pioneering force and that I should introduce myself to her as he was sure we'd get along. I wondered if I'd got the wrong day. Did four stalls make a market? That was all there was, selling next to nothing and not a crowd in sight. I asked one of them where everyone was and he just shrugged his shoulders. "This is Montezuma", he said.

So instead of talking organics, I went for lunch. Carlos' place was the best in town and it was to there that I went. He was so pleased to see me that he hugged me like a bear, gave me a beer and said that he'd told his mum all about me. In a casual way, he said, that if I wanted to live in Costa Rica, he could marry me (at no charge, of course) and then we would have to live together in his house for a year and then I would get my residency and then, IF I wanted, we could get a divorce. He was so sweet and lovely. I wondered if he was genuine or had offered to do it for a million girls before. But in any case, I didn't have the heart to tell him that I was leaving on Monday for Casa Eddy. Instead, I agreed to go out for yet more drinks that night and to spend his first day off, in five months, with him the following day. I just hoped that he remembered that I had an imaginary boyfriend at home.

He didn't, unless constantly trying to snog someone else's girlfriend was normal in that part of the world. I had to remind him and once he realised his marriage proposal was futile, we went halves on the beer and rum and had a night, back on the wall, of very interesting conversation and an awful lot to drink.

He said that in Costa Rica, despite free contraception, most girls had children when they were young with numerous fathers who didn't support them. Sound familiar? BUT they received no support from the government either, so all I could surmise was that, contrary to popular belief, girls didn't get pregnant to get a house and a life on benefits, they got

217

pregnant because they wanted to be mothers and have children. It was the most natural thing in the world so why in Britain (and elsewhere) were they all vilified as scroungers and irresponsible? Every animal on the planet does it and we are, after all, only animals with supposedly bigger brains.

We also talked politics, education and everything else that I was dying to investigate. I'm not sure Carlos enjoyed it as much as I did, but he was polite enough to pretend. Finally, after a long time – I had no idea how long, we lay on the beach (never mind that I was decked out in silk) and looked at the stars. It was pitch black and there they all were, millions of them in no formation that was familiar to me and sitting aloft, was an upside down quarter of a moon hanging, once again, like a hammock in the sky. Perfect really.

****

I awoke with no head ache but what I did have was total confusion as to who I was, where I was and when I was. A good night then... I sat there on the veranda outside my room and savoured perhaps my last day in Montezuma and my last day of that outstanding, magnificent view, vista and soundscape. The Pacific Ocean was so loud it would compete with a grand prix circuit in decibels and yet it didn't pierce the ears or numb the senses. It just ceaselessly thundered in and then, when it was ready, it thundered out with the regulation of time itself. Everything yielded to it and occasionally, birds flew past on the thermal with such synchronicity, human beings couldn't emulate it if they practised all their lives. The first bird dipped down to the waves and all the other birds followed like a magical airborne dance and then they banked and swooped back up.

There was a lone fisherman out on the rock catching his supper and just a bit further out, there was a fishing boat bobbing patiently and in no hurry. Much further out, nearer the horizon, there was a giant cruise ship – where had it been and where was it going? They sailed past, maybe docked for

218

a day and said that they'd been to Costa Rica but that wasn't the Costa Rice I was discovering. Living the Pura Vide meant no stress, no worry or hurry, eating good food from rich soil and having the time to give to other people and to nature.

In Costa Rica, they didn't use chemical fertilisers, they didn't have to. They didn't have an army, they didn't need one. Education and health care were free and the people lived longer than almost anywhere else on the planet. And as I sat there contemplating whether or not it was a paradise in which I could live, I remember the boiling heat and the 90% humidity – maybe not...

Carlos called by – he'd left his wallet at home in Cobano – ten miles away up a dirt track and had been too embarrassed to call earlier since he couldn't afford to take me out. I said that I would have paid; after all he'd treated me to, it would have been fair, but he just shook his head and told me that wasn't how he did things. I was relieved that, in my state, I hadn't had to go anywhere. I admitted that I was leaving and in truth, I think he was relieved. Until men are distanced from their libido through age or whatever, if there is nothing on offer in that department they soon lose interest. He didn't want me as a friend (I presume) he wanted me as a lover. So we had a farewell chat and a big hug and promised not to forget one another.

And then, for the last time, I sat looking out over the Pacific from the fan cooled luxury of my room. The following day, I would leave for Santa Teresa and Casa Eddy and maybe, just maybe, some fun and another adventure...

SANTA TERESA

I woke with my last sunrise and headed for the kitchen and coffee. I bumped into the German couple who had arrived the day before. Imagine; they were riding a tandem from Alaska to Tierra del Fuego – the tip of South America!!!!!!! I registered my amazement at the idea of it and he just shrugged and said "I am professional sportsman". Oh, so that was normal then was it? I looked into doing that trip a few years ago by motorbike, but by tandem – that sounded like pure lunacy. I wished them well and endeavoured to ring Eddy of Casa Eddy. I couldn't make any sense of it and finally asked the lady in the souvenir shop for help. She just pointed to her phone and moments later, I was talking to him. He seemed surprised but pleased to hear from me and we agreed to meet that afternoon. I was almost sad to be packing away all my things again and leaving my beautiful room, but it just felt right to be moving on and I needed a change.

I walked into town to book my shuttle – not the clapped out people carrier of last week, but a proper one. Bang on time, he arrived and off we all went along not so treacherous a road across the peninsula. If it wasn't for the palm trees, Nicoya looked very much like England – lots of grass, trees and COWS. They were all lying down without a cloud in sight so that old adage that sitting cows were a sign of rain, was most certainly not true. The driver told me that all the surrounding land belonged to just two families and it was hard to imagine how they'd acquired it all. Did they buy it or was it given to them as a favour or was it just purloined long ago when no one owned anything and all you had to do was fence it off? He also told me that hi-tech firms were moving in, lured by

221

the no tax policy of the Costa Rican government – the times were certainly changing. I wondered how much longer Ticos would live to be over a hundred when the strife of modern living began to hit.

We pulled up outside Casa Eddy and he gave me a big hug. My room wasn't quite ready so he showed me around. He'd bought the land as a plot and seemingly, like everyone else, he built when he could afford to. Through the main gates on the right was his "office" and above that, two rooms (one of which was mine) with their own staircases. Further on to the left and right were more rooms, some self contained and housing long-stay families and some just for tourists. All were made of wood and all were different and individually designed and decorated. There was a laundry room with an old twin tub, a big old barbeque area, an open space in the middle and trees everywhere.

Whilst we waited for my room to have its face lifted, he led me into a small, stuffy attic space with just a single bed. I wondered why he'd taken me there until he sat me down on the bed and started to give me a back rub which turned into a full massage. Odd. When I objected, he told me not to be shy and that I had a byoodiful body. I told him that I wasn't shy, I just didn't want to show it to him and felt uncomfortable with him sitting astride me trying to undo everything that I had on especially as all I did have on at that point was my bikini. I bet he didn't do that for all of his guests.

It made me think of all those older ladies who headed off to The Gambia or cheap Caribbean islands on package deals in search of love but all they found were young studs who told them they loved them, took their money and convinced them that their love was for real. I felt quite sorry for those women; so lonely for love and desperate to be touched that they would believe anything. I was suddenly aghast that Eddy might see me as one of those women rather than the "attractive older woman" I'd hoped I was. OK, I was on my

222

own but not because I had no choice, but because I never settled for anything but the best (for me), no matter how long that might take... Not that Eddy knew that though – I mentioned my imaginary boyfriend again and hoped it would keep him at bay for at least a while. I wasn't quite sure how it would end but I was hoping that I wouldn't be leaving in a huff and a hurry with nowhere else to go.

After an hour or so my room was ready. Eddy picked my bag up, threw it over his mighty shoulder and led me up the stairs. I'd forgotten how beautiful it was. (It was room number 69 – there was no 67, 68 or 70 or indeed any rooms with any numbers at all – slightly ominous. I wondered if, in reality, it was Eddy's room.)

The walls were white washed rough stone with a blue skirting board exactly the same shade as one I had at home – was it just familiarity that makes us instantly like something (or someone)? It had a huge wooden bed hand-made by Eddy from old tree trunks and topped with a mosquito net which I hoped I wouldn't need. On the left hand side was a sink and drainer, a fridge and a little Calor gas cooker sitting above its cylinder. Beyond, was another door leading to my very own bathroom.

To the right of the bed, there was a door that opened onto the roof below and then a full wall of blue louvre windows which opened onto the garden and what seemed like a million trees and a big blue sky. A desk and chairs sat beneath the window and some ramshackle door-less cupboards lined the remaining wall. The sun was streaming in the window, it was bright and it was airy and it was mine all mine and I loved it. I was slightly worried about mosquitoes dive bombing me in the night without an ocean breeze to keep them away, but I'd coped in Mexico and I would cope there.

Unlike Montezuma, the water there was not for drinking – something about too much calcium, so I walked to the supermarket. It was like the Tardis, seemingly tiny on the outside but labyrinthine on the inside full of everything you could possibly need including buckets of ice cream, engine oil, cake mix, booze, pasta of every description, jars of olives and pickles to suit every taste and great big containers of water. I hefted one onto my shoulder and walked it home. Suddenly, I was ravaged by thirst – was it just the idea that I might run out that made me desperate for it, or was it the INTENSE heat, humidity and lack of an ocean and its breeze on the doorstep?

I decided to try out my "kitchen" and loaded up my little coffee pot. It turned out that the gas ring didn't work, so it was down to Eddy for him to make me one. He said he'd like it if I **always** used his cooker -that way we could spend more time together. He also mentioned a few day trips he'd like to take me on and how much he would love to cook for me – quite sweet really. It made me wonder who was lonelier – Eddy or me. And then for the shower. I lathered up and suddenly the water just stopped. Did anything work? I had to go back down the stairs and rinse off out in the open under a make shift shower by Eddy's make shift kitchen. It was all turning into a shambles but you know what, I really didn't care. The place just had a good relaxed feel to it – so what if nothing worked?

I found a "soda" cafe and once again, ate like a king for next to nothing and almost too full to move, headed for the beach to watch my first sunset since the ferry. It was of course spectacular. Give me a sunset over a sunrise any day – it was almost like a reward. The beach was peppered with people of all descriptions and ages but mostly, they were young surfer dudes living the Pura Vida. I could never understand how they afforded it but maybe in real life they were all entrepreneurs inventing apps like one for finding your surf board once it's clonked you on the head and knocked you senseless.

Every nationality was there, from Europe to South, Central and North America and even Australians. Some had made a

224

home for themselves and some were just visiting and apart from the quad bikes and motorbikes tearing up the road and the dust, there was a tranquillity, as there was all over Costa Rica, that just made me want to kick off my shoes and stay for awhile – Eddy permitting of course. He wanted me to join him downstairs in his lair but I just wanted to settle in to my super new room and find a place for everything, so I told him not to boss me about and he took the hint. He did however reassure me that if I needed anything or got scared in the night, he was just down the stairs any time I needed him. He really was a very lovely man.

When it was time for sleep, I didn't know which doors to close and which I could leave open. It's a terrible thing to say but there were Nicaraguans nearby and all that anyone said, was that you couldn't trust them. I didn't know if you could or you couldn't but it was a little worrying. In the end, I left the door next to my bed open – it only led out onto a corrugated iron roof anyway and locked the one into the room and even though I felt relatively secure, I slept really badly and dreamt the Mafia were coming to get me – luckily one of them was Robert de Niro, so I knew it was only a dream. Weird all the same.

✳✳✳✳✳✳✳✳✳✳✳✳✳✳

Eddy had suggested I go to the port town of Punteranas with him, which was where I'd taken the ferry from, whenever it was (I had totally lost track of time) but the idea of catching the bus at 6am decided that one for me. There was no ocean to wake to, but what there was, was a dawn chorus of hundreds of birds and, rather oddly, a Mad Max style truck; all bashed up, broken lights and all, which appeared to have parked over night under the awning of trees, only to start up and thunder out at day break. Some things just didn't make sense. I sat on the steps, surrounded and serenaded by nature. It wasn't the might of the ocean but it was just as wonderful and if anything, a whole lot calmer. Strange, the ease with which your perspective changes.

225

The beach at Montezuma involved a walk into town and out the other side. In Santa Teresa, I only had to cross the road, walk the path through the trees and there it was. I wasn't sure if I'd ever seen such a long beach. It was practically deserted save for a few early morning dog walkers and the inevitable serious surfers who started at dawn and finished at dusk. I decided to walk to an abutment of rocks which I presumed was the end. It wasn't – before me lay another totally deserted beach and beyond that another and another and another.   Apparently, it just goes on for miles and miles and miles. There were a few tiny birds playing near the rocks and as nature intended, just like the deer camouflaged to blend in with the boulders, those little birds were exactly the same colour as the rocks. So clever.

The surf, although not huge, rolled in all day and it was as pretty a sight as I had ever seen. It wasn't noisy and threatening, it was playful and inviting. Needing no more than that, I left my bag with a French woman and plunged in. It was so much fun to just body surf the waves to shore and then just swim out and do it all over again. Some slapped into you with more force than you expected and others were whimsical and just gathered you up and carried you forth. When I'd finally had enough, the French woman was gone but luckily my bag wasn't. I couldn't bear being security conscious and I wondered if I really needed to be, despite the warning from the Colorado boys.

I thought I'd walked back to where I'd started and headed off to the road only to find myself still way out of town. I remembered Eddy saying that a new law forbade building between the beach and the road, but I passed at least a dozen up-market seriously expensive developments which, when I Googled them, turned out to be as expensive as they looked – upwards of £100 per night per person. So it seemed that once again, if you had the money, you could have anything you wanted...

226

Another advantage of emerging so far out of town was that I discovered yet another Tardis type supermarket and a wonderful Soda restaurant. Built entirely from wood, it had an upstairs floor where big fans whirred but which, for some reason, was deserted. Unperturbed, I walked up the stairs and sat down alone. Downstairs, it was filled with Ticos there for an early lunch. Like Colombians, lunch was the main meal of the day. Yet again, I had a Casado and yet again, I was amazed at the quality and the quantity. I worried I was eating TOO much but justified it by all my walking and swimming and the fact that I ate only one big meal a day. It seemed to work – if anything I was getting slimmer and with all the exercise, I felt as fit as a feline.

Back at Casa Eddy, with the place to myself, I did a mound of washing. It was cheap to have your clothes laundered but I was always suspicious as to whether they really washed it or just rinsed it in some fragrant fabric conditioner. It made me laugh to hang all my bright and colourful clothes on Eddy's line alongside his monotone stuff. I thought of going for a bicycle ride on the pink bike he'd pointed out to me only to find it had a flat tyre. I thought of borrowing his but (with all those Nicaraguans) I was afraid of getting it stolen. I really hated the way nationalities were demonised but I presumed it went on everywhere and everyone did it – sad really.

And so to the sunset. I wandered back to the beach and that day, it was packed. People on bicycles with and without dogs, people juggling (see, I knew I should had brought my clubs), people just being people and one girl, sitting on a log, singing her heart out and playing a ukulele. I thought I'd have to sneak a photo of her but she just waved me over and carried on, as if it was the most normal thing in the world. I wasn't sure if she could sing or play – I had my doubts, but who cared, she was enjoying herself and so was I. The sun began to set but disappeared behind clouds. I thought the show was over and turned to go but then it reappeared like a ball of red fire reflected in the water and then slowly without fan fare, the huge majestic ball just vanished into the sea as if it was the most ordinary thing in the world. Which, of course, it was.

＊＊＊＊＊＊＊＊＊＊＊＊＊＊＊

I thought that as a joke, someone had either turned on a really noisy fan or even an electric vacuum cleaner next to my bed. What was that noise? RAIN! It clattered on the corrugated roof outside my window, it pounded on the roof above my bed and it beat down like a waterfall that you could barely see through. This was the rain that everyone had been waiting for. The rain that would wash away the dust piled up onto everything, hose down the grass, the plants and the forests, fill the rivers, the drinking puddles and pools for all the animals and lift the weight of humidity from all of our beings. The air was suddenly crisp and fresh and for once, I didn't need two fans running at once just to be able to breathe. Wonderful! Who could imagine that I would ever celebrate rain? And the birds were crazy. You should had seen them; darting, swooping, playing, bathing, chattering – they were as excited as everyone around them. It was a celebration as important as Christmas.

Eddy was already outside, lying in his hammock, just watching it. He was relieved and happy – I'm not sure I would feel the same if I was a home owner where nothing seems as if it was built to last, but he'd owned one for a long time, so it couldn't be that threatening. We sat in the dry and drank coffee. He'd already been out to buy us almond cakes, which was so thoughtful but even so, I had to decline (allergies – such a bore) and we got talking again. I was so used to practically always having breakfast on my own, (even when I am with someone – it's just my way), that I'd forgotten what it was to have company – it was interesting. Well, at least it was with Eddy but then he had a head start in that his stories had no precedent for me and he, in himself, was a remarkable man.

First he showed me his family photos. His Jamaican father

228

looked like a handsome 60's crooner – slicked back hair and an easy smile. His mother was a sassy looking lady who told him as a child that if he shouted, no one would listen, but if he spoke quietly they would have to listen just to hear him – wisdom indeed. And then there was one of his daughter. I asked if he saw her. He said not as often as he would like but it seemed that all along the line, the story was the same; that men in those parts didn't make good fathers for whatever reason which was odd because Eddy seemed to have so much love to give.

He told me that I should go over to the Caribbean coast of Costa Rica because it was full of black men who loved blonde women. I told him I was happy where I was. I really enjoyed his company. I liked his easy laugh and his big smile. I liked the big scar that ran down the side of his face which he insisted was the result of a surfing accident – I had my doubts, and I just liked the way that he cared and that he had ambition. He used to own a fishing boat but could see where the future lay and that it was there in Santa Teresa. He bought his land 17 years ago and began to build. He wanted to add a pool, a gym (he used to be a boxer) and a bar. We talked for so long, that when we'd finished, the rain had stopped and it was time for him to go to the main town, Cobano, to do business. He invited me to have dinner with him that night and that he'd cook. I happily accepted.

He leant me a pair of enormous flip flops to save ruining my already ruined moccasins and I tramped through massive puddles back up the stairs to my room. I realized it was a bit ridiculous, but even having his shoes in my room gave me a sense of security. But even more than that, it gave me the sense of togetherness which I'd missed from nearly three months on my own. Loneliness was hard to cope with when travelling solo and when given the chance, I embraced company more than at any other time. When you are at home, a friend is just a phone call away; there, a friend was like a Faberge Egg – to be coveted and adored.

229

Despite or because of the rain, the air once again grew heavy. Clouds regrouped and the only sense of the sun was a shrouded heat moving across the sky. It was as much as I could do to walk to the restaurant and the shops. Sweat just poured off me and it was as if when I drank water, it didn't pass through my body, it simply washed straight out through my pores like some sort of cartoon colander – think of the Tin Man full of holes and that was what it was like. I gave in to it and slept and read.

When Eddy returned, buckling under the weight of food to cook (yes honestly) I said how strange it was that the rain had seemed to make things worse. "That wasn't the rain". He gestured to the blackening sky "this will be the rain", he said. It was only 5.30pm, half an hour before sunset and already, the night, or what resembled it, had come. I poured myself some wine, felt a chill of fearful expectation and sat and watched as Eddy cleaved away at chicken and vegetables, some I'd never seen before, with something akin to a mini machete.

And then BOOM! An almighty crash of thunder was instantly followed by a flash, and cracks of lightening so bright it was like floodlights being turned on directly overhead. It was as if the sky gods were at war hurling fire bombs at one another. Rain emptied down like a waterfall from the heavens. Rivulets flowed fast and everywhere. The pebbled ground at the edge of the tiled patio was soon a lake and huge palm tree leaves, sodden and heavy with rain lashed around like a giant, ghoulish, skeletal, Tyrannosaurus Rex threatening to bite our heads off. I'm not one to be scared of anything, but when it comes to the unpredictability of nature, nothing was either safe or sacred. At one point, I mentioned that I needed to go up to my room for more wine and he told me just how many people he knew who had been killed by lightening. I could just imagine the gossip - "It was the drink what killed her." I decided to at least wait until the cataract on the stairs had subsided but when it didn't, I risked it anyway...

It rained, thundered and lightninged all night. Eddy cooked to the sound of it, we ate to the sound of it and we talked to the sound and sight of it, the light from above constantly silhouetting everything around us like flash bulbs popping. Ultimately, I got used to it – Eddy didn't have to, he lived with it every year. And when our evening was over; my belly filled with chicken stew seasoned with his very own secret mix of spice and herbs and my mind filled with forthcoming adventures – like the bull riding festival at the weekend, I paddled through the lake, sloshed up the stairs and for the first night in months, I didn't need a fan to keep me cool. The mosquito net around my bed billowed like sails in the frantic breeze, and to the clatter of rain, I fell to sleep like an exhausted, satiated, child.

****

The sky was still overcast and the sun as dull as the bottom of an unwashed milk bottle. Eddy left for town early but not before he gave me the information I needed about his bike – the combination of the lock, which gears not to use lest the chain fell off and which break not to be too heavy on. My mission was to cycle the 15 kilometres to Mal Pais and back before the mid day heat set in.

I left early with hardly anyone around, steering his mountain bike around the pot holes and through the gravel. I was reminded of the ludicrous motorbike ride up the mountain to Minca and how I could envisage my skin turning into coleslaw if I fell off. It was similar. The road was like a road when it's had its surface removed for resurfacing except there was never a surface to remove and there would never be a new surface to be laid. That was it. Just bare gravel and rocks, glistening after the rain and even more slippery than usual.

I cycled through Santa Teresa, south past Playa Carmen and then forked right along the coast. My guide book described Mal Pais as a paradise for nature lovers. Eddy elaborated by

231

saying there was nothing there – "it was just for taking pictures". There were seriously expensive villas along the way with serious security gates and lavish hotels and spas all looking fairly empty. The month of May was out of season and it had the feel of any seaside town at the end of the summer when all of the people had gone, but they'd left a couple of lights on just in case.

Nature was ever present and huge trees with orange flowers, like enormous orchids lined the road. Sadly, the indigenous iridescent blue shelled yellow legged crabs lay squashed in their thousands. They used to leave the beach in their millions to breed in the woods but since the road had pushed through, the numbers were falling fast. So few survived the crossing and even fewer made it back, that there was a danger they would become extinct. It was such a terrible shame, but the same story in so many parts of the world, where man takes precedence.

It felt slightly eerie with monkeys screaming in the jungle and no one else around save for the odd SUV and motorbike. Warm rain kept me and my orange sarong moist and the breeze kept me cool until finally, I freewheeled down a little hill and into the mostly deserted fishing village of Mal Pais. It had a church, a cemetery, a school and a shop and a little further along, a fishery with weighing scales and fridges, and boats moored on the shore. No one was around save for two fishermen repairing their nets.

There were perilous rocks everywhere, a vicious ocean and steep cliffs all of which would never offer shelter to anyone from anything. It was the place where the mile upon mile of beach ran out. It felt remote and barren and to be honest, I couldn't see why anyone would ever want to live there. I looked back along the coast – the wind and rain had picked up, the sky and sea merged into a murky grey and the palm trees sagged as if being pulled down by a heavy weight. I shivered with foreboding.

I wandered around, pushing the bike over fallen palm leaves and found a derelict hotel right on the isthmus. It must once have been a thing of awe, way out there on the rocks with a mighty, menacing cliff behind it and all the rooms facing out to sea. Now it just stood there with all of its windows broken, its blue and white awning hanging like a dislocated arm from its socket and its once sun coloured walls covered in graffiti. I wanted to find out about it, but at that moment, during a lifeguard training session (couldn't they have picked somewhere less deadly) one of the students had been caught on the rocks. I initially thought it was role play, but as they carried him ashore on a surf board, the instructors were charging bare foot across the razor rocks for the first aid kit and I just knew it was serious.

I didn't stay to find out just how serious, I just cycled away with the feeling that I'd left a somehow cursed land behind me. When I looked up the meaning in my dictionary, it meant "bad country or land". I could believe it and wondered how it has/had ever become popular. Was it just that the land was cheaper? I asked Eddy about the deserted hotel – he said a "gringo" had bought the land even though it should never had been for sale, built it without permission and was forced to abandon it. Such a shame but maybe it was just Mal Pais claiming its own.

Back in Playa Carman, I took the time to look around. It was where I had originally turned up the week before under the impression that I was in Santa Teresa. Suddenly, it all became clear. This new addition, with its bars called "Frank's Place" and the like, was the American end of town. The accent was everywhere and there was a wholesome cleanliness and feeling of order and safety which there wasn't in Santa Teresa. The supermarket wasn't full of pasta and salami and, instead of quality chocolate in the fridge, there were Hershey bars which, in case you don't know, bear little resemblance to real chocolate.

Just to prove this hypothesis, I rechecked the supermarket in

Santa Teresa proper and sure enough, it was like an Italian delicatessen. And not only that, in the soda cafe's, they had olive oil and balsamic on the tables. Whilst "casado" was a totally filling meal, it was utterly bland without seasoning or dressing, and Italians need good dressing – both on their food and on their bodies. I was delighted to be staying in the Italian end of town, not only for the food but also because the people were a lot better looking than they were in Playa Carmen. There were only so many baseball caps I could stand and even fewer (or none) when they were turned back to front.

I think Eddy had been in a bit of a sulk since I spurned his advances (claiming the imaginary boyfriend amendment) but I was there to have fun and he had promised to take me to the "disco" for reggae night, so I reminded him of his obligation, got as dressed up as was possible in the heat and off we went. He, as a local, didn't have to pay an entry fee and me, as his guest (or imaginary girlfriend) I didn't have to pay either. It was a bit of a shambles but it had a dance floor, it had music and we did indeed dance. I think he was surprised that not only was I familiar with the music but was also familiar with the moves. I explained that I'd been dancing to reggae since I was 11 and there wasn't much that I didn't know about it. He was impressed and even though I preferred to dance on my own, he insisted that we dance together. I don't know, but when you're slippery with sweat, it sort of takes the fun out of it. But nonetheless, we were a good team even if the dancing was, at times, a little too close for comfort and decency – when in Rome and all that... The following Saturday it would be Latin American music night and as previously mentioned, he intended to teach me many, many, many, more moves – hopefully strictly limited to the dance floor.

****

The rain eased but it had left something in its wake I hadn't imagined – the birth of a million flying insects. They were

234

everywhere and it was deeply unpleasant. Think of flying ants, multiply them in size by 10 and that's what I had. The whole of the insect world seemed to have come out to play and many of them were in my room. And I thought Palomino in Colombia might be a bad bet. I doubt if they all carried a deadly disease, but I bet some of them did. I was at the stage where anything that touched me – a strand of cotton or hair, a grain of sand, an ant, my mosquito net and I was leaping in alarm and batting it away.

In one corner of the room I could see a commotion going on and it was a swarm of tiny ants carrying a great big orange ant off for dinner. They were ferocious and they were hungry and even when I whacked them with a book, they just laughed. They were impervious and not only that, some were invisible giving me no chance at all – UNBELIEVABLE.

In an effort to put some distance between me and them, I again hit the road on Eddy's bike. The plan was to cycle north to Manzanillo. Eddy said there were a few hills and it was about the same distance as Mal Pais. I looked on the rubbish map I had and it looked even nearer – no problem. I set off early again and with no rain, I just wore my bikini, moccasins, sunglasses and a smile.

It wasn't as easy as he'd said and at some points, I was clearly out of control, screaming down hills through gravel, afraid to apply his dodgy brakes in case they tipped me off. At some points, I had to stand up on the pedals because it was so bumpy and I just had to take my chances and hope that level ground was just around the bend rather than something perilous. Half the time, I was bumping over stones like a cartoon character, my smile a silent scream praying that there wouldn't be a car coming the other way as I tried to negotiate pot holes and boulders. I'd pass people cycling up the hill and they were all completely kitted out, Lycra, goggles, helmets and a look of incredulity as I tore past them. Part of me was totally exhilarated whilst the other part just shouted "for christ's sake, slow down!!!!!"

Somehow, without injury, I clattered into the town you would miss if you blinked; Hermosa. With enormous relief, I stopped and rethought my plan. There were some workmen nearby looking wide eyed at me. I asked, in my rubbish Spanish, how far it was to Manzanillo? Four more kilometres they said. There were some serious hills behind me that I would have to climb on the way back and I wondered if it was worth the danger and the effort of going further. It took about a second to decide that it wasn't. I saw a sign that pointed to the beach and so headed that way.

Apparently, Hermosa was an international hamlet with an international school, megga rich villas, a bakery, a tapas restaurant, surf schools and not much else. I still couldn't quite understand how it all worked. In October and November, it rained all day every day and everything was closed and deserted. So what happened then? I simply couldn't imagine living through that – the humidity of May was unbearable and it would only get worse. The only thing to do there was surf but surely that wasn't the only reason to be there. Maybe it was just a case of one man's paradise was another man's poison.

The beach was, of course, spectacular. They were all spectacular. White powder sand, endless waves and as usual, practically deserted. There were several SUVs, a few motorbikes with specially adapted racks to carry surf boards and me and my bike. At Santa Teresa, the surfers look fairly amateurish, but in Hermosa, they looked serious. Even a little kid with a tiny board looked serious. They were all greased up with total sun block but even so, some of them looked as if their skin was something you would wash the car with. Somehow, I knew I could trust them and without even locking the bike, I just dumped it in the sand and went for a swim. It was perfect. The beach had the usual rip current warning but I wasn't going too far out. Just enough to be knocked over and carried ashore, time and time again.

I lay out in the sun for just long enough to vaguely dry off and got back on the bike for the journey home. I asked some surfers to help me lower the saddle of the bike before I did myself irreparable damage and in a more comfortable position, cycled off. Within a minute, the saddle collapsed and swung precariously to the left and there was nothing I could do to rectify it. So instead of sitting up high, my knees were more or less parallel with my chin and I looked like a grown up on a kids BMX – not what I had in mind and it just made things all the harder with no downward thrust to get me back up those hills. I thought that if the going got too tough, I would just flag someone down and pretend I had a puncture or something, but in the end, I didn't need to and when I finally pulled up outside the lovely wooden Soda Tiquicia, my favourite restaurant and locked up the bike, I really felt as if I'd earnt my enormous lunch. It tasted just fine, especially drenched in olive oil, balsamic vinegar, black pepper, salt and chilli sauce. Again, I thanked god that I was in the Italian end of town.

The midday heat was so exhausting, I wondered if I would even make it back before I simply fell asleep in the saddle. Luckily, it wasn't far to Casa Eddy. I just dropped the bike on the floor, crawled under my netting onto my great big bed and slept as if drugged for two hours and even then, it was hard to find the energy to get up. Like a zombie I paced down to the beach and like a thirsty man finding an oasis, there was the ocean surging with positive ions. I raced in and the relief was just tremendous! All the grime, sweat and dust of the day was just sand blasted off and standing braced in the surf, it was easy to feel more like a mighty statue than a mere mortal. And then the sun began to vanish, not into the sea but behind storm clouds and I had the strangest sensation – I was COLD!

Back at Casa Eddy, he **had** a cold – it was easy to get caught out going from being baking hot to being cooled by a breeze. Neither of us had much, if anything to do, so we sat and talked – him with his grape juice (he gave up drinking and all

237

bad habits seven years ago) and me with my wine (I doubt I will ever give up my bad habits, at least whilst I don't even consider them to be bad). I got my laptop down to show him photos and posted the one of him making me dinner and in seconds, a myriad of girls responded. He'd told me about one girlfriend who used to carry a gun everywhere (!) and I just hoped that she wouldn't be turning up any minute soon to claim her man. But I must say, Eddy was a good man, he'd worked hard to establish his business and even if he did keep trying to look up my skirt, down my top or yank me into his hammock with him, he was funny, interesting, open, stoical, philosophical and true AND tremendously good company. Sometimes, I wondered why I just didn't give in...

****

Yet another unfamiliar racket woke me early. Not that it wasn't a joy to wake early. Usually, I would just look out of the door right next to my bed which was open day and night and looked out onto the jungle and the morning sky and listened to the birds. But that morning, the birds were drowned by a different cacophony. I crawled out from beneath the netting and peeked down. Eddy and another man/boy were slashing with huge machetes all the dead wood and clearing the yard. He had his authorisation to open a tourist hub and he wanted to start work on building his new office. The soil was so fertile, all he had to do was lop off a cutting, stick it in the ground and it would flourish in hours. That was how his garden grew.

I used his cooker to brew my coffee and as I did so, I watched them work - like Trojans. There was one strange idiosyncrasy of Ticos - the back of their heads were flat. I noticed it with Carlos in Montezuma – I thought he was having a bad hair day but no, they all had it or rather didn't have it – a curved skull. It made me think of the Easter Island statues which also had flat heads. Yes, I know they were statues, but it bears some thinking about, like why? Answers on a postcard please.

238

I thought it was probably time to sort out my ticket out of there. It seemed unbelievable that in a couple of days time, I would leave the town, travel back to the airport and then very early on Thursday morning, I would fly out of Central America and the bulk of my journey would be over. I didn't want to reflect on it, preferring to remain in the moment for as long as possible. So I got Eddy to readjust the saddle of his bike and off I went, back to Playa Carmen and the travel shop.

It was so blissful to be cycling along in the early morning before the heat piled up and to just enjoy the journey. I usually cycled at top speed – I usually do everything at top speed, but that morning, I took my time. Maybe for the first time, I realised just how beautiful Santa Teresa was. I noticed everything. I'd seen it all before, but I'd never paid it any attention.

There were so many quirky little bars and cafes along the road which normally, I just sped past. There was a little "sweet shop" where everything was made with "love", a cafe that said "if we are what we eat then we were all cannibals", a micro brewery bar, restaurants from all over the world, ice cream parlours, surf board shops that repaired "dings", laundry places that "separate colours", specialised coffee shops, an Indonesian furniture shop, various pizzerias, a supermarket which I'd never even seen before (and it turned out to be the best one) and even a pet grooming parlour. And then all along, on the beach side of the road there were signs for bars and restaurants with an ocean view. I recalled Chase and Spencer the Colorado boys, saying that they liked to wander from bar to bar and me wondering what on earth they were talking about, because on first sight, it didn't look as if there were any. Seemed I was mistaken. I suppose that's the thing when you travel on your own – there isn't the same necessity to go out exploring at night, especially when everyone was half your age and you had an interesting sex maniac at home for company.

Anyway, I cycled to the American end of town and the travel shop was shut. I was told he'd be back in an hour or so but that could mean anything so I cycled back again. I did try another travel shop and was told that the 2.45pm shuttle to the airport didn't exist. I tried to explain that I was told that it did. Well not anymore it didn't. I didn't believe him and carried on home thinking I'd recheck it later.

I meant to go for a swim but Eddy said the tide was high and when it was that high, it swamped the beach, carried fallen trees out to sea and it was just as likely that they would be brought back in to bash you on the head. I went anyway but he was absolutely right. The tide was so high and the waves so big, that there wasn't a single surfer or swimmer in the water, nor a piece of idle flotsam or jetsam left on the beach. I retraced my steps and with nothing else to do amongst the hard work going on at Casa Eddy – whole rows of flowers had been planted and the whole place reorganised, that I just got back on the bike and cycled the whole way back to Playa Carmen.

I seemed to have been there so long by then, that people saw me as something of a local and gave me a greeting. We hola'd and buenos'd and raised a finger in recognition. It was really rather a pleasant thing to do. Having a feeling of belonging was such a warm feeling, no matter how transient.

But to the matter in hand – my shuttle to the airport. He was very sorry, he said, but the afternoon shuttle was definitely cancelled and there was only one a day at 6am. That's not so bad in itself – I wake early, but what on earth would I do all day once I got to the airport – sit there for 15 hours? I asked what the option was. Easy, he said, use public transport. Catch the 2pm bus and I would arrive at 10pm and it would cost me a fraction of what the shuttle would. I asked if there was a downside. Yes, he said, it's public transport and my bag might not turn up with me because someone might steal it! I was reminded of all the long distance buses I'd caught in India where the threat was the same but also remembered that my bag was the size of a small child (as it was then) and would not be the first thing you would want to run off with, if indeed, you had the strength to lift it in the first place.

I cycled back, bought yet another huge container of water and consulted Eddy. He said that the 2pm local bus was a good connection and there was nothing to worry about. He then climbed onto my roof, hacked down some coconuts, cleaved off the ends to reveal the fruit within and we sat and drank the milk straight from the shell. And then we waited for the water truck to arrive – the tank had emptied earlier in the day and grubby as I was, there was no way I was going to wash in drinking water at almost £1 a litre! When it finally did arrive, once again, I was reminded of *Mad Max* the movie and whilst we take water for granted, there will come a day when we can't and as I said to my Canadian friend Andree back in Mexico, with all the fresh water they had in Canada – more than anywhere else in the world, when the water finally ran out, they would have to mount the stockades. I couldn't help but notice that a news posting on line said that the prices of houses in Toronto were rising faster than anywhere else on the planet. It seemed I wasn't the only one thinking that way.

So showered and clean, I asked Eddy if we were going dancing? He mumbled something about his cold and a fever and I thought sod it, I'll go on my own. I got dressed up and even if I do say so, I looked byoodiful. When he saw me coming down the steps, he instantly changed his mind. I'd never seen anyone get ready so quick in my life – so what happened to the cold?

Saturday night was party night at the "disco", it was free to get in for everyone and beer was £1.50 – what more could I ask for. Eddy was high-fiving everyone and slipping his arm around me at every opportunity and in no time, was twirling me around the dance floor. I loved it! Of course, he insisted on dancing up close with me as often as was possible and with all the heat and the sweat, I wondered if he hugged me close enough, would I shoot up in the air like a bar of soap and get cut to ribbons by the overhead fans.

But I didn't and we had a whole lot of fun. At the end, I said "see, that wasn't so bad, was it?" and he sheepishly grinned at me. I thought I'd have a fight on my hands when we got back to his place but he was a perfect gentleman and just kissed my hand (and then both cheeks) and before he could close in for the lip smacker, I trotted up the stairs to my room, calling "Buenos noches," over my shoulder. Saturday night fever indeed.

****

I was up and out early to the beach for a very long walk. Again, it was deserted. The tide was on the way out and little rock pools had formed everywhere, some deep enough to sit in. I found a stretch of beach beyond the red flags and plunged in. Instantly, there was someone blowing a whistle and motioning me to get out of the water. Apparently BETWEEN the red flags was the only safe place to swim, near the rocks – how was that possible? I walked further on, out of his sight and swam in peace. Yes, I could feel an undertow, but if I stayed in the shallows, which I did, where was the harm?

Back at Casa Eddy we had coffee together and talked. It was so weird that I've been going on about an imaginary boyfriend for so long, I actually believed I was still going out with him. For example, when Eddie asked me if my boyfriend was fat I laughed out loud when I envisaged my former man who was as slim and lithe as a cat. Suddenly, I remembered that I was in fact single and found myself sneaking surreptitious looks at him – he was a very handsome man... The trouble was that my idea of sex was that it should be like a fine wine – enjoyed and explored over several hours not just necked in a gulp and I couldn't see Eddy as the type of man who would take his time. Most men, unfortunately, seemed to fall into that category.

242

He was supposed to be taking me to the bull riding fiesta the next day – he used to be one – a bull rider, not a fiesta, and had the gore marks to prove it. But for that day, it was a time of relaxation, lunch, napping, more swimming, more undertows, more alarmed life guards and the promise of watching a film in English with no dubbing! And that's exactly what we did. Eddy did manage to yank me in the hammock with him but as well as being a squash, it seemed too intimate. I think Eddy thought it would be like a cinema date and we'd kiss and cuddle in the metaphorical back row – it reminded me of a first date as a naive 14 year old. I thought that when you went to the cinema, you went to see a film and couldn't understand why my "boyfriend" kept trying to kiss me. I still think the same now.

****

Rain stopped play on the bull riding front. Rain had stopped play on most things apart from the verdure – were things growing before my eyes? The heat and humidity were becoming stifling and I really didn't know how any one coped with it. Would it be like that until the rain proper arrived in October? Plus I was being bitten night and day. I was becoming seriously relieved that I was leaving and then it occurred to me that as I was, I really ought to finalise a plan.

Eddy started to have doubts about using public transport (as did I) as to whether or not it was reliable enough. If the bus was cancelled or broke down I would miss the plane which relied on me actually turning up on time. After some deliberation and another hair raising break neck cycle ride to the other end of town I was booked on the 6.30am bus and not being able to bear the idea of sitting in the airport for hours, I also booked a hotel with an airport shuttle. I couldn't stand the idea of having to get up so early twice in a row, but I really had no option.

So my time was really coming to an end and it just felt right.

I went through my belongings deciding which to jettison –
three lots of sun cream for one and bits of material I
laughingly referred to as my wardrobe. My five year old
moccasins, which I'd worn every day for three months and
which were now completely full of holes, I would cast out to
sea (with a tear or two) and then struggle with the rest. My
next stop was New York and unless I went to a fancy dress
party, there probably wouldn't be much use for a snorkel... I
just didn't want to arrive in the fabled city and have to
navigate the subway with my massive bag which was as
unwieldy as a fully grown drunk.

Eddy had promised to cook me a last supper, which hopefully,
wouldn't be a mass of aphrodisiacs. But for all his outrageous
flirting, he really had been delightful company and his happy
optimistic outlook had been curiously refreshing plus his
English was superb and he even got my jokes. I just hoped
he wouldn't get carried away on the romance/seduction
stakes.

****

Finally, it was my last full day in Santa Teresa. I went for a
very long last walk along the still deserted beach. I swam
and dived through the waves with a terrible sense of longing.
I would miss them. I had no idea when I would ever swim in
the Pacific Ocean again, or indeed, a sea that warm. I slipped
out for provisions both for the journey and the evening and
that was when it really felt as if I was leaving. I'd been there
so long, even the shop girls recognised me.

I threw away as much as I could bear to, but even then,
found myself sneaking things back in as if I wouldn't notice. I
took photos of my toes sticking out through my moccasins
just to show how utterly worn out they were and then I went
to the beach for my final sunset. I photographed my
moccasins in the surf and waited for them to drift off out to
sea except the tide was coming in and so were they. I lobbed
them out and a dog ran after them and brought one back for

244

me. It wasn't quite the ceremonious goodbye I was expecting. I lobbed it again. Same thing. On my third attempt, I watched it sail out and it didn't come back. The sun set, not as spectacularly as I'd hoped but it wasn't as if I hadn't seen many, many, many before, and I walked back to Casa Eddy.

True to his word, he turned up at 6 but rather than cook he invited me out for dinner – to my favourite restaurant. I got dressed up, but not too much, not wanting to lead him on, and we had such a great evening. He told me about a night at the "disco" when Mel Gibson, (who had the place in Mal Pais which Dominic Champagne of Hotel Lucy had landscaped) and Matthew McConaughey helicoptered in. Gibson was well known but not McConaughey and as the night played out, the latter got so drunk (not falling down, but riotously) he stripped down to his boxers and everyone else did too and then having such a good time, he paid the owner (Eddy's cousin) to keep it open for another three hours and all the drinks were his treat. The bill was $5000 and Eddy said it was the greatest night they'd ever seen.

Back at Casa Eddy, he went off to have a shower and when he came back, wearing just a towel, he asked again if I was sure that I didn't want to have sex and that no one need know, especially my (imaginary) boyfriend. He said I wouldn't regret it and let his towel fall. I thought it was women who were supposed to do that, but no. He stood before me and I can report that everything that you've heard about black men is entirely true. He said that as a child, he and his brothers, who were equally well endowed, would play on the beach naked and a crowd would gather to gawp – apart from his mother, who was always trying to cover them up. When he was just a teen, he said, his mother's friends would pay him to babysit and then have sex with him and he said that he'd been frightening girls with the size of it for as long as he could remember.

And there he was standing right beside me, totally

245

unabashed, as if it was the most normal thing in the world to stand there, in company, totally naked, like a body builder in a competition except it was only one specific enormous part of his body that he was displaying to me. He even got hold of my arm so that he could measure it up against it. I am not even exaggerating when I say that it was the length and breadth of my arm, from elbow to wrist and I'm no tiny Barbie. It was so astonishing and unprecedented, I didn't even know how to react and just sat there, as stiff as an ironing board whilst he stood there as stiff as a stallion, my arm feeling as if it belonged to a mannequin dummy rather than to me. I won't elaborate on what happened but will say that he just scooped me up and carried me shrieking with laughter up the stairs to my room but suffice to say, that try as we might, square peg round hole comes to mind…   .

****

I was up at five with the sun, dosing myself with caffeine and really getting rid of things. For some reason, I kept the snorkel. You just never know. Eddy carried my bag down for me as if it weighed nothing, the shuttle arrived and he gave me a big hug and a big kiss. He said he wouldn't say goodbye because that was too final and he just knew that I'd be back. Instead, we said "hasta luego", hugged again and we both had a tear in our eyes. As the bus pulled away, we waved and blew kisses until we were out of sight.

Eddy. I had never met anyone like him before and I wondered if I ever would again.

The minibus collected other people and we began the journey to the ferry. By coincidence, they were all English girls who'd been volunteering for Operation Raleigh all over Costa Rica. They were mostly doctors or charity workers and all very interesting. Again, I was reminded that I hadn't spoken to any English people since Lisa walked off nearly two weeks ago. Instantly there was that familiarity that I missed.

246

When we were on the ferry, I got talking to the social worker. I told her my theory - that if young Afro Caribbean boys were probably descended from slaves, no wonder that they never ever wanted to be told what to do again and were rebellious. She'd never thought about it like that but said that she would from then on. And then I spoke to one of the doctors and likened the coastline to that of the Carrick Roads near Falmouth and by sheer coincidence that's where she came from and had sailed there with her father many, many times. Between three of us, we covered South Africa, Sardinia, the Isle of Wight, Clapham, Twickenham, Streatham and obviously Costa Rica and our experiences of all of them. It was so easy to have things in common with your countrymen regardless of age and background. They were bound for recreation, their term of volunteering over and we parted at Punteranus. I wished them Pura Vida and meant it.

Alajuela was the airport town of San Jose. It was built on a hill and I kept expecting to see the sea over the brow, but I couldn't – it was the mountains. It was so much cooler and I finally stopped sweating. Such a relief. I was dropped at the Hotel Trotamundo (I'm not sure I would eat there...) and shown my little unbeautiful room with a window that opened onto the lounge and so had no air, but it was only for a few hours and did at least have a fan. There was a TV and the only English speaking channel was, as usual, CNN so I watched it anyway.

I went out to explore and to just get some exercise and found myself idly looking in shop windows. To be specific, shoe shop windows. Somehow, I bought ANOTHER pair of shoes. How did that happen? Back at the hostel I wandered out to the smoking area – a small patio between the kitchen and more rooms. I chatted to a young American couple who had their flight delayed by the volcano (what volcano?) and a Dutch couple who amazingly were listening to a CD of a friend of mine *Johnny G*. I think it got lost in translation that I knew him but they were glad I liked it.

247

I intended to sleep really early but one interesting person after another came out to talk. A French couple told tales of bus rides in Guatemala, an American told of how he was slowly trying to re-educate South America (and beyond) into sustainable agriculture and before long, there we all were, swapping stories. It was the most conversationally interesting evening I'd had for ages but as usual, it was not to last. We were all in transit and I had to go to bed. Reluctantly, I left them to it, set my alarm for 2.30am, turned out the light and tried to sleep in an airless room.

****

In the morning I packed for the last time in Latin America. It had been such a tremendous experience. I and the Dutch girl left at 3.30am for the airport in our free taxi. I paid my airport departure tax which was supposed to go to maintaining the roads – what roads were they then? On the five hour flight ahead of me no food was to be served so I complained – apparently United Airlines didn't serve food on internal flights. I asked how long they thought that Costa Rica had been in America when it wasn't even on their border.

I then went in search of coffee only to find an Italian "Lavazza" stall. I love the brand and drink it all the time in England, but in a land awash with coffee, why did they allow an Italian concession in its airport? I then complained in the duty free shop because they couldn't just give me the bottle of rum, oh no, that would be too easy. They had to manually walk it to the departure gate and give it to me there – ridiculous. And so, it was with little surprise that I was told I had been "especially selected" for and all over body and luggage search. It was very early, I hadn't slept properly for two days and I was a little tetchy – IT HAPPENS SOMETIMES! I can report though that the poor security girl, when she'd finished, really wished it wasn't me who'd been selected. I even apologised to her. I realized it wasn't her fault but after three months of nothing making sense, it seemed like the

248

final straw!

We crossed the tarmac by bus, climbed aboard and I sat in the very back row with a window seat hoping that by being in the back, any spare seats would be mine. There were no spare seats and so on a tiny aircraft with no refreshments, we ramped up speed, took off and beneath me, the lush and verdant land of Costa Rica dropped away.

Adios South and Central America HELLO NEW YORK!

NEW YORK

MANHATTAN AND HAMILTON HEIGHTS

The New York skyline – we've all seen pictures of it and many of you have seen it for yourselves. For the first time in my life (how did it take so long when I'd even had two plays on there?), I was seeing it too! We landed at Newark and then took an hour to clear customs. Just like Houston three months before on my way through, it was third world with massive queues and toilets that didn't work – welcome to the USA.

I was told by everyone that the quickest way into Manhattan was to take the sky train ($5) and then the Amtrak train into Penn Station ($12.50). I tried to phone Christian (my new airbnb host) to let him know I was there, except my phone didn't work. I asked a member of staff for help and she just looked at my antique of a phone, said "what is that?" and just said "use mine" and even dialled the number for me. Instantly wowed, I said that if she ever went to London, I hoped that someone would show her a similar kindness. What a great way to start my journey.

From the busy terminus of Penn, I transferred to the subway. Just thinking of the word "subway" was thrilling. For my whole life I'd wanted to travel on it and finally, I was there. Excitement was too limp a word to describe what I was feeling. If I'd just landed on the moon, I wouldn't have been as euphoric. I'd even owned a map of New York for over twenty years – that's how long I'd been meaning to go. I'd lapped up location after location in every New York Film from *Goodfellas* to *Taxi Driver* to *The Godfather* to *The French Connection* to *Manhattan* and *The Warriors.* The number of films I'd seen based in that city you couldn't count on a hundred hands. So even though it was my first time, I felt as though I already knew it and yet still, I was tingling with elation as the A train thundered into view. I'd arrived!

The subway doesn't have names, it has letters or numbers and the A train was the express, speeding through lesser used stations but stopping at mine - 145th Street. I came up onto street level and the first thing I saw were the iconic green street signs and yellow traffic lights. I walked a block west and turned left onto Convent Way and suddenly, it was like being in leafy heaven with gorgeous red and brown brick buildings and trees in purple bloom. I'd read that Hamilton Heights was an oasis and it was true. There were trees everywhere and a calmness I hadn't expected. I walked a couple of blocks south, counting the house numbers and came to a block of seven storey brown stone apartments. I rang the bell and was buzzed in and took the lift to the third floor. It was my airbnb apartment for the next week and very lovely it was too.

In the photo on the website, my room looked like a closet but in reality it was bigger and certainly big enough for me. Even if it had been the size of a closet I wouldn't have cared, I was in New York and at £30 a night – the YMCA or a hostel was £80 a night – it was a bargain. Christian showed me around, gave me some keys and vanished to take a phone call. Not quite what I expected but I was tired anyway, so just napped. When I woke, I went out to explore my new neighbourhood. Known as West Harlem, it was on a hill and still a bit down at heel - except for Convent Avenue. I found a cheap Hispanic diner. I said hola, they said hola, I said casado and they said si and that was that. I could still be in Latin America. I said I didn't know about tipping and was 85 cents (for an $8 meal) enough. She seemed surprised I was giving anything. I then crossed the road to the "wine specialist" not knowing what to expect and sure enough, it was a shop totally devoted to wine – good wine and it was in my neighbourhood – perfect.

I went "home" and met Nicolette, Christian's girlfriend. She was African American but as I later found out, not the usual type. Her dad emigrated from Nigeria to Dallas and, she said, as far as it was possible to come from royal blood when you were still carrying water on your head, she was from royal blood. (I retold the story of my dad, my great great grandfather and me being a princess too.) So as a couple of princesses, we hit it off straight away. She started in finance and then disenchanted, transferred to teaching and you could just tell that she was the type of teacher that ALL teachers should aspire to be. She said that in an ideal world, all the money in the private education sector should be ploughed into the public sector and then EVERY child could have a decent education. She was sure it would happen, probably somewhere liberal like Seattle. I suggested she should go into politics and she said that's what she was afraid of. I said maybe it was her destiny and to think about it – she wasn't a princess for nothing.

Her and Christian went out and then in came Sable, another African American but born in Brooklyn. She had to be 6' tall and she too was a teacher and she too was an exceptional person. She won a scholarship to study, as did Nicolette and she said that it was only in Philadelphia, at a private school that she realised how good education could be. She'd also studied in Brazil and as a New Yorker, took no stick from anyone, and had empowered black women to just stand up for their rights both as women and as blacks. Between them, they seemed to be revolutionising education in the very poor district of Washington Heights nearby. I was desperate to write up my day but I just couldn't stop talking. Of all the people I could have ended up sharing with and I was sharing with two of the most dynamic black women I had ever met – fantastic.

I slipped out to smoke a cigarette on the front steps and was surprised at the diversity of the tenants; from "preppies" in expensive clothes to long term tenants in slippers and curlers, all living alongside one another, and to each and every one of

255

them, I said hello and they all smiled back and said hi. I also noticed a police van parked outside. I wasn't sure if there was anyone in it or whether it was just there for show, but it seemed to work. At 10pm, people were out walking their dogs and just enjoying the evening without even a whiff of danger. I did hear something that could have been gun shots followed by sirens but you know what, I just didn't care. I was in New York!

ROCKAWAY BEACH – BROOKLYN BRIDGE – FINANCIAL DISTRICT - STATEN ISLAND

I was out by 10am and heading for the subway with my map and my Rough Guide. I bought my week's pass for $30 which gave me unlimited subway and cross town buses – compared to other cities it was a bargain. I intended to explore the Financial District in the far south of Manhattan until I looked at the subway map on the wall. On just that one train, I could go all the way through Brooklyn, into Queens and finally out the other end to Rockaway Beach. The song *Rock, Rock, Rockaway Beach* by the Ramones came into my head and it just stayed there, as I changed my mind, and rode all the way to the end of the line. At each stop, the driver announced the station "Aqueduct - Horse Race Track and Casino" – I imagined I was in a film of my very own and that this was the voice over. I loved it!

Most of the journey was underground, but when it did emerge it was to a green, leafy and pleasant land that I just didn't expect. Little clapboard houses with stoops and steps stood in line and as we rolled on to West Hamilton Beach, there was water everywhere and some of the houses literally stood on the water's edge with little jetties instead of verandas. I got talking to the man in the next seat who fortunately lived in Rockaway and he told me the history of it.

First it was just a swamp and then it was turned into a "Project" town – public housing for the roughest people in New York. I said "what, like a prison island?" He thought for a minute and said "Yes, I suppose it was." Never mind, I was

257

still going to go there and as we clattered over the bridge across Jamaica Bay with JFK airport behind us, he said that Rockaway caught the worst of Hurricane Sandy a couple of years ago and a lot of it had been destroyed. He said houses were literally blown away and the concrete foundations they stood on were just piled up like plates. It must have been like Hurricane Katrina in New Orleans.

And what the two storms had in common was that a lot of old shanty houses were washed away and replaced with desirable buildings that could be sold for a fortune. There were rows and rows of lovely new buildings and beyond them were the boardwalk and then the beach. You could see it from the train and it all looked chocolate box sweet. When we reached the terminus of Far Rockaway, the man said that what I should do was walk to the beach and have a good look around. And I was all for it, until another man from the train, with a mouthful of gold teeth, said "Don't go telling this lady she can walk around with all these crazies". **Crazies**! Down on the street, I looked around me and they did all look, well, crazy in that inbred out of control sort of way. Suddenly I lost all interest in the beach and the buildings. I bought some coffee which a huge man, who told me I was very "byoodiful" - there's that word again, asked me for a sip of – I gave him the whole cup and just got back on the train, trying not to look conspicuous and failing totally. It was a relief when the train pulled out even though at least 20 pairs of weird looking eyes were on me.

I thought of going to Coney Island as I was deep in the south, but by that time it was midday and the subway seemed to be full of loonies. There was a sign on the train saying that "the poles were for your safety, not your latest routine" with a drawing of a person swinging on one. There were signs all over the tubes about politeness and manners. It all suddenly made sense. I remembered how appalled I had been by the lack of manners in Colombia where people would block the pavement, or just stop in front of you with absolutely no regard for you or anyone other than themselves.

I presumed that it was similar all over Latin America and when you think that many of those people had, for reasons of poverty or war or famine or disaster, ended up in New York, it was not surprising that their manners had arrived with them. If I hadn't just come from down that way, I would never had understood it and would have just thought that all New Yorkers were bad mannered, but it was a cultural thing and cultures were VERY different. Anyway, three black kids got on the train with a ruckus and an attitude and then started their dance routine and just like the drawing, one of them began to swing around the pole nearly kicking one old lady in the face. My instinct was to complain on her behalf but I didn't and neither did anyone else but it put me off going all the way back down south to Coney Island, even if was an important venue in one of my favourite films - *The Warriors*.

Instead, I jumped out at Brooklyn Bridge. I couldn't find decaffeinated coffee anywhere and with all the caffeine I was drinking, I was constantly dying for a pee. No wonder it was called "The City That Never Sleeps" – they're all dosed up on the stuff. I asked a man in a car with a siren on top where I could go. "In the Court House", he said – "it's a public building, anyone can go in there". I loved the idea that public meant public – that was what a republic meant – well, at least that was what it was *supposed* to mean. I loved the freedom of it. I walked in and all right, I had to go through metal detectors and god knows what and then leave my camera with a guard, but no one stopped me. When I returned three minutes later he winked at me – we both knew what I was there for.

And so. The Brooklyn Bridge. What a mighty miracle of engineering. To my mind, it wasn't as beautiful as London's Tower Bridge but then no bridge was as beautiful as Tower Bridge. But it was MAGNIFICENT! It had a walkway above the traffic which was divided for pedestrians and cyclists and had police men and women hollering at you to keep to one side. There's no reason for me to describe it to you – surely we have all seen it either in real life, in photos or in movies.

It joined Manhattan to Brooklyn across the East River and crossing that bridge was my first view of the Financial District.

It was a monster of skyscrapers some old, most new and mostly, quite ugly (to me) with the odd, old majestic outline bursting through like a flower amongst weeds. I presumed it was once old dock land which was bought up cheap and then totally transformed. Curiously, just to the west of the bridge there was a little enclave of low rise buildings which sat almost awkwardly at the feet of the pomp of the surrounding high rises. I asked a policeman about it and he said that it was the old docks and port district which were still partially in use and also home to important museums (and bars). He urged me to go and have a look and buy myself a drink.

I wandered down that way and came across a stall selling bags. A man who looked curiously like Morgan Freeman asked me how much I would give him for one. I said I didn't want a bag. He said but how much would you give me if you *did* want a bag. $30, I said. $30 he shrieked – you cain't buy a bag for $30. But I don't want a bag. This went on for a good five minutes and I really didn't want a bag but somehow, he said he was doing me a favour and I said that no, I was doing him a favour. Finally, I gave him $30 and he gave me a gorgeous red, knock off Dolce & Gabbana bag, muttering something about daylight robbery and I wandered off wondering how all that had happened.

My feet were already killing me in my new pink Mexican moccasins so I found a massive chemist and stocked up on plasters. There was a man collecting a prescription – his bill was over $1000 – I wanted to say to him "if you were in England, that would cost you £8.50". Never underestimate just how great the National Health Service of England is. I then remembered what the policeman had said about getting a drink and, only following orders, I went in search of one.

"The Iron Horse" on Pearl Street was a sort of bikers' bar that played LOUD heavy rock music, had a pool table and men with muscles, moustaches and attitude. It also has beer at $2 – I went in dressed in my lovely white floral print dress, squeezed myself through a slightly agog crowd, crushed up to the bar and bought one. I imagined I would take it outside where I could drink and smoke in peace but it was New York and no, I couldn't drink in the street, the growly bar man told me. So I hoisted myself up onto a bar stool, smiled at the two hairy grizzlies either side of me, took a long slug of beer and told them that I too rode motorbikes. They almost spat their beer out in surprise, yelled "this little lady rides bikes!" and when I finally left the bar, several free beers later, I was a minor celebrity, promising to come back "real soon".

In something of a blur, I went in search of Wall Street. I asked directions of a smartly dressed woman who said "Wool Street"? Suddenly I was right back there in Minca with the "menoo". No, "Wall Street", I said – "the most famous street in America". "Oh, just head that way and you'll bump into it", she said. Flabbergasted, I walked off but did indeed bump into it very nearby and also the New York Stock Exchange.

There were posters everywhere claiming that it was the most important financial district in the world. I wondered if that was still true. Buildings crowd out even the sun and apart from Tiffany's and a few other Arte Nouveau designs, it was all rather bland. Just to see some beauty, I went into Tiffany's and in my very finest English accent, said that I wanted to have a "jolly good look around". I was very warmly welcomed. The jewellery wasn't as inspiring as the building, which was a surprising disappointment, but then I couldn't afford any of it anyway so what did it matter? Opposite was the Trump Tower. I expected to be as garish and ludicrous as the man himself, but it wasn't. I don't know if I was delighted or disappointed.

From there I went to Trinity Church which looked totally out of place – it was a building of Gothic wonderment amongst a slew of Gotham ugliness. It had incredible ornate bronze sculpted doors, a stained glass nave and a vaulted ceiling reminiscent of any European cathedral and there it was, standing aloof and majestic, worshipping something other than Mammon.

By that time it was 5pm and there was only one place to go – the Staten Island Ferry. I walked down Broadway "The Canyon of Heroes" and there it was, the great big glass and stainless steel structure that housed the terminal. Someone told me that there used to be a charge for the ferry but as the conductor kept getting robbed, they made it free. I asked a woman what to do and she just said "Get in line and when the gates open you just get on and if you want to see the Statue of Liberty, stand on the right".

I stood on the right. It was a hot 76F or 24C day, the sky was without cloud and the view was spectacular. Looking behind me was New Jersey to the left, Manhattan directly behind me and Brooklyn to the right. We cruised past the Statue of Liberty and Ellis Island and then I got talking to the man next to me who lived on the island. He said that initially, it was just a garbage dump for New York but gradually, it had become something of a recreational haven. After all, it was just a 30 minute boat ride away from the chaos of Manhattan and a total respite of parks and woods and a fraction of the price for housing. I got the feeling that, as with any city, when the centre gets too expensive, the locals look for somewhere, anywhere, to decamp to, but with Staten Island, it wasn't a long laborious expensive train journey to upstate New York, it was a wonderful 30 minute FREE boat journey. I was surprised that more people didn't live there.

As we came into dock, the island looked like it couldn't possibly be that close to New York. It was covered in trees and had an old world look and feel to it. It's 20 miles from north to south and had a train that ran the line. I was disappointed that I didn't have time to ride it and have a proper look but I did have time for dinner. I found a Mexican restaurant with all sorts of things I recognised but first I needed to pee. I asked if they had a "rest room", no she said but I could use the one in the police station. What? Could that be possible? I walked a block along, up the steps to the NYPD building and with incredulity, was pointed to their own personal policemen's toilet which had a sign saying PLEASE FLUSH and that was that – I was peeing with New York's finest.

I went back to the restaurant, ate an enormous plateful of meatballs (though how much "meat" was in them was debatable), black beans and brown rice and coffee for $8 and just gawped at the view of New York in the distance – outstanding!

Back on the ferry and back on the subway, I got talking to a lady who wanted to tell me EVERYTHING that I should see. The funniest thing though was that after each suggestion, she added "but don't go there alone and don't go after dark" as if it was some kind of zombie land. We were so busy talking that I missed my stop but no matter, I could change elsewhere and she seemed amazed that I already had the hang of the subway – I was from London I told her. "Oh my uncle lives near London, in Manchester" she said. I know Americans aren't that big on geography, hardly knowing which oceans border their country so I didn't point out just how far apart the two cities are and when I finally changed at Columbus onto the A train, she shook my hand with such warmth, as did everyone that day, that I wondered why people say New Yorkers were unfriendly.

And so I wandered back to Convent Way and another thoroughly interesting evening with Nicolette and Christian, but mainly Nicolette. She seemed so well informed that it made me think; paradise was only really paradise if you had conversation and stimulation. Otherwise, it was just beauty and for all the beauty of where I'd just been – untamed beaches, wild oceans and wilder people, give me a cupboard in New York any day.

CHELSEA TO CHINA TOWN

People were raving about the Hi Line Park so that's where I went.   First, I took the subway and then hoofed it west to the Hudson River. I climbed the wrought iron steps not sure what I'd find. It was an old railroad track that had been renovated and ran north to south but as far as I could make out, it was just an old rail road track with some plants and a bit of a view. I walked two blocks south and gave up, but not before a Buddhist monk had given me a bracelet for good Karma, but when I explained I had no change for a donation, he whipped back the bracelet and walked off in a huff. Was that good Karma then?

Yet again, I was dying for a pee but seemed to be in an area of old warehouses but it didn't make sense. Very up town people were coming and going and being Saturday, I wondered why. I consulted my map – I was in Chelsea, the old meat packing warehouse part of town, which was now home to all the art galleries. I was astonished at the apparent wealth which could sustain an entire district dedicated entirely to art. But with galleries, come open doors and of course, toilets. I spied an open doorway and went to investigate. Instantly, a smiling girl handed me a glass of wine and welcomed me. Who was I to refuse? I downed the wine, spent about a minute looking at the art which seemed as pretentious as the people, ducked into the toilet and back out onto the street.

I had no real plan so walked to the Hudson and took a seat as people cycled, roller bladed, skate boarded or simply jogged past, whilst on the river, small sailboats buzzed past and cruisers ferried tourists. My map had become part of me and I opened and closed it all day long. I wasn't far from Greenwich Village, so off I went. What surprised me most about New York was just how many apartment blocks there are. New York was full of people but what on earth did they all do? Surely they couldn't all work in the service industry or the Financial District, or maybe they did.

Greenwich Village was very pretty and old with gorgeous renovated brown stone buildings with steps up to the front doors and a lot of wrought iron work going on. This was a serious-money village with swanky shops, exclusive boutiques, pavement bars and cafes and everyone was out to be seen. It had narrow cobbled streets, trees, and not even a whiff of danger or edge.

From there I walked to Fifth Avenue, perhaps the most famous and most opulent of the avenues – No1 had a massive awning that just oozed success and had an "I've made it" feel to it, with porters to match. Just south, through a marble arch, was Washington Square Park. Being Saturday, it was full of buskers and people just out for a stroll in the sunshine. From there it was on to Soho which literally meant south of Houston (pronounced Howston). This area was famous for its wrought iron work and every building had those iconic exterior fire escape ladders which were really rather beautiful and a testament to geometric wizardry. Again, it was a very civilised area full of bijou shops and cafes but nothing of any real character. It was what Soho in London will be once they've got rid of all the super little cafes and sandwich bars which give the place its character.

From Soho, I walked across to Little Italy. Apparently all the Italians had moved out to cheaper areas but it was still full of what looked like bona fide restaurants and it was, of course, packed with diners. All the waiters were clad in long white aprons and it could be anywhere in any Italian city and just in case you were in any doubt as to where you were, there was a little neon sign saying "Welcome to Little Italy". From there

I more or less crossed the street into China Town. All the guide books said that it was all a sham but it looked pretty realistic to me. There were hundreds of shops, restaurants and stalls selling all things Chinese from meat to fish to vegetables to lampshades, so what was the sham in that? All right, probably the Chinese had also moved somewhere cheaper but if everything was Chinese, I think it can legitimately hang up a sign saying "Welcome to China Town". Maybe New Yorkers were just a bit too cynical for their own good.

I never ate Chinese food in London because it was swamped in MSG, but there in New York, I thought I'd give it a go. I found Bo Ky on Bayard Street with Peking ducks hanging in the window (always a good sign) and lots of Chinese people inside (another good sign). The lady cashier asked if I wanted the food to go and seemed surprised when I said no, I wanted to eat in. I was banished to a table behind a pillar set for two and a surly waiter came up to take my order.

It must have been obvious I had no idea what anything was and somehow, he developed patience and waited. Finally I asked for the "country meat" with rice and he gravely shook his head. I raised my hands in a "why" formation and he pointed to his tongue and his stomach and said a word I recognised – intestines. He could have just let me order that (like the waiter in Amsterdam) and then watched as I pushed it around my plate wondering whether to chance it or not, so I am blessed that he warned me. Instead, I ordered "leg pork" and he even gave me a free bowl of soup and lashings of jasmine tea. The plate was massive and even had a helping of pak choy and, including tax was $6.50 – I loved that city.

Back on the streets I made the mistake of looking in a jewellery shop, more specifically a pearl shop. I don't know why, other than that I have always wanted pearl earrings. Within ten minutes, I had a pair... The price (like my bag) started at $85 but I got her down to $30. I didn't even know

267

what the price of South Sea Island Pearls was, but as she said "if you can't spend your money, then it's not yours." Plus they were very beautiful... I absolutely marvel at the salespeople in that city especially if they can get me, who never buys anything, to buy whatever they want to sell me.

From there I took the subway to Union Square but arrived as everything was being packed away. It was full of organic meat and other produce so New Yorkers didn't have to eat junk food all the time. Nicolette (my host) said New York was seriously under served in the fresh food stakes but everywhere I went that day, there were big delis with wonderful looking food on a par with any other city, so I wasn't sure what she meant.

I was looking for coffee and found it in yep, a deli. I couldn't believe they had my favourite – Sumatran AND soya milk and all for $1.45 – unbelievable. I ducked around the corner and found a deserted brown stone with steps, a For Sale sign and three young men already sitting there. I asked if I could join them and sat down on the top step. We got talking – they were from Venezuela, said the country was ruined – i.e. Communist, everyone with any money had left and did I want a puff on their spliff. When in Rome...

Not surprisingly, the journey home took on a bit of a surreal feel. The "L" line which ran east to west along 14th street was out of order so it was back up to the street, a walk of one block and then the "C" line "uptown". I was getting really good at navigating the subway and people were asking **me** for directions. On the train there was even a good looking man holding a bunch of flowers. In my mind, I asked who the lucky lady was and he replied that it was his mother (it was Mother's Day) and then I said, who's the other lucky lady and he said you, but for some reason I didn't say that. Instead, we got into a bit of a conversation and he said he never usually went uptown and that downtown was the place to be. It was then my stop and there was that significant moment when you want to say more but don't. Ships in the night and all that...

When I finally made it back to 145th street, I called in at the wine shop and to try to cut my expenses, I bought a big bottle of wine hoping that I wouldn't be tempted to just drink more, but to be honest, I was too **tired** to drink more. I didn't know how many miles I was walking in a day but it was a lot. When I told Nicolette how many districts I'd covered she was shocked. Obviously, I still had a whole lot more to go and I hadn't even been to Central Park but as I knew I could rent bikes there, I'd whip round it in no time. Tomorrow was another day and I didn't even know where I was going yet. It was all just such a huge adventure!

NEW YORK SHOPPING FRENZY!

I seemed to have gone berserk! My plan was to look around the Flea Market and then cycle the whole of Central Park. It was a boiling hot, cloudless day and I headed south on the subway. I got off at the stop for the Natural History Museum but as I worked in London's museum, I had no need to look around theirs. Besides, who wanted to be inside looking at dead things when I could be outside looking at live things?

First up were really expensive stalls selling designer this and that - like a PVC coat for $350 – obviously, I didn't buy it. Then I found the Flea market but it wasn't the cornucopia that I was expecting and slightly shambolic. I heard someone talking about another market. I asked the Boys in Blue what and where it might be and they said down on Columbus Avenue, literally a few streets away, so that was where I went.

The road was blocked off and it was heaving. One of the shops – an Aids charity "Housing Works Thrift Shop" (it has branches everywhere and a web site) was my first stop. It was FULL of lovely things for the house and home and lots of lovely clothes. I rummaged through and found a beautiful orange silk dress for $15 (£10) and that would have done me, except I caught sight of a suit designed by Steve Fabrikant (New York's answer to Chanel). It was gorgeous, it was my size, it was $25. What I needed with a woollen suit was beyond me but you know how it is. Then I looked at accessories and came across a belt that was just so irresistible, well, again, you know how it is. In a blink, I'd spent $55- more than I would spend in a week in Colombia

271

for everything!

From there, I was into the market proper. Was it the sun? Was it the fact that in England I never went shopping and even when I did, found nothing that I liked? Well that day I liked everything. I bought four gorgeous patterned pashminas, two fabulous lipsticks with their own little mirrors and even a bottle of face foundation – I couldn't believe how dark my skin was! And then, like a magpie distracted by all that sparkles, I spotted a jewellery stall. Not only did I find the loveliest red crystal necklace I had ever seen, (and I've been looking for years), but also a bracelet to match AND a pearl necklace to match the earrings I'd bought the day before – they were cultured and not South Sea Island naturals but they looked good enough to me. I had to walk all the way to the Rockefeller Center just to find a bank (they only accepted cash) and in my haste to get back, I didn't even realise that the Center was linked to the Opera House. I could have taken a look around but what did I care about opera when I had jewels to buy? I was even oblivious to the architecture. Oh look, some more tall buildings, was about all I thought.

People say that New York is a shoppers' paradise and I can honestly say that I was hooked. I felt like a victim of Stockholm Syndrome and I'd fallen in love with my consumer habit kidnapper. One thing for sure though, if I lived there, I would have to get a job or sell a serious number of books, plays and poetry to afford my new giddy shopping habits. I wondered whether, if I'd discovered shopping in my 20's, I'd have been more career minded – with all the things there I'd want to buy, I would probably be running a huge corporation or even the country. Maybe an incentive was all I ever needed...

So pausing with yet another outstanding coffee from a simple deli, I sat in a side street full of brown stone buildings and one of them had Wisteria in bloom right up to the roof. It was the simple beauty of New York that astounded me rather

272

than all those monolithic glass buildings that did nothing except crowd the skyline. Along a side street, I spotted one building that had what looked like Roman temples on the top. I went for a closer look and discovered it to be the *San Remo* apartment building. I was so enthusiastic about it, the concierge even let me in to see the lobby. It was homage to Tiffany and everything Arte Nouveau. A four bedroom apartment cost $15 million!

I had intended to cycle the park but laden with bags, it didn't seem feasible so instead, I just sat on a bench, like thousands of other New Yorkers and enjoyed the sunshine and RELAXED. It was so pleasant to sit and do nothing rather than being on a mission to see everything that New York had to offer. What's that saying about taking time to smell the flowers – it was one of those moments. Heaven really.

Back at Chez Christian and Nicolette's, I showed her all my goodies like a little kid and she said that when she first arrived there from Dallas, she ran up an overdraft of $1000 in a matter of weeks from just buying everything that she wanted.

Sunday being the day of dining out, I went to Pinky's Jamaican restaurant which was about as ethnic as you can get in that part of town – it was all jerk this and jerk that, curried goat and even "Sex Tonic" – I wasn't sure if it was to give you energy or replace it. It wasn't fancy but it was fun; food to be eaten and not savoured but it was great all the same. And then it was back to my box to get on with some writing lest I forgot the dizziness of the day.

MIDTOWN TO CONEY ISLAND

Back on the sight-seeing track, I took the A train to Times Square on 42nd Street. I wasn't that interested in going there but as it was iconic, I felt I should. It was tacky, it was loud, it was bright, it was noisy – it was New York. It had its own mini NYPD booth and also one for Army Recruitment – maybe the fellas remembered the famous photo of the sailor kissing the girl there all those years ago and figure they'd be in with more of a chance if they were in uniform.

It was a photographer's delight. There were so many great photo opportunities – neon signs were everywhere from "Buba Gump Shrimp Company" to one that just said, rather enigmatically, "REALNESS". I snapped some shots, and when surrounded by Mini Mouse and friends, who was I to say no? I splashed out and gave them some money – never mind that they did complain that it wasn't enough... I even got someone to take one of me standing next a mini Statue of Liberty – the nearest I got to going there.

From there I walked south east to 34th Street and the Empire State Building. It was big and it was beautiful both inside and out. Even the floor was an Art Deco masterpiece. I only went up to the 2nd floor where I had my Swiss Army knife confiscated but later returned to me when I left – they seemed surprised a "lady" would carry one. I didn't bother telling them I'd just been to two of the most dangerous countries in the Americas and it had become second nature for me to carry it everywhere.

But what baffled me was just how many people worked in

275

security in each and every one of those buildings. Since 9/11 the whole city was patrolled and there was a presence everywhere from police to army and even to some kind of Mounties – or at least that's what they looked like. I wondered if the terror that so called Al Qaeda began was being continued by and for the American government to keep the army coffers full and unfounded bullying wars around the globe affordable, viable and votable.

That part of Manhattan was full of skyscrapers so the sun was blocked out most of the time. The only time it got through was via a cross street and when it did, it lit up the glass facades which then reflected everything around, including the sky and clouds. Those bolts of light were magnificent.

Trucks, buses, yellow taxis and traffic poured past all day but for some reason, there weren't the stationary traffic jams of most big cities – unless I was just lucky. When it was safe to cross, the walking legs sign came up and when it wasn't, the big red hand came up – people, including me, crossed whenever it looked safe or took a chance when the seconds counted down even though you could be prosecuted for "jay walking".

Then it was back up to 42nd Street in search of the Chrysler Building – my favourite Art Deco extravaganza replete with gargoyles. A lady on the sidewalk told me to zip up my bag because you could never be too careful "I'm New Yoik, born and bred", she said. I asked about the Chrysler Building and she didn't know – so much for that one then... I asked a man for directions and he turned out to be Irish and from Cork City. I told him about my heritage being Irish and we got into a chat. He told me De Valera was born in a brownstone on the former site of the Chrysler Building and I said I was more of a Collins man myself. He gave me a big bear hug and said that, of course, so was he. When I said that I'd tended his grave, I swear a little tear formed. We talked for as long as we could but the Oriental man he was with, kept eyeing his watch and sadly, he had to go.

276

So into the Chrysler Building and it was exquisite. If Chrysler had designed their cars the way they designed their building they would all look like a Vintage Rolls Royce with clean, clear lines and superb synchronicity. The lobby was chromed steel and homage to all things tasteful. It wasn't possible to go anywhere other than the foyer but that was enough for me. I was almost relieved incase the attention to detail fizzled out, although I very much doubted that it would – it was built when money was abundant and architecture reflected, in both senses of the word, identity and class. That was what Midtown Manhattan was, and for me, it was the most outstanding District of them all, echoing a time when taste oozed from every building and every building was, and still is a beacon of flair, panache and individuality.

From there, it was Grand Central Station and a more beautiful station I have never seen in my life and I've seen a lot and slept in many. The interior was marble and chandeliers, stained glass windows, brass fittings, gleaming polished wood and vast chambers of movement. It was a monument to the very idea of a united America when trains were the means of transport and anyone who was anyone would have travelled through that station – and everyone else besides. It was a temple to transport and I was in awe. Never mind that, once again, there were police and army officers everywhere. The threat was horrendously palpable.

Onwards then along 42nd Street to the Public Library which was as grand a building as any I had seen. Logia of learning – it had giant columns in a Grecian style, a parade of steps leading up to it and inside it was a vast vault of knowledge. It had a temporary photographic exhibition – 175 years through the lens and I must say, it was the first time I'd spent time inside for longer than a few moments. Strangely, despite how interesting the photos were – cataloguing American development both socially and architecturally, I couldn't wait to get back out into real life.

Behind the library was Bryant Square – a little Eden of

277

greenery and fountains, packed with people taking a break.
It was perfectly positioned to get a 360 degree view of
Midtown New York so I took yet more photos. It was a
photographers' paradise. I felt as if I were a tiny child lying
on the floor at a very exciting party looking up at the adults
all dressed up in sparkly gowns looming above me.

Back on ground level, people were hurrying everywhere.
There were jewellers, pawn shops, in fact shops selling
everything – expensive and cheap all crammed in together.
There were food trucks on every street selling hot dogs, halal
meat, kosher meat, pretzels and ice cream. Old fashioned
deli's stood cheek to cheek with new chain coffee and
sandwich bars and everyone at lunch time was eating. Sitting
inside, sitting on steps and any available space and believe it
or not, everyone seemed to smoke! That surprised me.
There was a smoking ban (of course) but people smoked
everywhere and no one seemed to mind – what a relief.

Next on my list was the Algonquin. I wished I could have
been there, with or instead of, Dorothy Parker. I was sure I
would have loved it although I wouldn't have loved the room
– it was dark and dingy and I just couldn't image it being
conducive to lavish wit or frivolity. I didn't stay long and was
back on the street in search of the Rockefeller Center by way
of Radio City which again, was a lovely old preservation of a
time gone by – a confection of glass and chrome, like a giant
Wurlitzer Juke Box.

I asked a man on the sidewalk if I was going the right way
and he very sweetly said those words I've come to love
"You're so byoodiful" and he added "You've still got it – in
spades". I thanked him – you can never get too many
compliments, and continued up 6th Avenue – Avenue of
Americas. The Rockefeller Centre was big. NBC has a studio
there and dozens of other things besides like shops and
offices and god knows what. There was a viewing platform
"The Top of the Rock" but having spent so much money on
clothes and accessories, I couldn't convince myself that to see

New York from above, when it looked so great from below, was worth the money.

I'd noticed earlier that at Delmonico's (not a subsidiary of its more famous counterpart near Wall Street) had a half price buffet between 4 and 7pm. All I had to do was get all the way back down to Lexington. I asked a lady at a bus stop what my best option was – get on the bus. So I got on my first New York bus, also covered by my Metrocard of unlimited travel, and we got talking. She told me about Mayor Bloomberg, the billionaire philanthropist who served for three terms – one more than he was technically supposed to, and that he'd cleaned up the city into what it had become – SAFE. She was a native New Yorker, obviously loaded and lived in a glass apartment building on 1st Avenue with floor to ceiling windows which she said had so much sunlight and such a great view, there was no need to go out. I made the mistake of presuming that it was on the East Side – apparently not, although when I looked on my map, it looked pretty much East Side to me. But she was really sweet and we had a great chat proving yet again that New Yorkers weren't grumpy; you just needed to talk to them.

At Delmonico's, the food was all laid out buffet style in big, deep stainless steel trays. You took a plastic receptacle of the size you wanted and filled it from a choice of about 30 different dishes and then paid by the weight. But it wasn't ordinary food. It was total Cordon Bleu cookery – sea bass and other fish in the most delicate of sauces, meats of all kind from melt in the mouth beef to buttered chicken and piles of vegetables from asparagus to mange tout. Everything was fantastic and it was almost impossible to choose.

Most people filled piddly little containers but I was starving and craving vegetables. I had a taste of almost every single one of them and buckling under the weight of my container, I went to pay and my food weighed nearly two pounds and cost $7.50 – it was a bargain of monumental proportions. The food was outstanding and I would recommend everyone and

279

anyone to go there – you won't get a finer meal in New York no matter how much you pay and the clientele was totally varied from the rich to me...

I finished with a take away coffee and almost unable to walk, sat on the steps near Grand Central Station. The filtered sun, which was disappearing for the day behind the sky scrapers, still offered light and it was bathed in that warmth that I sat and made a great big roll up and smoked – I just loved the idea that no one cared.

By then it was 5pm and fuelled up with food and caffeine, I knew that there was only one place that I wanted to be – Coney Island. Ever since I'd seen the film *The Warriors*, I'd wanted to see it. So back to Grand Central, onto the 5 Line, changed onto the D and off I went. Before, when I went to Rockaway, the train stayed underground below the East River. Imagine my surprise when the train came up above ground and we were still on the island. I asked the lady next to me where we went next and she told me "straight over Manhattan Bridge". I was wedged in the middle of the carriage and desperate to get to a window to see it. She saw my plight and just shouted "outta the way, this lady wants to see the bridge" and as if by magic, everyone moved and ushered me through as we clattered across. It was just so fantastic! I just couldn't believe it and as I turned, my face and entire presence was lit with joy. They all maybe realised just how remarkable their journey was, even though they'd done it so many times. Familiarity breeds contempt, as they say, but suddenly, they lit up too with such a blush of pride I wanted to cry and I bet one or two of them did too – grumpy New Yorkers – what grumpy New Yorkers?

When the train emptied out a bit, I got talking to Sal, a Coney Islander born and bred. He filled me in on the history and told me that property there now went for a fortune and that the Russian mafia was buying most of it. He shrugged and said had he known, he'd had bought years ago. The beauty of hindsight is a precious thing. He seemed surprised that I

280

was there on my own and astonished when I told him I'd been to Mexico and Colombia too. "You're one brave lady", he said. I flexed my muscles in a Popeye pose and he laughed. When he got off, we had a huge hand shake and he told me to take care and not to stay out after dark – as if I would.

The train pulled into its final stop and off I got and followed the sign for the Boardwalk and the Beach. I knew there was a fun fair there but apart from that, I had no idea. Coney Island was a total joy. It was like any tacky seaside town anywhere in the world. It had fast food joints, Nathan's International Hot Dog Eating Competition with past winners listed in a Hall of Fame (eating over 200 in one go was the record!), bucket and spade shops, a Boardwalk that ran for miles, the fun fair (closed until the season started) which boasted Ferris Wheels and all sorts of death defying rides and it had a BEACH.

There was an old dilapidated pier long since out of use falling into the sea and little waves tickling the beach. It was so lovely and so kitsch and it was just a subway ride away from Manhattan – unbelievable. There were, of course, Project type buildings everywhere. Like Rockaway, it had never been used for recreation and the only thing to do with it was to house problem people you didn't want anywhere else. Except now, EVERYONE wanted to live there. As Sal said "Everyone likes the beach" and they do. And so did I. Coney Island – what a dream. It did baffle me though that it had been so under used in the past. If everyone did enjoy the beach, how come no one used to go there? Was New York, in fact, ultimately territorial and you didn't stray that far from your patch?

The sun was going down and it was time to turn back but not before I'd photographed a crazy looking lady with hair past her bottom and a cool Coney dude on his motorbike. Both were really happy to have their photo taken. Everyone in New York seemed really happy to have their photo taken. I

281

didn't know whether they thought that one day they would be famous like the aforementioned kissers in Times Square or maybe they're just all born entertainers – even earlier by Bryant Square there were a couple of big black shoe shine men (yes, they still had them) in red berets, muscles, shades and attitude; I thought they'd be too cool to have their photo taken but when I asked them, they were delighted and we did a big high five afterwards. And they say New York's dangerous – as New Yorkers would say "Get outta here". And to prove this point once again, a tough young man got on the train with a big bouquet of flowers with a tag saying "Happy Birthday" and when I asked him if I could take a picture, he went all bashful but posed anyway. And I know I've said it before, but I'll say it again – I loved that city.

COLUMBUS CIRCLE, CENTRAL PARK BY BIKE, QUEENS AND THE BRONX

My feet needed a rest. They were covered in plasters from all the walking so it seemed like a good day for Central Park – by bike. I left the Subway at Columbus circle which had a column to commemorate him. It was in the middle of one of the few roundabouts in town and was awash with fountains. There were several expensive organised bike rental places but I knew there were people renting for less and that was what I wanted.

I asked a big black dude what the deal was and he led me to a Chinese man who insisted it would take me three hours to cycle around the park. I told him I could walk around the park in that time. We fell out and he walked off in a huff telling me to take a Citibike which were free but if you didn't know where to dock them, they would cost you a fortune. I just said, "Would you PLEASE go and get me a bike," and off he went. He didn't want another argument so told me to pay him later and I pedalled off. It took me awhile to discover where the gears were but then I was powering around the park, overtaking everyone and not even stopping at red lights – much the way I cycle everywhere.

Central Park was massive. It was in the middle of the city surrounded by phenomenal wealth in the shape of apartment buildings and had lakes, boating ponds, rocks, a castle, an enormous reservoir, a lido, a bowling green and a mini zoo. It had hills, rocks, meadows and woods. It was full of people, joggers and cyclists and for the really mad, horse drawn carriages or men who would pedal you around in rickshaw type carriages for $1 per three minutes – I couldn't even begin to calculate how much a tour would cost, if my man was right, and it would take three hours to cycle round. (Well actually I can - $60 which between two was really rather reasonable...)

Of course he wasn't right and with all my cycling in Santa Teresa, I whipped round it in half an hour despite the sneezing and streaming eyes from all the grass being cut. I screeched up in front of the Chinese man, he said $15 and we settled on $10. I was sure you could spend an entire day in Central Park if you wanted to, but why would you, when time was short and there was so much else to see?

Paul from Costa Rica who grew up in Queens, suggested I went to Flushing Main Street at the end of the 7 line and I'd get a glimpse of multi-cultural New York the way it would have been in the beginning. I was curious to see what he meant so I went. The Subway surfaced across the river and at the beginning of Queens. It didn't look good. It was a great big wasteland of trains and tracks, but then trees appeared and it was much the same as Brooklyn except more down at heel with not much in the line of beauty. It was, however, also the home of the New York Mets baseball team and had a huge stadium – Citifield. I doubt there was ever room in Manhattan to build stadiums so it made sense to put them elsewhere – just across the East River and that's where it was.

The train rattled above the street which was like one long market selling everything you could ever imagine. Every shop had an awning proudly proclaiming the owners name and I was struck that New York was a nation of shop keepers. I then took it further – when immigrants arrived all hankering for something from home, whole neighbourhoods would import and supply treats to satisfy that need and that was just what it was still like now.

Not far into the borough, it took on a definite Hispanic feel –

everything was written in Spanish and everyone who got on and off the train spoke Spanish. There was graffiti everywhere, one proclaiming it to be "Mexico, New York". But as it rattled on through along the winding tracks, Chinese symbols began to appear and so did Chinese people. When I finally reached the last stop – Main Street, I might as well have been in China.

Everything was **in** Chinese and everyone **was** Chinese. I was really surprised. When I was in Chinatown at the weekend, it looked like China but this made that look false. Now I knew what they meant. And then I thought about what Paul meant by New York's multiculturalism. Yes it did have many different cultures from all over the world. It was, after all, a nation of immigrants (notwithstanding the native Indians), but each of them had their own distinctive neighbourhoods – like Coney Island, and stood guard to preserve their own identity. Imagine if you'd just got off the boat from, say, France, wouldn't you want to be with your own people who spoke your language? It was like a mini "world" in one city. Suddenly, it made sense to call all American sports meeting "The World Series" because in New York, the whole world was there! And in Flushing, that world was Chinese.

There were entire shops selling just ginseng and menus with absolutely no English – there was no point gauging the quality of the food on the amount of Chinese people eating there, because there were **only** Chinese people eating there. This was not what I expected and to be honest, I was a bit disappointed. There was garbage everywhere and people openly spat all over the street. It even put me off the idea of going to China if that was what it would be like – there's a reason Bird Flu and all those other deadly epidemics arise in the Far East.

I decided to head back into town and eat at Delmonico's again. It was quickly becoming my favourite restaurant and was so convenient being right next to Grand Central station – the centre of New York's transport hub. I opted for the cold buffet and to my utter delight, they had a Brussels sprout salad. I know there are few people who enjoy this vegetable as much as I do but I can only tell you how exquisite it was. But that's not all I had folks. I cannot believe just how good that food was. It needed no extra seasoning whatsoever – it was all perfect and once again, I ate nearly 2lb of it. The owner just happened to be in there and I was so gushing, he may have thought I was mad. Maybe I was. But please, take my word for it and when you are next in New York, go there. It's on Lexington Avenue at 42nd street almost beneath the Chrysler building and then you can make up your own mind but I promise, you will not be disappointed.

There was only one Borough that I hadn't been to and that was The Bronx. We've seen it in movies – always made out to be the bad boy of the Boroughs with runaway trains, danger where ever you look and not a place to be after dark, or even in daylight. So I went there anyway. It was still light out after all. We all crammed on the 4 line and headed Uptown. I must say though that the Subway trains were at least twice as long as any other city trains I've ever been on so carry twice the amount of people and they just keep howling through. I doubt I'd waited more than three minutes for one the whole time I'd been there. It optimises the mass movement of people to get them to and from work as quickly as possible. I was an instant fan – they work and they were cheap - that's all that mattered.

So The Bronx – why that name for one? The land was bought centuries ago by a Swedish man called Jonas Bronck and it was abbreviated from there. It was almost all apartment buildings with the metal fire escapes adorning the outside – more geometric glory. It went on and on for miles and miles. It wasn't broken up by delightful streets of brown stone houses like parts of Brooklyn were, but it did have parks and it did have trees and here and there you could see attention to detail in the architecture which was just so endearing; like a child dressed up especially for a birthday party.

Someone pointed out Lehman College and I was astonished. It looked centuries old but had been there for less than 100 years. It was part of the City University of New York and just looked so out of place. The Bronx was not a pretty borough but surprisingly, it did had a lot of hills which interrupt the monotony and it also had the new Yankee Stadium – the old one was close by and now a park. The New York Yankees was the team that Babe Ruth and Joe di Magio (husband of Marilyn Monroe) played for. It was big, it was bold and it was brash – just like The Bronx itself. You couldn't help but love its bravado.

And once again, I got talking to New Yorkers and they talked to me. They were such lovely people and even though living in the outer Boroughs must be a bit like living in East Berlin before the Wall came down – you could see the glitz of the big city but you couldn't live it, they were happy to be where they were – home. And as for danger – forget it. I hadn't seen or been in one (really) dodgy moment. I don't know if it was because there was more equality or more policemen these days, but whatever it was, it worked.

EAST VILLAGE AND BROADWAY

The only place on my list I hadn't been to was the East Village. It was supposed to be hip, cool and trendy and where the people who couldn't afford Greenwich Village anymore had opted for. It had been adopted by arty types who suffered for their art i.e. they will brave it out in rough areas to live closer to the centre feeding on the urgency and depravity of the long term residents. It was also supposed to be full of thrift shops but I only saw a handful so I don't know where they'd gone but I supposed it was for the best – I had no more money to waste nor room in my bag. And no need of anything anyway.

I arrived early and as an omen, a cold east wind was blowing in off the river. I sat in a little park full of down and outs and drank bitter $1 coffee and the whole place seemed to be still asleep. St Marks Place was supposed to delineate the area and true, it was full of chic bars and restaurants but they were all either closed or empty. It had a feeling of sorrow to it – scruffy and run down and although it was once home to the Stuyvesants, that glory was long gone and so was a lot of the original architecture. Where ever there was a space, the local community filled it with a park, which they tended collectively but the further east you went, the worse it got.

I stopped for a break at Tompkins Square Park and saw real poverty – it just seemed so out of place on the island of Manhattan where real estate was at such a premium. I knew that in many cities it was the same and poverty was everywhere, but it just seemed so sad, abandoned and gloomy. The park was well kept and pretty enough but there were people standing in line for the local food bank, people

289

sleeping rough and people just sleeping. All were dressed in rags. But the strangest thing was, juxtaposed with this, were middle class people walking their dogs and their children as if the desperate didn't exist, as if they would go away if you ignored them (a bit like Bogota).

My guide book said that only the really brave went east of Tompkins Square, so feeling brave, as always, I carried on walking. It was slightly intimidating but I went further on through Alphabet City – so called because the avenues were called A B C and D – named and built on reclaimed swamp land long after 1st Avenue had been named. It made me think of how Manhattan had grown; from a palatial island home, to an island so crammed with people that every inch was precious.

I'd intended to walk through to the East River but was beginning to feel conspicuous. The few people about at that hour looked at me with resentment more than anything, in that I was relatively well dressed and I was invading their privacy; there to see how the down and outs lived. I didn't exactly feel threatened but I did feel unwelcome and uncomfortable and when I finally reached Avenue D and saw police vans parked up and an elevated mobile police observation tower, I knew that that was as far as I would and should go. Even the police were wagging their fingers at me. One of them said "What choo doing down here lady?" and he was right – what was I doing down there?

Beyond was a very bleak colourless housing estate that ran down to the water's edge. One day it would probably be redeveloped and all the people moved out of the Borough – can't be having all those poor people making the place look shabby... But for the time being, and as long as the impoverished remained, the rents would stay lower and all the hipsters could enjoy living there and swanking it up.

And the hipsters, where they had encroached, did make a difference. Some of the old buildings had been bought and cleaned up and a new wine retailer had a sign proudly proclaiming that it had been there since 2007. Before that, I can only imagine that the wine being consumed would have been some sort of deadly hooch. There was even a mural depicting Joe Strummer of *The Clash* urging people to "Know Your Rights".

Heading back to 1st Avenue, the many cafes and restaurants were waking up and little bedecked tables had appeared on the pavements. The tinkle of fine crockery and glassware could be heard and the clicking of high heels sang on the sidewalk. The place had taken on a totally new vibe and the ghost town of earlier was suddenly full of people and idle gossip. The hiccup of broken shopping trolleys filled with people's belongings suddenly faded like the remnants of a bad dream.

I crossed back west to Bowery and the old Merchants House Museum which hadn't been refurbished and looked a bit tatty, but the one next door had and looked fantastic – it sold for $12 million – that's how fantastic it looked. This was on 4th Street West – I wondered if this was the 4th Street Bob Dylan had sung about? North up 4th Avenue was a mix of old and new – the old were of red brick and housed the Public Theatre and various architectural gems like The Puck Building. It once housed and printed the *Puck* Magazine but was now mostly apartments that sold for up to $35 million. It was literally just a few blocks west of the depravity of Tompkins Square - sort of unbelievable. Others were architectural curiosities like the Cooper Union and others were the overly common glass fronted high rises that reflected the sky. But what I really wanted to see was The Strand bookshop which boasted 18 miles of books. It was near the university and it was vast and spectacular. It looked like a theatre and in a way it was – what was writing if not theatre of the mind?

With theatre on my mind, I took the subway to Broadway. It was slightly underwhelming, surrounded, as it was, by high rise buildings. I thought it would be one long stretch of ornate buildings like a true theatre land but it wasn't and had all the allure of a row of multi storey car parks. Odd, that as writers, we all aspire to one day being there, but the only building that really caught my eye was The Playwright Tavern and Celtic pub. I went in but it had about as much promise as a flat pint. I was slightly astonished at how lack lustre it all was. It had such a fabulous history of careers being made or broken, of Marlon Brando in Tennessee Williams' *Street Car Named Desire* or Miller's *Death of a Salesman* with Lee J Cobb. Now it was all musicals and fairly heart breaking. Oh well, perhaps I won't see you on Broadway after all.

On my way back to the subway at Times Square, I passed a mass meditation/silent protest against the Chinese government. Considering the Chinese crushed protestors with tanks, I couldn't see how a protest that they couldn't even hear would ever make an impact and even if it could, they still wouldn't care.

I was flagging and starving and could feel my third Delmonico's moment in three days coming on, so it was back to Grand Central and Lexington. How it happened I don't know, but I chose over 2lbs in weight of food – that's eight quarter pounder burgers. I couldn't understand how I'd turned into such a total glutton. There was just so much tantalizing food, especially vegetables which you hardly ever see anywhere, that when I did see them, I just went berserk. I simply couldn't choose and so ended up having a little of everything. Plus, of course, I was walking miles with barely a pause and if anything, I was getting slimmer.

Energised, I was onto the A train up to 168th Street and then onto the 1. The only part of Manhattan I hadn't seen was the very northern tip and to be honest, there wasn't much to see but I was determined to see it anyway. From there, the subway train crossed the Broadway Bridge and I was back into The Bronx. The East River was so narrow there, you could almost swim across but the gap was huge. I supposed as usual, it was location, location, location...

And as the sun began to set, it was back to my leafy neighbourhood of Hamilton Heights. A man giving away free copies of *Time Out said* "Happy Wednesday Sister" and I really felt as if I was home and I really wished that it was my home. I packed for the very last time. It was impossible to believe that my adventure was finally coming to an end. I then headed down the stairs with my wine and cigarettes and just sat out on the steps on a balmy May evening and talked to everyone and anyone who passed by. And talk we did. Did all New Yorkers like to talk? I really couldn't say, but that night, they all wanted to talk to me and me to them. Wonderful really.

MADISON AVENUE, CENTRAL PARK ON FOOT AND HARLEM

My flight wasn't until the evening and with shock, I realised that I hadn't seen Madison Avenue and the advertising district made so famous by "Madmen" on TV. So it was south on the A train to Columbus. I asked which bit of Madison Avenue was the bit I wanted and two New Yorkers said it didn't exist anymore. The big agencies were long gone and Madison Avenue was just full of big expensive stores. They said to walk across the south end of the park and just have a look. I couldn't imagine how many miles I had walked around New York but the idea of walking another step was almost more than I could bear. I had blisters on my blisters, the ligaments that held my hips to my thighs were shredded and the cartilage that supported my knees was tissue thin.

Walking was not really what I wanted to do but you know what, once I got going, there was no stopping me. I walked to Madison Avenue and had a wonder moment – I saw a building which just said "650 MAD". So the people in Mad Men weren't actually mad, they just worked on MADison Avenue. Sometimes I can't understand where the computer brain of my youth went to...

Having taken photos of the iconic street signs, I ducked back into Central Park. I'd whisked around it on the bike like a whirlwind, whenever that was, but hadn't stopped to really see anything – it was my chance to put that right. And what a beautiful place it was. Imagine, with all those apartment blocks, no one had a garden. Central Park was New York's garden and that was where everyone went.

It was roughly the size of 400 football pitches and had been there for over 150 years. When you considered the price of real estate in Manhattan, the land alone must have been worth an absolute fortune and yet it was still there – unbelievable. Not so long ago, it had become shabby, neglected and unsafe but not anymore. The beds were full of flowers, shrubs and trees, the grass was cut and every inch was tended. It had hills, woods, lakes, rivers, bridges, follies and miles of paths. There was a castle, a zoo, a carousel and an amphitheatre. It had ornamental clocks, statues, little parks, a tiny boating lake with tiny remote controlled boats, an Alice in Wonderland Garden and New York's Reservoir.

The reservoir held a billion gallons of water and was circled by a running/jogging track and was the most superb way to see the buildings around the park. And the greatest thing about Central Park, apart from being full of people just enjoying the weather or simply themselves, was that there were signs everywhere saying THIS IS YOUR PARK, WE ARE JUST LOOKING AFTER IT FOR YOU. I got that message everywhere – that New York belonged to New Yorkers and once again, I really wished I was one of them.

I'd intended to see Harlem and as it was such a beautiful day and I'd lost the feeling in my feet anyway, there didn't seem any reason not to walk to the end of the park and out onto 125th Street. I did detour out to see the Metropolitan Museum of Art which was, of course, exquisite. It was as beautiful a building as you would find in New York despite the rear end which looks like a rear end – big and fat and round – an add on that for me didn't work but hey, Guggenheim seemed to think it did so who am I to argue. A few words of advice though – if you want to buy ANY paintings of, or in, New York – local scenes, little framed photos etc, buy them there – there were rows of stalls outside and you had a better selection than anywhere else and they weren't even expensive. I would have bought some but my bag was FULL.

Back into the park, it was just a meander north on as lovely a day as you could ever have in a city, especially New York City. It was just full of people; it was New York's playground and breath of air. It was the place to go just to sit and think or play or even pray and I am so glad that it still held centre stage in a city that appeared, at times, like an avaricious monster and yet the whole area was totally free in every sense of the word.

When I finally left the park, it was just a short walk to 125th Street - better known as Harlem. I presume we all have an idea of what Harlem used to be like – jazz city, home of Billie Holiday, Speak Easys and definitely a no go area for the white folk unless they arrived in a limo and left in a limo or knew people – or just wanted to score drugs and were willing to risk it. I was told that that Harlem was long gone and the Apollo Theatre, where it all used to happen, had gone to the dogs. I'd hoped to spend a couple of hours there, wandering around but that's not what happened.

I crossed the road and almost instantly the air and everything else changed.   It was desperation city. One old beggar man was just standing there with his hand out saying, as if it was all one word, "mama needs a hot dog, dollar for a hot dog", over and over again and indeed, opposite was a hot dog diner where you could buy a Halal beef hot dog for the said $1. The place was crazier than Rockaway Beach and that really was saying something, the only difference being that Rockaway was deserted so there was no one really there to bother you. But on 125th it was crowded with people, many of whom seemed bonkers. They walked along raving to themselves and everyone else besides. There were old and young walking with strange seat type strollers and many many many people were enormously fat. I know the whole world is getting obese, but I hadn't seen that anywhere else in Manhattan and of course, the whole area was full of total junk food outlets – and religion.

There were people of all religions but mostly they were either Christians or Muslims. The Christians, mostly Evangelical, had set up stalls on the side of the road and apparently, they were all going to heaven – at least if they believed. The Muslims were not there to convert but to present and proudly proclaim their faith. But what they both had in common was a celebration of Black identity. There were the avenues and photos devoted to Marcus Garvey, Malcolm X, Martin Luther King and even Barack Obama although, in comparison, he looked and probably felt like an interloper.

There were big cheap tacky malls and people with mad staring eyes and I felt that most of them were staring at me. Not for the first time, I felt as if I was in the wrong part of town. I barely looked left or right and lost all interest in looking around. But the most surprising revelation for me was that the avenues of Fifth, Lexington and Madison all ran that far north. Number 1 Fifth Avenue was perhaps the most prestigious address in Manhattan but up there in Harlem, it would count for nothing. The whole area seemed rundown and for all of its so called gentrification, it didn't feel safe and it didn't feel welcoming. I just felt, and was, an outsider with no business being there – much the same as in Alphabet City. So rather than linger, I ducked down into the subway and shuffled one stop home and a million miles away to 145th street and Hamllton Heights.

With time to spare I thought I'd find out what the outstanding building I'd seen towering over the area every day for a week was. If only I'd known. Just 100 yards from the entry to my apartment building was the New York City College and it was as fine a group of buildings as you would ever see. (It was the main part of the gorgeous building I'd seen up in the Bronx.) It was up there with Oxford or Cambridge, albeit much smaller and only a toddler on the historic front. And the funniest thing was that I had sat on the steps of my building in the mornings and evenings watching so many people walking that way, and I never once bothered to find out where they were all going until an hour before I was leaving for good.

It was pure chance that I'd decided to stay on Convent Way – well, chance and the fact that it was laughably cheap, but you know what? It was a really great area, high up on the hill in Hamilton Heights; full of trees and splendid architecture, almost everything that you could need (provided you didn't need much) and just 20 minutes to the centre of town. I could see why people were moving up there. And so back to my "home" to collect my things, bid farewell to Christian and start my journey, to the airport at Newark that would finally take me home - somewhere that I didn't really want to be anymore. What would I do there? Where would the adventure be?

When I got to the subway, a girl offered to help me carry my even bigger bag than when I arrived, down the stairs. Once again, I marvelled and commented on the kindness of New Yorkers, only to discover that she was just avoiding the fare by helping me through - I admired her ingenuity and the ingenuity of all New Yorkers to make that fantastic wonderful stupendous city work for them.

The train was packed but when I got to Penn Station, somehow, they knew that I was getting off, and despite the crush, they made way for me. With yet another flight of steps to lug my bag up, a man with no agenda asked if I would like some help – "I would love some," I said. He helped me to the ticket booths, which I would have had a job to find – signs in the subway were the least helpful aspect, and with the last of my dollars, I bought my ticket back to Newark airport for less than it cost me on the way there – odd.

A train had been derailed that day so frustrated travellers were everywhere trying to find an alternative way home – one woman told me she was going to the airport simply to hire a car to drive the 200 miles home. So we all packed onto the train and as it pulled out of the station and crossed the bridge, I watched the fantastic fabled city of New York disappear behind me, gradually getting smaller and finally

299

vanishing from view.

I would miss that city more than any other I had ever been to. I would miss the accents, I would miss the skyline – the old reflecting a time when exquisite detail could be afforded and the new simply reflecting the sky. I would miss the people who started out being grumpy and then turned into sweethearts. I would miss the energy, generosity of spirit and the sheer confidence that New Yorkers exuded at just being part of that proud metropolis. But most of all, I would miss the idea that all those people were once immigrants and had made that city their own multicultural home which no one race could really lay claim to. As Sable, one of my hosts, said; in New York City, there were places where speaking English was of no use to you. I applauded New York and all who lived there. They were wonderful people in a wonderful city – WONDER being the operative word.

And so I began my journey home. The check-in was the usual palaver and with a sinking feeling, I saw my flight announced as "boarding". It just didn't seem real that it was over. I didn't feel excited at the thought of going home or that it was even time to be going home and I'd never felt that before. I was so full of thoughts about where I'd been which were still so raw as to not even be memories yet. As luck would have it, I found myself sitting next to a young Scandinavian media consultant who asked what I'd been doing in New York. It's a long story, I said. It's a long flight, he said.

So I told him how I'd arrived in Oaxaca, hung like a hammock high above the hills in the Sierra Madre, travelled on the bone shaking bus to Puerto Escondido, spent 10 glorious days in San Agustinillo, back up the mountain and onto Mexico City. How I'd walked everywhere, barged my way onto the macho food stalls and fiestad with the best in Coyoacan. I told him about the bleakness of Bogota where they'd airbrushed out the desperately poor and how I'd walked into the wrong end of town in search of the Bogota bicycle tour.

I described the colour and beauty of Cartagena and laughed as I recounted dancing at Fidel's club with Alexander and his mum and how I'd gone on then to Santa Marta and Aracataca to see the home of Gabriel Garcia Marquez – the reason I was there in the first place. I described Easter at Taganga and how mad Colombians were when they turned up to holiday and then the mad motorbike ride to Minca; all in the name of chocolate. I described the beautiful house in Getsemani and the opulence of The Ranch replete with horses and maids and swimming pool. I described my beautiful room in Montezuma which was like sleeping on a boat with the waves crashing beneath me and then to Casa Eddy and the endless beaches of Santa Teresa. I didn't elaborate on Eddy – some things were best kept secret. And then I told him about the glory of New York.

He said it must had been a wonderful adventure and I said "yes, it was", and I really meant it. It's easy to be blasé about travelling, but when you realise just where you've been, what you had to do to get there, how you dealt with problems and worries and the very fact that you did it all on your own and by yourself - that's when you realise just what an adventure you've had. And it's not just about seeing new things, it's about challenging yourself to even have the determination to do it in the first place – to change a whim into a reality and also change a part of you forever.

And I *was* changed, forever. I just knew that my travelling wouldn't end there. Why would it and why should it when the rest of the world was still out there to discover?

If you have enjoyed this book, please leave a review.
THANKYOU

20921365R00177

Printed in Great Britain
by Amazon